Making Sense of

SALVATION

Works by Wayne Grudem

Bible Doctrine: Essential Teachings of the Christian Faith

Christian Beliefs: Twenty Basics Every Christian Should Know

Counterpoints: Are Miraculous Gifts for Today? (General Editor)

Politics According to the Bible

Systematic Theology

Systematic Theology Laminated Sheet

Making Sense of Series

Making Sense of the Bible

Making Sense of Who God Is

Making Sense of Man and Sin

Making Sense of Christ and the Spirit

Making Sense of Salvation

Making Sense of the Church

Making Sense of the Future

Making Sense of

SALVATION

One of Seven Parts from Grudem's
Systematic Theology

Wayne Grudem

ZONDERVAN

Making Sense of Salvation
Copyright © 1994, 2011 by Wayne Grudem

Previously published in *Systematic Theology*

This title is also available as a Zondervan ebook. Visit www.zondervan.com/ebooks.

Requests for information should be addressed to:

Zondervan, *Grand Rapids, Michigan 49530*

This edition: ISBN 978-0-310-49315-0 (softcover)

The Library of Congress has cataloged the complete volume as:

Grudem, Wayne Arden.
    Systematic theology: an introduction to biblical doctrine / Wayne Grudem.
       p.   cm.
    Includes index.
    ISBN 978-0-310-28670-7
    1. Theology, Doctrinal. I. Title.
BT75.2.G78 — 1994
230'.046—dc20   94-8300

Cover design: *Rob Monacelli*
Interior design: *Mark Sheeres*

Printed in the United States of America

HB 11.13.2023

CONTENTS

PREFACE

I have not written this book for other teachers of theology (though I hope many of them will read it). I have written it for students—and not only for students, but also for every Christian who has a hunger to know the central doctrines of the Bible in greater depth.

I have tried to make it understandable even for Christians who have never studied theology before. I have avoided using technical terms without first explaining them. And most of the chapters can be read on their own, so that someone can begin at any chapter and grasp it without having read the earlier material.

Introductory studies do not have to be shallow or simplistic. I am convinced that most Christians are able to understand the doctrinal teachings of the Bible in considerable depth, provided that they are presented clearly and without the use of highly technical language. Therefore I have not hesitated to treat theological disputes in some detail where it seemed necessary.

Yet this book is still an *introduction* to systematic theology. Entire books have been written about the topics covered in each chapter of this book, and entire articles have been written about many of the verses quoted in this book. Therefore each chapter is capable of opening out into additional study in more breadth or more depth for those who are interested. The bibliographies at the end of each chapter give some help in that direction.

The following six distinctive features of this book grow out of my convictions about what systematic theology is and how it should be taught:

1. A Clear Biblical Basis for Doctrines. Because I believe that theology should be explicitly based on the teachings of Scripture, in each chapter I have attempted to show where the Bible gives support for the doctrines under consideration. In fact, because I believe that the words of Scripture themselves have power and authority greater than any human words, I have not just given Bible references; I have frequently quoted Bible passages at length so that readers can easily examine for themselves the scriptural evidence and in that way be like the noble Bereans, who were "examining the scriptures daily to see if these things were so" (Acts 17:11). This conviction about the unique nature of the Bible as God's words has also led to the inclusion of a Scripture memory passage at the end of each chapter.

2. Clarity in the Explanation of Doctrines. I do not believe that God intended the study of theology to result in confusion and frustration. A student who comes out of a course in theology filled only with doctrinal uncertainty and a thousand unanswered questions is hardly "able to give instruction in sound doctrine and also to confute those who contradict it" (Titus 1:9). Therefore I have tried to state the doctrinal positions of this book clearly and to show where in Scripture I find convincing evidence for those positions. I do not expect that everyone reading this book will agree with me at every point of doctrine; I do think that every reader will understand the positions I am arguing for and where Scripture can be found to support those positions.

This does not mean that I ignore other views. Where there are doctrinal differences within evangelical Christianity I have tried to represent other positions fairly, to explain why I disagree with them, and to give references to the best available defenses of the opposing positions. In fact, I have made it easy for students to find a conservative evangelical statement on each topic from within their own theological traditions, because each chapter contains an index to treatments of that chapter's subject in thirty-four other theology texts classified by denominational background.

3. Application to Life. I do not believe that God intended the study of theology to be dry and boring. Theology is the study of God and all his works! Theology is meant to be lived and prayed and sung! All of the great doctrinal writings of the Bible (such as Paul's epistle to the Romans) are full of praise to God and personal application to life. For this reason I have incorporated notes on application from time to time in the text, and have added "Questions for Personal Application" at the end of each chapter, as well as a hymn related to the topic of the chapter. True theology is "teaching which accords with godliness" (1 Tim. 6:3), and theology when studied rightly will lead to growth in our Christian lives, and to worship.

4. Focus on the Evangelical World. I do not think that a true system of theology can be constructed from within what we may call the "liberal" theological tradition—that is, by people who deny the absolute truthfulness of the Bible, or who do not think the words of the Bible to be God's very words. For this reason, the other writers I interact with in this book are mostly within what is today called the larger "conservative evangelical" tradition—from the great Reformers John Calvin and Martin Luther, down to the writings of evangelical scholars today. I write as an evangelical and for evangelicals. This does not mean that those in the liberal tradition have nothing valuable to say; it simply means that differences with them almost always boil down to differences over the nature of the Bible and its authority. The amount of doctrinal agreement that can be reached by people with widely divergent bases of authority is quite limited. I am thankful for my evangelical friends who write extensive critiques of liberal theology, but I do not think that everyone is called to do that, or that an extensive analysis of liberal views is the most helpful way to build a positive system of theology based on the total truthfulness of the whole Bible. In fact, somewhat like the boy in Hans Christian Andersen's tale who shouted, "The Emperor has no clothes!" I think someone needs to say that it is doubtful that liberal theologians have given us any significant insights into the doctrinal teachings of Scripture that are not already to be found in evangelical writers.

It is not always appreciated that the world of conservative evangelical scholarship is so rich and diverse that it affords ample opportunity for exploration of different viewpoints and insights into Scripture. I think that ultimately we will attain much more depth of understanding of Scripture when we are able to study it in the company of a great number of scholars who all begin with the conviction that the Bible is completely true and absolutely authoritative. The cross-references to thirty-four other evangelical systematic theologies that I have put at the end of each chapter reflect this conviction: though they are broken down into seven broad theological traditions (Anglican/Episcopalian, Arminian/Wesleyan/Methodist, Baptist, Dispensational, Lutheran, Reformed/Presbyterian, and Renewal/Charismatic/ Pentecostal), they all would hold to the inerrancy of the Bible and would belong to what would be called a conservative evangelical position today. (In addition to these thirty-four conservative evangelical works, I have also added to each chapter a section of cross-references to two representative Roman Catholic theologies, because Roman Catholicism continues to exercise such a significant influence worldwide.)

5. Hope for Progress in Doctrinal Unity in the Church. I believe that there is still much hope for the church to attain deeper and purer doctrinal understanding, and to overcome old barriers, even those that have persisted for centuries. Jesus is at work perfecting his church "that he might present the church to himself in splendor, without spot or wrinkle or any such thing, that she might be holy and without blemish" (Eph. 5:27), and he has given gifts to equip the church "until we all attain to the unity of the faith and of the knowledge of the Son of God" (Eph. 4:13). Though the past history of the church may discourage us, these Scriptures remain true, and we should not abandon hope of greater agreement. In fact, in this century we have already seen much greater understanding and some greater doctrinal agreement between Covenant and Dispensational theologians, and between charismatics and noncharismatics; moreover, I think the church's understanding of biblical inerrancy and of spiritual gifts has also increased significantly in the last few decades. I believe that the current debate over appropriate roles for men and women in marriage and the church will eventually result in much greater understanding of the teaching of Scripture as well, painful though the controversy may be at the present time. Therefore, in this book I have not hesitated to raise again some of the old differences (over baptism, the Lord's Supper, church government, the millennium and the tribulation, and predestination, for example) in the hope that, in some cases at least, a fresh look at Scripture may provoke a new examination of these doctrines and may perhaps prompt some movement not just toward greater understanding and tolerance of other viewpoints, but even toward greater doctrinal consensus in the church.

6. A Sense of the Urgent Need for Greater Doctrinal Understanding in the Whole Church. I am convinced that there is an urgent need in the church today for much greater understanding of Christian doctrine, or systematic theology. Not only pastors and teachers need to understand theology in greater depth—the whole church does as well. One day by God's grace we may have churches full of Christians who can discuss, apply, and live the doctrinal teachings of the Bible as readily as they can discuss the details of their own jobs or hobbies—or the fortunes of their favorite sports team or television program. It is not that Christians lack the ability to understand doctrine; it is just that they must have access to it in an understandable form. Once that happens, I think that many Christians will find that understanding (and living) the doctrines of Scripture is one of their greatest joys.

> *"O give thanks to the LORD, for he is good; for his steadfast love endures for ever!"*
> *(Ps. 118:29).*

"Not to us, O LORD, not to us, but to your name give glory" (Ps. 115:1).

WAYNE GRUDEM
Phoenix Seminary
4222 E. Thomas Road/Suite 400
Phoenix, Arizona 85018
USA

ABBREVIATIONS

BAGD	*A Greek-English Lexicon of the New Testament and Other Early Christian Literature.* Ed. Walter Bauer. Rev. and trans. Wm. Arndt, F. W. Gingrich, and F. Danker. Chicago: University of Chicago Press, 1979.
BDB	*A Hebrew and English Lexicon of the Old Testament.* F. Brown, S. R. Driver, and C. Briggs. Oxford: Clarendon Press, 1907; reprinted, with corrections, 1968.
BETS	*Bulletin of the Evangelical Theological Society*
BibSac	*Bibliotheca Sacra*
cf.	compare
CRSQ	*Creation Research Society Quarterly*
CT	*Christianity Today*
CThRev	*Criswell Theological Review*
DPCM	*Dictionary of Pentecostal and Charismatic Movements.* Stanley M. Burgess and Gary B. McGee, eds. Grand Rapids: Zondervan, 1988.
EBC	*Expositor's Bible Commentary.* Frank E. Gaebelein, ed. Grand Rapids: Zondervan, 1976.
ed.	edited by, edition
EDT	*Evangelical Dictionary of Theology.* Walter Elwell, ed. Grand Rapids: Baker, 1984.
et al.	and others
IBD	*The Illustrated Bible Dictionary.* Ed. J. D. Douglas, et al. 3 vols. Leicester: Inter-Varsity Press, and Wheaton: Tyndale House, 1980.
ISBE	*International Standard Bible Encyclopedia.* Revised edition. G. W. Bromiley, ed. Grand Rapids: Eerdmans, 1982.
JAMA	*Journal of the American Medical Association*
JBL	*Journal of Biblical Literature*
JETS	*Journal of the Evangelical Theological Society*
JSOT	*Journal for the Study of the Old Testament*
KJV	King James Version (Authorized Version)
LSJ	*A Greek-English Lexicon,* ninth edition. Henry Liddell, Robert Scott, H. S. Jones, R. McKenzie. Oxford: Clarendon Press, 1940.
LXX	Septuagint
mg.	margin or marginal notes
n.	note
n.d.	no date of publication given
n.p.	no place of publication given

NASB	New American Standard Bible
NDT	*New Dictionary of Theology.* S. B. Ferguson, D. F. Wright, J. I. Packer, eds. Leicester and Downers Grove, Ill.: InterVarsity Press, 1988.
NIDCC	*New International Dictionary of the Christian Church.* Ed. J. D. Douglas et al. Grand Rapids: Zondervan, 1974.
NIDNTT	*The New International Dictionary of New Testament Theology.* 3 vols. Colin Brown, gen. ed. Grand Rapids: Zondervan, 1975–78.
NIGTC	New International Greek Testament Commentaries
NIV	New International Version
NKJV	New King James Version
NTS	*New Testament Studies*
ODCC	*Oxford Dictionary of the Christian Church.* Ed. F. L. Cross. London and New York: Oxford University Press, 1977.
rev.	revised
RSV	Revised Standard Version
TB	*Tyndale Bulletin*
TDNT	*Theological Dictionary of the New Testament.* 10 vols. G. Kittel and G. Friedrich, eds.; trans. G. W. Bromiley. Grand Rapids: Eerdmans, 1964–76.
TNTC	Tyndale New Testament Commentaries
TOTC	Tyndale Old Testament Commentaries
trans.	translated by
TrinJ	*Trinity Journal*
vol.	volume
WBC	Word Biblical Commentary
WTJ	*Westminster Theological Journal*

INTRODUCTION TO SYSTEMATIC THEOLOGY

What is systematic theology?
Why should Christians study it?
How should we study it?

EXPLANATION AND SCRIPTURAL BASIS

A. Definition of Systematic Theology

What is systematic theology? Many different definitions have been given, but for the purposes of this book the following definition will be used: *Systematic theology is any study that answers the question, "What does the whole Bible teach us today?" about any given topic.*[1]

This definition indicates that systematic theology involves collecting and understanding all the relevant passages in the Bible on various topics and then summarizing their teachings clearly so that we know what to believe about each topic.

1. Relationship to Other Disciplines. The emphasis of this book will not therefore be on *historical theology* (a historical study of how Christians in different periods have understood various theological topics) or *philosophical theology* (studying theological topics largely without use of the Bible, but using the tools and methods of philosophical reasoning and what can be known about God from observing the universe) or *apologetics* (providing a defense of the truthfulness of the Christian faith for the purpose of convincing unbe-

---

[1]This definition of systematic theology is taken from Professor John Frame, now of Westminster Seminary in Escondido, California, under whom I was privileged to study in 1971–73 (at Westminster Seminary, Philadelphia). Though it is impossible to acknowledge my indebtedness to him at every point, it is appropriate to express gratitude to him at this point, and to say that he has probably influenced my theological thinking more than anyone else, especially in the crucial areas of the nature of systematic theology and the doctrine of the Word of God. Many of his former students will recognize echoes of his teaching in the following pages, especially in those two areas.

lievers). These three subjects, which are worthwhile subjects for Christians to pursue, are sometimes also included in a broader definition of the term *systematic theology.* In fact, some consideration of historical, philosophical, and apologetic matters will be found at points throughout this book. This is because historical study informs us of the insights gained and the mistakes made by others previously in understanding Scripture; philosophical study helps us understand right and wrong thought forms common in our culture and others; and apologetic study helps us bring the teachings of Scripture to bear on the objections raised by unbelievers. But these areas of study are not the focus of this volume, which rather interacts directly with the biblical text in order to understand what the Bible itself says to us about various theological subjects.

If someone prefers to use the term *systematic theology* in the broader sense just mentioned instead of the narrow sense which has been defined above, it will not make much difference.[2] Those who use the narrower definition will agree that these other areas of study definitely contribute in a positive way to our understanding of systematic theology, and those who use the broader definition will certainly agree that historical theology, philosophical theology, and apologetics can be distinguished from the process of collecting and synthesizing all the relevant Scripture passages for various topics. Moreover, even though historical and philosophical studies do contribute to our understanding of theological questions, only Scripture has the final authority to define what we are to believe,[3] and it is therefore appropriate to spend some time focusing on the process of analyzing the teaching of Scripture itself.

Systematic theology, as we have defined it, also differs from *Old Testament theology, New Testament theology,* and *biblical theology.* These three disciplines organize their topics historically and in the order the topics are presented in the Bible. Therefore, in Old Testament theology, one might ask, "What does Deuteronomy teach about prayer?" or "What do the Psalms teach about prayer?" or "What does Isaiah teach about prayer?" or even, "What does the whole Old Testament teach about prayer and how is that teaching developed over the history of the Old Testament?" In New Testament theology one might ask, "What does John's gospel teach about prayer?" or "What does Paul teach about prayer?" or even "What does the New Testament teach about prayer and what is the historical development of that teaching as it progresses through the New Testament?"

"Biblical theology" has a technical meaning in theological studies. It is the larger category that contains both Old Testament theology and New Testament theology as we have defined them above. Biblical theology gives special attention to the teachings of *individual authors and sections* of Scripture, and to the place of each teaching in the *historical development* of Scripture.[4] So one might ask, "What is the historical development of the teaching about prayer as it is seen throughout the history of the Old Testament and then of the

---

[2]Gordon Lewis and Bruce Demarest have coined a new phrase, "integrative theology," to refer to systematic theology in this broader sense: see their excellent work, *Integrative Theology* (Grand Rapids: Zondervan, 1996). For each doctrine, they analyze historical alternatives and relevant biblical passages, give a coherent summary of the doctrine, answer philosophical objections, and give practical application.

[3]Charles Hodge says, "The Scriptures contain all the Facts of Theology" (section heading in *Systematic Theology,* 1:15). He argues that ideas gained from intuition or observation or experience are valid in theology only if they are supported by the teaching of Scripture.

[4]The term "biblical theology" might seem to be a natural and appropriate one for the process I have called

New Testament?" Of course, this question comes very close to the question, "What does the whole Bible teach us today about prayer?" (which would be *systematic theology* by our definition). It then becomes evident that the boundary lines between these various disciplines often overlap at the edges, and parts of one study blend into the next. Yet there is still a difference, for biblical theology traces the historical development of a doctrine and the way in which one's place at some point in that historical development affects one's understanding and application of that particular doctrine. Biblical theology also focuses on the understanding of each doctrine that the biblical authors and their original hearers or readers possessed.

Systematic theology, on the other hand, makes use of the material of biblical theology and often builds on the results of biblical theology. At some points, especially where great detail and care is needed in the development of a doctrine, systematic theology will even use a biblical-theological method, analyzing the development of each doctrine through the historical development of Scripture. But the focus of systematic theology remains different: its focus is on the collection and then the summary of the teaching of all the biblical passages on a particular subject. Thus systematic theology asks, for example, "What does the whole Bible teach us today about prayer?" It attempts to summarize the teaching of Scripture in a brief, understandable, and very carefully formulated statement.

2. Application to Life. Furthermore, systematic theology focuses on summarizing each doctrine as it should be understood by present-day Christians. This will sometimes involve the use of terms and even concepts that were not themselves used by any individual biblical author, but that are the proper result of combining the teachings of two or more biblical authors on a particular subject. The terms *Trinity, incarnation,* and *deity of Christ,* for example, are not found in the Bible, but they usefully summarize biblical concepts.

Defining systematic theology to include "what the whole Bible *teaches us* today" implies that application to life is a necessary part of the proper pursuit of systematic theology. Thus a doctrine under consideration is seen in terms of its practical value for living the Christian life. Nowhere in Scripture do we find doctrine studied for its own sake or in isolation from life. The biblical writers consistently apply their teaching to life. Therefore, any Christian reading this book should find his or her Christian life enriched and deepened during this study; indeed, if personal spiritual growth does not occur, then the book has not been written properly by the author or the material has not been rightly studied by the reader.

3. Systematic Theology and Disorganized Theology. If we use this definition of systematic theology, it will be seen that most Christians actually do systematic theology (or at least make systematic-theological statements) many times a week. For example: "The Bible says that everyone who believes in Jesus Christ will be saved." "The Bible says that Jesus Christ is the only way to God." "The Bible says that Jesus is coming again." These are all summaries of what Scripture says and, as such, they are systematic-

---

"systematic theology." However, its usage in theological studies to refer to tracing the historical development of doctrines throughout the Bible is too well established, so that starting now to use the term biblical theology to refer to what I have called systematic theology would only result in confusion.

theological statements. In fact, every time a Christian says something about what the whole Bible says, he or she is in a sense doing "systematic theology"—according to our definition—by thinking about various topics and answering the question, "What does the whole Bible teach us today?"[5]

How then does this book differ from the "systematic theology" that most Christians do? First, it treats biblical topics in a *carefully organized way* to guarantee that all important topics will receive thorough consideration. This organization also provides one sort of check against inaccurate analysis of individual topics, for it means that all other doctrines that are treated can be compared with each topic for consistency in methodology and absence of contradictions in the relationships between the doctrines. This also helps to ensure balanced consideration of complementary doctrines: Christ's deity and humanity are studied together, for example, as are God's sovereignty and man's responsibility, so that wrong conclusions will not be drawn from an imbalanced emphasis on only one aspect of the full biblical presentation.

In fact, the adjective *systematic* in systematic theology should be understood to mean something like "carefully organized by topics," with the understanding that the topics studied will be seen to fit together in a consistent way, and will include all the major doctrinal topics of the Bible. Thus "systematic" should be thought of as the opposite of "randomly arranged" or "disorganized." In systematic theology topics are treated in an orderly or "systematic" way.

A second difference between this book and the way most Christians do systematic theology is that it treats topics in *much more detail* than most Christians do. For example, an ordinary Christian as a result of regular reading of the Bible may make the theological statement, "The Bible says that everyone who believes in Jesus Christ will be saved." That is a perfectly true summary of a major biblical teaching. However, it can take several pages to elaborate more precisely what it means to "believe in Jesus Christ," and it could take several chapters to explain what it means to "be saved" in all of the many implications of that term.

Third, a formal study of systematic theology will make it possible to formulate summaries of biblical teachings with *much more accuracy* than Christians would normally arrive at without such a study. In systematic theology, summaries of biblical teachings must be worded precisely to guard against misunderstandings and to exclude false teachings.

Fourth, a good theological analysis must find and treat fairly *all the relevant Bible passages* for each particular topic, not just some or a few of the relevant passages. This often means that it must depend on the results of careful exegesis (or interpretation) of Scripture generally agreed upon by evangelical interpreters or, where there are significant differences of interpretation, systematic theology will include detailed exegesis at certain points.

---

[5]Robert L. Reymond, "The Justification of Theology with a Special Application to Contemporary Christology," in Nigel M. Cameron, ed., *The Challenge of Evangelical Theology: Essays in Approach and Method* (Edinburgh: Rutherford House, 1987), pp. 82–104, cites several examples from the New Testament of this kind of searching through all of Scripture to demonstrate doctrinal conclusions: Jesus in Luke 24:25–27 (and elsewhere); Apollos in Acts 18:28; the Jerusalem Council in Acts 15; and Paul in Acts 17:2–3; 20:27; and all of Romans. To this list could be added Heb. 1 (on Christ's divine Sonship), Heb. 11 (on the nature of true faith), and many other passages from the Epistles.

Because of the large number of topics covered in a study of systematic theology and because of the great detail with which these topics are analyzed, it is inevitable that someone studying a systematic theology text or taking a course in systematic theology for the first time will have many of his or her own personal beliefs challenged or modified, refined or enriched. It is of utmost importance therefore that each person beginning such a course firmly resolve in his or her own mind to abandon as false any idea which is found to be clearly contradicted by the teaching of Scripture. But it is also very important for each person to resolve not to believe any individual doctrine simply because this textbook or some other textbook or teacher says that it is true, unless this book or the instructor in a course can convince the student from the text of Scripture itself. It is Scripture alone, not "conservative evangelical tradition" or any other human authority, that must function as the normative authority for the definition of what we should believe.

4. What Are Doctrines? In this book, the word *doctrine* will be understood in the following way: *A doctrine is what the whole Bible teaches us today about some particular topic.* This definition is directly related to our earlier definition of systematic theology, since it shows that a "doctrine" is simply the result of the process of doing systematic theology with regard to one particular topic. Understood in this way, doctrines can be very broad or very narrow. We can speak of "the doctrine of God" as a major doctrinal category, including a summary of all that the Bible teaches us today about God. Such a doctrine would be exceptionally large. On the other hand, we may also speak more narrowly of the doctrine of God's eternity, or the doctrine of the Trinity, or the doctrine of God's justice.[6]

Within the major doctrinal category of this book, many more specific teachings have been selected as appropriate for inclusion. Generally these meet at least one of the following three criteria: (1) they are doctrines that are most emphasized in Scripture; (2) they are doctrines that have been most significant throughout the history of the church and have been important for all Christians at all times; (3) they are doctrines that have become important for Christians in the present situation in the history of the church (even though some of these doctrines may not have been of such great interest earlier in church history). Some examples of doctrines in the third category would be the doctrine of the inerrancy of Scripture, the doctrine of baptism in the Holy Spirit, the doctrine of Satan and demons with particular reference to spiritual warfare, the doctrine of spiritual gifts in the New Testament age, and the doctrine of the creation of man as male and female in relation to the understanding of roles appropriate to men and women today.

Finally, what is the difference between systematic theology and *Christian ethics?* Although there is inevitably some overlap between the study of theology and the study of ethics, I have tried to maintain a distinction in emphasis. The emphasis of systematic theology is on what God wants us to *believe* and to *know*, while the emphasis in Christian ethics is on what God wants us to *do* and what *attitudes* he wants us to have. Such a distinction is reflected in the following definition: *Christian ethics is any study that answers*

---

[6]The word *dogma* is an approximate synonym for *doctrine*, but I have not used it in this book. *Dogma* is a term more often used by Roman Catholic and Lutheran theologians, and the term frequently refers to doctrines that have official church endorsement. *Dogmatic theology* is another term for *systematic theology*.

the question, "What does God require us to do and what attitudes does he require us to have today?" with regard to any given situation. Thus theology focuses on ideas while ethics focuses on situations in life. Theology tells us how we should think while ethics tells us how we should live. A textbook on ethics, for example, would discuss topics such as marriage and divorce, lying and telling the truth, stealing and ownership of property, abortion, birth control, homosexuality, the role of civil government, discipline of children, capital punishment, war, care for the poor, racial discrimination, and so forth. Of course there is some overlap: theology must be applied to life (therefore it is often ethical to some degree). And ethics must be based on proper ideas of God and his world (therefore it is theological to some degree).

This book will emphasize systematic theology, though it will not hesitate to apply theology to life where such application comes readily. Still, for a thorough treatment of Christian ethics, another textbook similar to this in scope would be necessary.

B. Initial Assumptions of This Book

We begin with two assumptions or presuppositions: (1) that the Bible is true and that it is, in fact, our only absolute standard of truth; (2) that the God who is spoken of in the Bible exists, and that he is who the Bible says he is: the Creator of heaven and earth and all things in them. These two presuppositions, of course, are always open to later adjustment or modification or deeper confirmation, but at this point, these two assumptions form the point at which we begin.

C. Why Should Christians Study Theology?

Why should Christians study systematic theology? That is, why should we engage in the process of collecting and summarizing the teachings of many individual Bible passages on particular topics? Why is it not sufficient simply to continue reading the Bible regularly every day of our lives?

1. The Basic Reason. Many answers have been given to this question, but too often they leave the impression that systematic theology somehow can "improve" on the Bible by doing a better job of organizing its teachings or explaining them more clearly than the Bible itself has done. Thus we may begin implicitly to deny the clarity of Scripture or the sufficiency of Scripture.

However, Jesus commanded his disciples and now commands us also to *teach* believers to observe all that he commanded:

> Go therefore and make disciples of all nations, baptizing them in the name of the Father and of the Son and of the Holy Spirit, *teaching them* to observe all that I have commanded you; and lo, I am with you always, to the close of the age. (Matt. 28:19–20)

Now to teach all that Jesus commanded, in a narrow sense, is simply to teach the content of the oral teaching of Jesus as it is recorded in the gospel narratives. However, in a broader sense, "all that Jesus commanded" includes the interpretation and application of his life and teachings, because in the book of Acts it is implied that it contains a narrative of what Jesus *continued* to do and teach through the apostles after his resurrection (note that 1:1 speaks of "all that Jesus *began* to do and teach"). "All that Jesus commanded" can also include the Epistles, since they were written under the supervision of the Holy Spirit and were also considered to be a "command of the Lord" (1 Cor. 14:37; see also John 14:26; 16:13; 1 Thess. 4:15; 2 Peter 3:2; and Rev. 1:1–3). Thus in a larger sense, "all that Jesus commanded" includes all of the New Testament.

Furthermore, when we consider that the New Testament writings endorse the absolute confidence Jesus had in the authority and reliability of the Old Testament Scriptures as God's words, and when we realize that the New Testament epistles also endorse this view of the Old Testament as absolutely authoritative words of God, then it becomes evident that we cannot teach "all that Jesus commanded" without including all of the Old Testament (rightly understood in the various ways in which it applies to the new covenant age in the history of redemption) as well.

The task of fulfilling the Great Commission includes therefore not only evangelism but also *teaching.* And the task of teaching all that Jesus commanded us is, in a broad sense, the task of teaching what the whole Bible says to us today. To effectively teach ourselves and to teach others what the whole Bible says, it is necessary to *collect* and *summarize* all the Scripture passages on a particular subject.

For example, if someone asks me, "What does the Bible teach about Christ's return?" I could say, "Just keep reading your Bible and you'll find out." But if the questioner begins reading at Genesis 1:1 it will be a long time before he or she finds the answer to his question. By that time many other questions will have needed answers, and his list of unanswered questions will begin to grow very long indeed. What does the Bible teach about the work of the Holy Spirit? What does the Bible teach about prayer? What does the Bible teach about sin? There simply is not time in our lifetimes to read through the entire Bible looking for an answer for ourselves every time a doctrinal question arises. Therefore, for us to learn what the Bible says, it is very helpful to have the benefit of the work of others who have searched through Scripture and found answers to these various topics.

We can teach others most effectively if we can direct them to the most relevant passages and suggest an appropriate summary of the teachings of those passages. Then the person who questions us can inspect those passages quickly for himself or herself and learn much more rapidly what the teaching of the Bible is on a particular subject. Thus the necessity of systematic theology for teaching what the Bible says comes about primarily because we are finite in our memory and in the amount of time at our disposal.

The basic reason for studying systematic theology, then, is that it enables us to teach ourselves and others what the whole Bible says, thus fulfilling the second part of the Great Commission.

2. The Benefits to Our Lives. Although the basic reason for studying systematic theology is that it is a means of obedience to our Lord's command, there are some additional specific benefits that come from such study.

First, studying theology helps us *overcome our wrong ideas.* If there were no sin in our hearts, we could read the Bible from cover to cover and, although we would not immediately learn everything in the Bible, we would most likely learn only true things about God and his creation. Every time we read it we would learn more true things and we would not rebel or refuse to accept anything we found written there. But with sin in our hearts we retain some rebelliousness against God. At various points there are—for all of us—biblical teachings which for one reason or another we do not want to accept. The study of systematic theology is of help in overcoming those rebellious ideas.

For example, suppose there is someone who does not want to believe that Jesus is personally coming back to earth again. We could show this person one verse or perhaps two that speak of Jesus' return to earth, but the person might still find a way to evade the force of those verses or read a different meaning into them. But if we collect twenty-five or thirty verses that say that Jesus is coming back to earth personally and write them all out on paper, our friend who hesitated to believe in Christ's return is much more likely to be persuaded by the breadth and diversity of biblical evidence for this doctrine. Of course, we all have areas like that, areas where our understanding of the Bible's teaching is inadequate. In these areas, it is helpful for us to be confronted with the *total weight of the teaching of Scripture* on that subject, so that we will more readily be persuaded even against our initial wrongful inclinations.

Second, studying systematic theology helps us to be *able to make better decisions later* on new questions of doctrine that may arise. We cannot know what new doctrinal controversies will arise in the churches in which we will live and minister ten, twenty, or thirty years from now, if the Lord does not return before then. These new doctrinal controversies will sometimes include questions that no one has faced very carefully before. Christians will be asking, "What does the whole Bible say about this subject?" (The precise nature of biblical inerrancy and the appropriate understanding of biblical teaching on gifts of the Holy Spirit are two examples of questions that have arisen in our century with much more forcefulness than ever before in the history of the church.)

Whatever the new doctrinal controversies are in future years, those who have learned systematic theology well will be much better able to answer the new questions that arise. The reason for this is that everything that the Bible says is somehow related to everything else the Bible says (for it all fits together in a consistent way, at least within God's own understanding of reality, and in the nature of God and creation as they really are). Thus the new question will be related to much that has already been learned from Scripture. The more thoroughly that earlier material has been learned, the better able we will be to deal with those new questions.

This benefit extends even more broadly. We face problems of applying Scripture to life in many more contexts than formal doctrinal discussions. What does the Bible teach about husband-wife relationships? About raising children? About witnessing to a friend at work? What principles does Scripture give us for studying psychology, or economics, or the natural sciences? How does it guide us in spending money, or in saving, or in tithing? In every area of inquiry certain theological principles will come to bear, and those who have learned well the theological teachings of the Bible will be much better able to make decisions that are pleasing to God.

A helpful analogy at this point is that of a jigsaw puzzle. If the puzzle represents "what the whole Bible teaches us today about everything" then a course in systematic theology would be like filling in the border and some of the major items pictured in the puzzle. But we will never know everything that the Bible teaches about everything, so our jigsaw puzzle will have many gaps, many pieces that remain to be put in. Solving a new real-life problem is analogous to filling in another section of the jigsaw puzzle: the more pieces one has in place correctly to begin with, the easier it is to fit new pieces in, and the less apt one is to make mistakes. In this book the goal is to enable Christians to put into their "theological jigsaw puzzle" as many pieces with as much accuracy as possible, and to encourage Christians to go on putting in more and more correct pieces for the rest of their lives. The Christian doctrines studied here will act as guidelines to help in the filling in of all other areas, areas that pertain to all aspects of truth in all aspects of life.

Third, studying systematic theology will *help us grow as Christians.* The more we know about God, about his Word, about his relationships to the world and mankind, the better we will trust him, the more fully we will praise him, and the more readily we will obey him. Studying systematic theology rightly will make us more mature Christians. If it does not do this, we are not studying it in the way God intends.

In fact, the Bible often connects sound doctrine with maturity in Christian living: Paul speaks of "*the teaching which accords with godliness*" (1 Tim. 6:3) and says that his work as an apostle is "to further the faith of God's elect and their knowledge of *the truth which accords with godliness*" (Titus 1:1). By contrast, he indicates that all kinds of disobedience and immorality are "contrary to sound doctrine" (1 Tim. 1:10).

In connection with this idea it is appropriate to ask what the difference is between a "major doctrine" and a "minor doctrine." Christians often say they want to seek agreement in the church on major doctrines but also to allow for differences on minor doctrines. I have found the following guideline useful:

> A major doctrine is one that has a significant impact on our thinking about other doctrines, or that has a significant impact on how we live the Christian life. A minor doctrine is one that has very little impact on how we think about other doctrines, and very little impact on how we live the Christian life.

By this standard doctrines such as the authority of the Bible, the Trinity, the deity of Christ, justification by faith, and many others would rightly be considered major doctrines. People who disagree with the historic evangelical understanding of any of these doctrines will have wide areas of difference with evangelical Christians who affirm these doctrines. By contrast, it seems to me that differences over forms of church government or some details about the Lord's Supper or the timing of the great tribulation concern minor doctrines. Christians who differ over these things can agree on perhaps every other area of doctrine, can live Christian lives that differ in no important way, and can have genuine fellowship with one another.

Of course, we may find doctrines that fall somewhere between "major" and "minor" according to this standard. For example, Christians may differ over the degree of significance that should attach to the doctrine of baptism or the millennium or the extent of the atonement. That is only natural, because many doctrines have *some* influence on other doctrines or on life, but we may differ over whether we think it to be a "significant" influence. We could even recognize that there will be a range of significance here and just say that the more influence a doctrine has on other doctrines and on life, the more "major" it becomes. This amount of influence may even vary according to the historical circumstances and needs of the church at any given time. In such cases, Christians will need to ask God to give them mature wisdom and sound judgment as they try to determine to what extent a doctrine should be considered "major" in their particular circumstances.

D. A Note on Two Objections to the Study of Systematic Theology

1. "The Conclusions Are 'Too Neat' to be True." Some scholars look with suspicion at systematic theology when—or even because—its teachings fit together in a noncontradictory way. They object that the results are "too neat" and that systematic theologians must therefore be squeezing the Bible's teachings into an artificial mold, distorting the true meaning of Scripture to get an orderly set of beliefs.

To this objection two responses can be made: (1) We must first ask the people making the objection to tell us at what specific points Scripture has been misinterpreted, and then we must deal with the understanding of those passages. Perhaps mistakes have been made, and in that case there should be corrections.

Yet it is also possible that the objector will have no specific passages in mind, or no clearly erroneous interpretations to point to in the works of the most responsible evangelical theologians. Of course, incompetent exegesis can be found in the writings of the less competent scholars in *any* field of biblical studies, not just in systematic theology, but those "bad examples" constitute an objection not against the scholar's field but against the incompetent scholar himself.

It is very important that the objector be specific at this point because this objection is sometimes made by those who—perhaps unconsciously—have adopted from our culture a skeptical view of the possibility of finding universally true conclusions about anything, even about God from his Word. This kind of skepticism regarding theological truth is especially common in the modern university world where "systematic theology"—if it is studied at all—is studied only from the perspectives of philosophical theology and historical theology (including perhaps a historical study of the various ideas that were believed by the early Christians who wrote the New Testament, and by other Christians at that time and throughout church history). In this kind of intellectual climate the study of "systematic theology" as defined in this chapter would be considered impossible, because the Bible would be assumed to be merely the work of many human authors who wrote out of diverse cultures and experiences over the course of more than one thousand years: trying to find "what the whole Bible teaches" about any subject would be thought nearly as hopeless as trying to find "what all philosophers teach" about some question, for the answer in both cases would be thought to be not one view but many diverse and often conflicting views. This skeptical viewpoint must be rejected by evangelicals who see Scripture as the product of human *and* divine authorship, and therefore as a collection of writings that teach noncontradictory truths about God and about the universe he created.

(2) Second, it must be answered that in God's own mind, and in the nature of reality itself, *true* facts and ideas are all consistent with one another. Therefore if we have accurately understood the teachings of God in Scripture we should expect our conclusions to

"fit together" and be mutually consistent. Internal consistency, then, is an argument for, not against, any individual results of systematic theology.

2. "The Choice of Topics Dictates the Conclusions." Another general objection to systematic theology concerns the choice and arrangement of topics, and even the fact that such topically arranged study of Scripture, using categories sometimes different from those found in Scripture itself, is done at all. Why are *these* theological topics treated rather than just the topics emphasized by the biblical authors, and why are the topics *arranged in this way* rather than in some other way? Perhaps—this objection would say—our traditions and our cultures have determined the topics we treat and the arrangement of topics, so that the results of this systematic-theological study of Scripture, though acceptable in our own theological tradition, will in fact be untrue to Scripture itself.

A variant of this objection is the statement that our starting point often determines our conclusions on controversial topics: if we decide to start with an emphasis on the divine authorship of Scripture, for example, we will end up believing in biblical inerrancy, but if we start with an emphasis on the human authorship of Scripture, we will end up believing there are some errors in the Bible. Similarly, if we start with an emphasis on God's sovereignty, we will end up as Calvinists, but if we start with an emphasis on man's ability to make free choices, we will end up as Arminians, and so forth. This objection makes it sound as if the most important theological questions could probably be decided by flipping a coin to decide where to start, since *different* and *equally valid* conclusions will inevitably be reached from the different starting points.

Those who make such an objection often suggest that the best way to avoid this problem is not to study or teach systematic theology at all, but to limit our topical studies to the field of biblical theology, treating only the topics and themes the biblical authors themselves emphasize and describing the historical development of these biblical themes through the Bible.

In response to this objection, much of the discussion in this chapter about the necessity to teach Scripture will be relevant. Our choice of topics need not be restricted to the main concerns of the biblical authors, for our goal is to find out what God requires of us in all areas of concern to us today.

For example, it was not the *main* concern of any New Testament author to explain such topics as "baptism in the Holy Spirit," or women's roles in the church, or the doctrine of the Trinity, but these are valid areas of concern for us today, and we must look at all the places in Scripture that have relevance for those topics (whether those specific terms are mentioned or not, and whether those themes are of primary concern to each passage we examine or not) if we are going to be able to understand and explain to others "what the whole Bible teaches" about them.

The only alternative—for we *will* think *something* about those subjects—is to form our opinions haphazardly from a general impression of what we feel to be a "biblical" position on each subject, or perhaps to buttress our positions with careful analysis of one or two relevant texts, yet with no guarantee that those texts present a balanced view of "the whole counsel of God" (Acts 20:27) on the subject being considered. In fact this approach—one all too common in evangelical circles today—could, I suppose, be called "unsystematic theology" or even "disorderly and random theology"! Such an alternative is too subjective and too subject to cultural pressures. It tends toward doctrinal fragmentation and widespread doctrinal uncertainty, leaving the church theologically immature, like "children, tossed to and fro and carried about with every wind of doctrine" (Eph. 4:14).

Concerning the objection about the choice and sequence of topics, there is nothing to prevent us from going to Scripture to look for answers to *any* doctrinal questions, considered in *any sequence.* The sequence of topics in this book is a very common one and has been adopted because it is orderly and lends itself well to learning and teaching. But the chapters could be read in any sequence one wanted and the conclusions should not be different, nor should the persuasiveness of the arguments—if they are rightly derived from Scripture—be significantly diminished. I have tried to write the chapters so that they can be read as independent units.

E. How Should Christians Study Systematic Theology?

How then should we study systematic theology? The Bible provides some guidelines for answering this question.

1. We Should Study Systematic Theology With Prayer. If studying systematic theology is simply a certain way of studying the Bible, then the passages in Scripture that talk about the way in which we should study God's Word give guidance to us in this task. Just as the psalmist prays in Psalm 119:18, "Open my eyes, that I may behold wondrous things out of your law," so we should pray and seek God's help in understanding his Word. Paul tells us in 1 Corinthians 2:14 that "the unspiritual man does not receive the gifts of the Spirit of God, for they are folly to him, and he is not able to understand them because they are spiritually discerned." Studying theology is therefore a spiritual activity in which we need the help of the Holy Spirit.

No matter how intelligent, if the student does not continue to pray for God to give him or her an understanding mind and a believing and humble heart, and the student does not maintain a personal walk with the Lord, then the teachings of Scripture will be misunderstood and disbelieved, doctrinal error will result, and the mind and heart of the student will not be changed for the better but for the worse. Students of systematic theology should resolve at the beginning to keep their lives free from any disobedience to God or any known sin that would disrupt their relationship with him. They should resolve to maintain with great regularity their own personal devotional lives. They should continually pray for wisdom and understanding of Scripture.

Since it is the Holy Spirit who gives us the ability rightly to understand Scripture, we need to realize that the proper thing to do, particularly when we are unable to understand some passage or some doctrine of Scripture, is to pray for God's help. Often what we need is not more data but more insight into the data we already have available. This insight is given only by the Holy Spirit (cf. 1 Cor. 2:14; Eph. 1:17–19).

2. We Should Study Systematic Theology With Humility. Peter tells us, "Clothe yourselves, all of you, with humility toward one another, for 'God opposes the proud, but gives grace to the humble'" (1 Peter 5:5). Those who study systematic theology will learn many things about the teachings of Scripture that are perhaps not known or not known well by other Christians in their churches or by relatives who are older in the Lord than they are. They may also find that they understand things about Scripture that some of their church officers do not understand, and that even their pastor has perhaps forgotten or never learned well.

In all of these situations it would be very easy to adopt an attitude of pride or superiority toward others who have not made such a study. But how ugly it would be if anyone were to use this knowledge of God's Word simply to win arguments or to put down a fellow Christian in conversation, or to make another believer feel insignificant in the Lord's work. James' counsel is good for us at this point: "Let every man be quick to hear, slow to speak, slow to anger, for the anger of man does not work the righteousness of God" (James 1:19–20). He tells us that one's understanding of Scripture is to be imparted in humility and love:

> Who is wise and understanding among you? By his good life let him show his works in the meekness of wisdom. . . . But the wisdom from above is first pure, then peaceable, gentle, open to reason, full of mercy and good fruits, without uncertainty or insincerity. And the harvest of righteousness is sown in peace by those who make peace. (James 3:13, 17–18)

Systematic theology rightly studied will not lead to the knowledge that "puffs up" (1 Cor. 8:1) but to humility and love for others.

3. We Should Study Systematic Theology With Reason. We find in the New Testament that Jesus and the New Testament authors will often quote a verse of Scripture and then draw logical conclusions from it. They *reason* from Scripture. It is therefore not wrong to use human understanding, human logic, and human reason to draw conclusions from the statements of Scripture. Nevertheless, when we reason and draw what we think to be correct logical deductions from Scripture, we sometimes make mistakes. The deductions we draw from the statements of Scripture are not equal to the statements of Scripture themselves in certainty or authority, for our ability to reason and draw conclusions is not the ultimate standard of truth—only Scripture is.

What then are the limits on our use of our reasoning abilities to draw deductions from the statements of Scripture? The fact that reasoning to conclusions that go beyond the mere statements of Scripture is appropriate and even necessary for studying Scripture, and the fact that Scripture itself is the ultimate standard of truth, combine to indicate to us that *we are free to use our reasoning abilities to draw deductions from any passage of Scripture so long as these deductions do not contradict the clear teaching of some other passage of Scripture.*[7]

This principle puts a safeguard on our use of what we think to be logical deductions from Scripture. Our supposedly logical deductions may be erroneous, but Scripture itself cannot be erroneous. Thus, for example, we may read Scripture and find that God the Father is called God (1 Cor. 1:3), that God the Son is called God (John 20:28; Titus 2:13), and that God the Holy Spirit is called God (Acts 5:3–4). We might deduce from this that there are three Gods. But then we find the Bible explicitly teaching us that God is one

(Deut. 6:4; James 2:19). Thus we conclude that what we *thought* to be a valid logical deduction about three Gods was wrong and that Scripture teaches both (a) that there are three separate persons (the Father, the Son, and the Holy Spirit), each of whom is fully God, and (b) that there is one God.

We cannot understand exactly how these two statements can both be true, so together they constitute a *paradox* ("a seemingly contradictory statement that may nonetheless be true").[8] We can tolerate a paradox (such as "God is three persons and one God") because we have confidence that ultimately God knows fully the truth about himself and about the nature of reality, and that in his understanding the different elements of a paradox are fully reconciled, even though at this point God's thoughts are higher than our thoughts (Isa. 55:8–9). But a true contradiction (such as, "God is three persons and God is not three persons") would imply ultimate contradiction in God's own understanding of himself or of reality, and this cannot be.

When the psalmist says, "The sum of your word is truth; and every one of your righteous ordinances endures for ever" (Ps. 119:160), he implies that God's words are not only true individually but also viewed together as a whole. Viewed collectively, their "sum" is also "truth." Ultimately, there is no internal contradiction either in Scripture or in God's own thoughts.

4. We Should Study Systematic Theology With Help From Others. We need to be thankful that God has put teachers in the church ("And God has appointed in the church

---

[7]This guideline is also adopted from Professor John Frame at Westminster Seminary.

[8]The *American Heritage Dictionary of the English Language,* ed. William Morris (Boston: Houghton-Mifflin, 1980), p. 950 (first definition). Essentially the same meaning is adopted by the *Oxford English Dictionary* (1913 ed., 7:450), the *Concise Oxford Dictionary* (1981 ed., p. 742), the *Random House College Dictionary* (1979 ed., p. 964), and the *Chambers Twentieth Century Dictionary* (p. 780), though all note that *paradox* can also mean "contradiction" (though less commonly); compare the *Encyclopedia of Philosophy,* ed. Paul Edwards (New York: Macmillan and The Free Press, 1967), 5:45, and the entire article "Logical Paradoxes" by John van Heijenoort on pp. 45–51 of the same volume, which proposes solutions to many of the classical paradoxes in the history of philosophy. (If *paradox* meant "contradiction," such solutions would be impossible.)

When I use the word *paradox* in the primary sense defined by these dictionaries today I realize that I am differing somewhat with the article "Paradox" by K. S. Kantzer in the *EDT,* ed. Walter Elwell, pp. 826–27 (which takes *paradox* to mean essentially "contradiction"). However, I am using *paradox* in an ordinary English sense and one also familiar in philosophy. There seems to me to be available no better word than *paradox* to refer to an apparent but not real contradiction.

There is, however, some lack of uniformity in the use of the term *paradox* and a related term, *antinomy,* in contemporary evangelical discussion. The word *antinomy* has sometimes been used to apply to what I here call *paradox,* that is, "seemingly contradictory statements that may nonetheless both be true" (see, for example, John Jefferson Davis, *Theology Primer* [Grand Rapids: Baker, 1981], p. 18). Such a sense for *antinomy* gained support in a widely read book, *Evangelism and the Sovereignty of God,* by J. I. Packer (London: Inter-Varsity Press, 1961). On pp. 18–22 Packer defines *antinomy* as "an appearance of contradiction" (but admits on p. 18 that his definition differs with the *Shorter Oxford Dictionary*). My problem with using *antinomy* in this sense is that the word is so unfamiliar in ordinary English that it just increases the stock of technical terms Christians have to learn in order to understand theologians, and moreover such a sense is unsupported by any of the dictionaries cited above, all of which define *antinomy* to mean "contradiction" (e.g., *Oxford English Dictionary,* 1:371). The problem is not serious, but it would help communication if evangelicals could agree on uniform senses for these terms.

A paradox is certainly acceptable in systematic theology, and paradoxes are in fact inevitable so long as we have finite understanding of any theological topic. However, it is important to recognize that Christian theology should never affirm a *contradiction* (a set of two statements, one of which denies the other). A contradiction would be, "God is three persons and God is not three persons" (where the term *persons* has the same sense in both halves of the sentence).

first apostles, second prophets, third *teachers* . . ." [1 Cor. 12:28]. We should allow those with gifts of teaching to help us understand Scripture. This means that we should make use of systematic theologies and other books that have been written by some of the teachers that God has given to the church over the course of its history. It also means that our study of theology should include *talking with other Christians* about the things we study. Among those with whom we talk will often be some with gifts of teaching who can explain biblical teachings clearly and help us to understand more easily. In fact, some of the most effective learning in systematic theology courses in colleges and seminaries often occurs outside the classroom in informal conversations among students who are attempting to understand Bible doctrines for themselves.

5. We Should Study Systematic Theology by Collecting and Understanding All the Relevant Passages of Scripture on Any Topic. This point was mentioned in our definition of systematic theology at the beginning of the chapter, but the actual process needs to be described here. How does one go about making a doctrinal summary of what all the passages of Scripture teach on a certain topic? For topics covered in this book, many people will think that studying the chapters in this book and reading the Bible verses noted in the chapters is enough. But some people will want to do further study of Scripture on a particular topic or study some new topic not covered here. How could a student go about using the Bible to research its teachings on some new subject, perhaps one not discussed explicitly in any of his or her systematic theology textbooks?

The process would look like this: (1) Find all the relevant verses. The best help in this step is a good concordance, which enables one to look up key words and find the verses in which the subject is treated. For example, in studying what it means that man is created in the image and likeness of God, one needs to find all the verses in which "image" and "likeness" and "create" occur. (The words "man" and "God" occur too often to be useful for a concordance search.) In studying the doctrine of prayer, many words could be looked up (*pray, prayer, intercede, petition, supplication, confess, confession, praise, thanks, thanksgiving,* et al.)—and perhaps the list of verses would grow too long to be manageable, so that the student would have to skim the concordance entries without looking up the verses, or the search would probably have to be divided into sections or limited in some other way. Verses can also be found by thinking through the overall history of the Bible and then turning to sections where there would be information on the topic at hand—for example, a student studying prayer would want to read passages like the one about Hannah's prayer for a son (in 1 Sam. 1), Solomon's prayer at the dedication of the temple (in 1 Kings 8), Jesus' prayer in the Garden of Gethsemane (in Matt. 26 and parallels), and so forth. Then in addition to concordance work and reading other passages that one can find on the subject, checking the relevant sections in some systematic theology books will often bring to light other verses that had been missed, sometimes because none of the key words used for the concordance were in those verses.[9]

(2) The second step is to read, make notes on, and try to summarize the points made in the relevant verses. Sometimes a theme will be repeated often and the summary of the various verses will be relatively easy. At other times, there will be verses difficult to understand, and the student will need to take some time to study a verse in depth

(just by reading the verse in context over and over, or by using specialized tools such as commentaries and dictionaries) until a satisfactory understanding is reached.

(3) Finally, the teachings of the various verses should be summarized into one or more points that the Bible affirms about that subject. The summary does not have to take the exact form of anyone else's conclusions on the subject, because we each may see things in Scripture that others have missed, or we may organize the subject differently or emphasize different things.

On the other hand, at this point it is also helpful to read related sections, if any can be found, in several systematic theology books. This provides a useful check against error and oversight, and often makes one aware of alternative perspectives and arguments that may cause us to modify or strengthen our position. If a student finds that others have argued for strongly differing conclusions, then these other views need to be stated fairly and then answered. Sometimes other theology books will alert us to historical or philosophical considerations that have been raised before in the history of the church, and these will provide additional insight or warnings against error.

The process outlined above is possible for any Christian who can read his or her Bible and can look up words in a concordance. Of course people will become faster and more accurate in this process with time and experience and Christian maturity, but it would be a tremendous help to the church if Christians generally would give much more time to searching out topics in Scripture for themselves and drawing conclusions in the way outlined above. The joy of discovery of biblical themes would be richly rewarding. Especially pastors and those who lead Bible studies would find added freshness in their understanding of Scripture and in their teaching.

6. We Should Study Systematic Theology With Rejoicing and Praise. The study of theology is not merely a theoretical exercise of the intellect. It is a study of the living God, and of the wonders of all his works in creation and redemption. We cannot study this subject dispassionately! We must love all that God is, all that he says and all that he does. "You shall love the LORD your God with all your heart" (Deut. 6:5). Our response to the study of the theology of Scripture should be that of the psalmist who said, "How precious to me are your thoughts, O God!" (Ps. 139:17). In the study of the teachings of God's Word, it should not surprise us if we often find our hearts spontaneously breaking forth in expressions of praise and delight like those of the psalmist:

> The precepts of the LORD are right,
>   rejoicing the heart. (Ps. 19:8)

> In the way of your testimonies I delight
>   as much as in all riches. (Ps. 119:14)

> How sweet are your words to my taste,

---

[9]I have read a number of student papers telling me that John's gospel says nothing about how Christians should pray, for example, because they looked at a concordance and found that the word *prayer* was not in John, and the word *pray* only occurs four times in reference to Jesus praying in John 14, 16, and 17. They overlooked the fact that John contains several important verses where the word *ask* rather than the word *pray* is used (John 14:13–14; 15:7, 16, et al.).

sweeter than honey to my mouth! (Ps. 119:103)

Your testimonies are my heritage for ever;
yea, they are the joy of my heart. (Ps. 119:111)

I rejoice at your word
like one who finds great spoil. (Ps. 119:162)

Often in the study of theology the response of the Christian should be similar to that of Paul in reflecting on the long theological argument that he has just completed at the end of Romans 11:32. He breaks forth into joyful praise at the richness of the doctrine which God has enabled him to express:

O the depth of the riches and wisdom and knowledge of God! How unsearchable are his judgments and how inscrutable his ways!

"For who has known the mind of the Lord,
or who has been his counselor?"
"Or who has given a gift to him
that he might be repaid?"

For from him and through him and to him are all things. To him be glory for ever. Amen. (Rom. 11:33–36)

QUESTIONS FOR PERSONAL APPLICATION

These questions at the end of each chapter focus on application to life. Because I think doctrine is to be felt at the emotional level as well as understood at the intellectual level, in many chapters I have included some questions about how a reader *feels* regarding a point of doctrine. I think these questions will prove quite valuable for those who take the time to reflect on them.

1. In what ways (if any) has this chapter changed your understanding of what systematic theology is? What was your attitude toward the study of systematic theology before reading this chapter? What is your attitude now?

2. What is likely to happen to a church or denomination that gives up learning systematic theology for a generation or longer? Has that been true of your church?

3. Are there any doctrines listed in the Contents for which a fuller understanding would help to solve a personal difficulty in your life at the present time? What are the spiritual and emotional dangers that you personally need to be aware of in studying systematic theology?

4. Pray for God to make this study of basic Christian doctrines a time of spiritual growth and deeper fellowship with him, and a time in which you understand and apply the teachings of Scripture rightly.

SPECIAL TERMS

apologetics

biblical theology

Christian ethics

contradiction

doctrine

dogmatic theology

historical theology

major doctrine

minor doctrine

New Testament theology

Old Testament theology

paradox

philosophical theology

presupposition

systematic theology

BIBLIOGRAPHY

Baker, D. L. "Biblical Theology." In *NDT*, p. 671.

Berkhof, Louis. *Introduction to Systematic Theology.* Grand Rapids: Eerdmans, 1982, pp. 15–75 (first published 1932).

Bray, Gerald L., ed. *Contours of Christian Theology.* Downers Grove, Ill.: InterVarsity Press, 1993.

_____. "Systematic Theology, History of." In *NDT*, pp. 671–72.

Cameron, Nigel M., ed. *The Challenge of Evangelical Theology: Essays in Approach and Method.* Edinburgh: Rutherford House, 1987.

Carson, D. A. "Unity and Diversity in the New Testament: The Possibility of Systematic Theology." In *Scripture and Truth.* Ed. by D. A. Carson and John Woodbridge. Grand Rapids: Zondervan, 1983, pp. 65–95.

Davis, John Jefferson. *Foundations of Evangelical Theology.* Grand Rapids: Baker, 1984.

_____. *The Necessity of Systematic Theology.* Grand Rapids: Baker, 1980.

_____. *Theology Primer: Resources for the Theological Student.* Grand Rapids: Baker, 1981.

Demarest, Bruce. "Systematic Theology." In *EDT*, pp. 1064–66.

Erickson, Millard. *Concise Dictionary of Christian Theology.* Grand Rapids: Baker, 1986.

Frame, John. *Van Til the Theologian.* Phillipsburg, N.J.: Pilgrim, 1976.

Geehan, E. R., ed. *Jerusalem and Athens.* Nutley, N.J.: Craig Press, 1971.

Grenz, Stanley J. *Revisioning Evangelical Theology: A Fresh Agenda for the 21st Century.* Downers Grove, Ill.: InterVarsity Press, 1993.

House, H. Wayne. *Charts of Christian Theology and Doctrine.* Grand Rapids: Zondervan, 1992.

Kuyper, Abraham. *Principles of Sacred Theology.* Trans. by J. H. DeVries. Grand Rapids: Eerdmans, 1968 (reprint; first published as *Encyclopedia of Sacred Theology* in 1898).

Machen, J. Gresham. *Christianity and Liberalism.* Grand Rapids: Eerdmans, 1923. (This 180-page book is, in my opinion, one of the most significant theological studies ever written. It gives a clear overview of major biblical doctrines and shows the vital differences with Protestant liberal theology at every point, differences that still confront us today. It is required reading in all my introductory theology classes.)

Morrow, T. W. "Systematic Theology." In *NDT*, p. 671.

Poythress, Vern. *Symphonic Theology: The Validity of Multiple Perspectives in Theology.* Grand Rapids: Zondervan, 1987.

Preus, Robert D. *The Theology of Post-Reformation Lutheranism: A Study of Theological Prolegomena.* 2 vols. St. Louis: Concordia, 1970.

Van Til, Cornelius. *In Defense of the Faith,* vol. 5: *An Introduction to Systematic Theology.* N.p.: Presbyterian and Reformed, 1976, pp. 1–61, 253–62.

_____. *The Defense of the Faith.* Philadelphia: Presbyterian and Reformed, 1955.

Vos, Geerhardus. "The Idea of Biblical Theology as a Science and as a Theological Discipline." In *Redemptive History and Biblical Interpretation,* pp. 3–24. Ed. by Richard Gaffin. Phillipsburg, N.J.: Presbyterian and Reformed, 1980 (article first published 1894).

Warfield, B. B. "The Indispensableness of Systematic Theology to the Preacher." In *Selected Shorter Writings of Benjamin B. Warfield,* 2:280–88. Ed. by John E. Meeter. Nutley, N.J.: Presbyterian and Reformed, 1973 (article first published 1897).

_____. "The Right of Systematic Theology." In *Selected Shorter Writings of Benjamin B. Warfield,* 2:21–279. Ed. by John E. Meeter. Nutley, N.J.: Presbyterian and Reformed, 1973 (article first published 1896).

Wells, David. *No Place for Truth, or, Whatever Happened to Evangelical Theology?* Grand Rapids: Eerdmans, 1993.

Woodbridge, John D., and Thomas E. McComiskey, eds. *Doing Theology in Today's World: Essays in Honor of Kenneth S. Kantzer.* Grand Rapids: Zondervan, 1991.

SCRIPTURE MEMORY PASSAGE

Students have repeatedly mentioned that one of the most valuable parts of any of their courses in college or seminary has been the Scripture passages they were required to memorize. "I have hidden your word in my heart that I might not sin against you" (Ps. 119:11 NIV). In each chapter, therefore, I have included an appropriate memory passage so that instructors may incorporate Scripture memory into the course requirements wherever possible. (Scripture memory passages at the end of each chapter are taken from the RSV. These same passages in the NIV and NASB may be found in appendix 2.)

Matthew 28:18–20: *And Jesus came and said to them, "All authority in heaven and on earth has been given to me. Go therefore and make disciples of all nations, baptizing them in the name of the Father and of the Son and of the Holy Spirit, teaching them to observe all that I have commanded you; and lo, I am with you always, to the close of the age."*

HYMN

Systematic theology at its best will result in praise. It is appropriate therefore at the end of each chapter to include a hymn related to the subject of that chapter. In a classroom setting, the hymn can be sung together at the beginning or end of class. Alternatively, an individual reader can sing it privately or simply meditate quietly on the words.

For almost every chapter the words of the hymns were found in *Trinity Hymnal* (Philadelphia: Great Commission Publications, 1990),[10] the hymnal of the Presbyterian Church in America and the Orthodox Presbyterian Church, but most of them are found in many other common hymnals. Unless otherwise noted, the words of these hymns are now in public domain and no longer subject to copyright restrictions: therefore they may be freely copied for overhead projector use or photocopied.

Why have I used so many old hymns? Although I personally like many of the more recent worship songs that have come into wide use, when I began to select hymns that would correspond to the great doctrines of the Christian faith, I realized that the great hymns of the church throughout history have a doctrinal richness and breadth that is still unequaled. For several of the chapters in this book, I know of no modern worship song that covers the same subject in an extended way—perhaps this can be a challenge to modern songwriters to study these chapters and then write songs reflecting the teaching of Scripture on the respective subjects.

For this chapter, however, I found no hymn ancient or modern that thanked God for the privilege of studying systematic theology from the pages of Scripture. Therefore I have selected a hymn of general praise, which is always appropriate.

"O for a Thousand Tongues to Sing"

This hymn by Charles Wesley (1707–88) begins by wishing for "a thousand tongues" to sing God's praise. Verse 2 is a prayer that God would "assist me" in singing his praise throughout the earth. The remaining verses give praise to Jesus (vv. 3–6) and to God the Father (v. 7).

> O for a thousand tongues to sing
> My great Redeemer's praise,
> The glories of my God and King,
> The triumphs of His grace.
>
> My gracious Master and my God,
> Assist me to proclaim,
> To spread through all the earth abroad,
> The honors of Thy name.
>
> Jesus! the name that charms our fears,
> That bids our sorrows cease;
> 'Tis music in the sinner's ears,
> 'Tis life and health and peace.
>
> He breaks the pow'r of reigning sin,
> He sets the prisoner free;
> His blood can make the foulest clean;

---

[10]This hymn book is completely revised from a similar hymnal of the same title published by the Orthodox Presbyterian Church in WW 1961.

His blood availed for me.

He speaks and, list'ning to His voice,
New life the dead receive;
The mournful, broken hearts rejoice;
The humble poor believe.

Hear him, ye deaf; his praise, ye dumb,
Your loosened tongues employ,
Ye blind, behold your Savior come;
And leap, ye lame, for joy.

Glory to God and praise and love
Be ever, ever giv'n
By saints below and saints above —
The church in earth and heav'n.

AUTHOR: CHARLES WESLEY, 1739, ALT.

COMMON GRACE

What are the undeserved blessings that God gives to all people, both believers and unbelievers?

EXPLANATION AND SCRIPTURAL BASIS

A. Introduction and Definition

When Adam and Eve sinned, they became worthy of eternal punishment and separation from God (Gen. 2:17). In the same way, when human beings sin today they become liable to the wrath of God and to eternal punishment: "The wages of sin is death" (Rom. 6:23). This means that once people sin, God's justice would require only one thing—that they be eternally separated from God, cut off from experiencing *any* good from him, and that they live forever in hell, receiving only his wrath eternally. In fact, this was what happened to angels who sinned, and it could justly have happened to us as well: "*God did not spare the angels when they sinned,* but cast them into hell and committed them to pits of nether gloom to be kept until the judgment" (2 Peter 2:4).

But in fact Adam and Eve did not die at once (though the sentence of death *began* to be worked out in their lives on the day they sinned). The full execution of the sentence of death was delayed for many years. Moreover, millions of their descendants even to this day do not die and go to hell as soon as they sin, but continue to live for many years, enjoying countless blessings in this world. How can this be? *How can God continue to give blessings to sinners who deserve only death*—not only to those who will ultimately be saved, but also to millions who will never be saved, whose sins will never be forgiven?

The answer to these questions is that God bestows *common grace.* We may define common grace as follows: *Common grace is the grace of God by which he gives people innumerable blessings that are not part of salvation.* The word *common* here means something that is common to all people and is not restricted to believers or to the elect only.

In distinction from common grace, the grace of God that brings people to salvation is often called "saving grace." Of course, when we talk about "common grace" and "saving grace" we are not implying that there are two different kinds of grace in God himself, but only that God's grace manifests itself in the world in two different ways. Common grace is different from saving grace in its *results* (it does not bring about salvation), in its *recipients* (it is given to believers and unbelievers alike), and in its *source* (it does not directly flow from Christ's atoning work, since Christ's death did not earn any measure of forgiveness for unbelievers, and therefore did not merit the blessings of common grace for them either). However, on this last point it should be said that common grace does flow *indirectly* from Christ's redemptive work, because the fact that God did not judge the world at once when sin entered it was primarily or perhaps exclusively due to the fact that he planned eventually to save some sinners through the death of his Son.[1]

B. Examples of Common Grace

If we look at the world around us and contrast it with the fires of hell that the world deserves, we can immediately see abundant evidence of God's common grace in thousands of examples in everyday life. We can distinguish several specific categories in which this common grace is seen.

1. The Physical Realm. Unbelievers continue to live in this world solely because of God's common grace — every breath that people take is of grace, for the wages of sin is death, not life. Moreover, the earth does not produce only thorns and thistles (Gen. 3:18), or remain a parched desert, but by God's common grace it produces food and materials for clothing and shelter, often in great abundance and diversity. Jesus said, "Love your enemies and pray for those who persecute you, so that you may be sons of your Father who is in heaven; for *he makes his sun rise on the evil and on the good, and sends rain on the just and on the unjust*" (Matt. 5:44–45). Here Jesus appeals to God's abundant common grace as an encouragement to his disciples that they too should bestow love and prayer for blessing on unbelievers (cf. Luke 6:35–36). Similarly, Paul told the people of Lystra, "In past generations he allowed all the nations to walk in their own ways; yet he did not leave himself without witness, for he did good and *gave you from heaven rains and fruitful seasons, satisfying your hearts with food and gladness*" (Acts 14:16–17).

The Old Testament also speaks of the common grace of God that comes to unbelievers as well as to believers. One specific example is Potiphar, the Egyptian captain of the guard who purchased Joseph as a slave: "*The Lord blessed the Egyptian's house* for Joseph's sake; the blessing of the Lord was upon all that he had, in house and field" (Gen. 39:5). David speaks in a much more general way about all the creatures God has made: "The Lord is good to all, and his compassion is over all that he has made. . . . The eyes of all look to you, and you give them their food in due season. You open your hand, you satisfy the desire of every living thing" (Ps. 145:9, 15–16).

These verses are another reminder that the goodness that is found in the whole creation is due to God's goodness and compassion.

---

[1]I have included this chapter in this book, not because common grace flows directly from Christ's redemptive work (it does not), but because it has a role of preparing for and assisting in God's work of the application of redemption to believers.

We even see evidence of God's common grace in the beauty of the natural world. Though nature itself is in "bondage to decay" and has been "subjected to futility" (Rom. 8:21, 20) because of the curse of the fall (Gen. 3:17–19), much beauty still remains in the natural world. The beauty of multicolored flowers, of grass and woodlands, of rivers and lakes and mountains and ocean shores, still remains as a daily testimony to the continuing common grace of God. Unbelievers deserve to enjoy none of this beauty, but by God's grace they can enjoy much of it for their whole lives.

2. The Intellectual Realm. Satan is "a liar and the father of lies" and "there is no truth in him" (John 8:44), because he is fully given over to evil and to the irrationality and commitment to falsehood that accompanies radical evil. But human beings in the world today, even unbelievers, are not totally given over to lying, irrationality, and ignorance. All people are able to have some grasp of truth; indeed, some have great intelligence and understanding. This also must be seen as a result of God's grace. John speaks of Jesus as "the true light that *enlightens every man*" (John 1:9), for in his role as creator and sustainer of the universe (not particularly in his role as redeemer) the Son of God allows enlightenment and understanding to come to all people in the world.[2]

God's common grace in the intellectual realm is seen in the fact that all people have a knowledge of God: "Although *they knew God* they did not honor him as God or give thanks to him" (Rom. 1:21). This means that there is a sense of God's existence and often a hunger to know God that he allows to remain in people's hearts, even though it often results in many differing man-made religions. Therefore, even when speaking to people who held to false religions, Paul could find a point of contact regarding knowledge of God's existence, as he did when speaking to the Athenian philosophers: "Men of Athens, I perceive that in every way you are very religious.... What therefore you worship as unknown, this I proclaim to you" (Acts 17:22–23).

The common grace of God in the intellectual realm also results in an ability to grasp truth and distinguish it from error, and to experience growth in knowledge that can be used in the investigation of the universe and in the task of subduing the earth. This means that *all science and technology carried out by non-Christians is a result of common grace,* allowing them to make incredible discoveries and inventions, to develop the earth's resources into many material goods, to produce and distribute those resources, and to have skill in their productive work. In a practical sense this means that every time

---

[2]Since the context of John 1 is talking about Christ coming into the world, it is better to take the phrase "was coming into the world" to modify the true light, Christ (so RSV, NASB, NIV), rather than every man (so KJV, NASB mg., NIV mg.), though both are grammatically possible. In either case, the verse still says that Christ enlightens every man. Though some have argued that this enlightening is just the shining of the light of Christ's incarnate presence in the world (so D. A. Carson, *The Gospel According to John* [Grand Rapids: Eerdmans, 1991], pp. 123–24), it is more likely that this enlightening is the light of general revelation that all people receive, the ability to observe and understand many true facts about God and the universe (so Leon Morris,

The Gospel According to John [Grand Rapids: Eerdmans, 1971], pp. 94–95). This is because (1) when John specifies that Christ "enlightens *every man*" (rather than "all men" or "the world") he suggests to us that this enlightening takes place for every individual, which would be true of general knowledge, but not of knowledge of Christ. (2) This sense allows the word "enlightens" to speak of an *actual* enlightening, not just a potential one: Christ here is said to enlighten, not just to offer enlightenment. (3) This sense heightens the ironic contrast in vv. 9–10: though Christ gives knowledge to all men, and though he created all men, yet they did not know him or receive him.

we walk into a grocery store or ride in an automobile or enter a house we should remember that we are experiencing the results of the abundant common grace of God poured out so richly on all mankind.

3. The Moral Realm. God also by common grace restrains people from being as evil as they could be. Once again the demonic realm, totally devoted to evil and destruction, provides a clear contrast with human society in which evil is clearly restrained. If people persist hard-heartedly and repeatedly in following sin over a course of time, God will eventually "give them up" to greater and greater sin (cf. Ps. 81:12; Rom. 1:24, 26, 28), but in the case of most human beings they do not fall to the depths to which their sin would otherwise take them, because God intervenes and puts restraints on their conduct. One very effective restraint is the force of conscience: Paul says, "When Gentiles who have not the law do by nature what the law requires, they are a law to themselves, even though they do not have the law. They show that *what the law requires is written on their hearts,* while *their conscience also bears witness* and their conflicting thoughts accuse or perhaps excuse them" (Rom. 2:14–15).

This inward sense of right and wrong that God gives to all people means that they will frequently approve of moral standards that reflect many of the moral standards in Scripture. Even those who are given up to the most base sin, Paul says, "Know God's decree that those who do such things deserve to die" (Rom. 1:32). And in many other cases this inward sense of conscience leads people to establish laws and customs in society that are, in terms of the outward behavior they approve or prohibit, quite like the moral laws of Scripture: people often establish laws or have customs that respect the sanctity of marriage and the family, protect human life, and prohibit theft and falsehood in speech.[3] Because of this, people will frequently live in ways that are morally upright and outwardly conform to the moral standards found in Scripture. Though their moral behavior cannot earn merit with God (since Scripture clearly says that "no man is justified before God by the law," Gal. 3:11, and "All have turned aside, together they have gone wrong; no one does good, not even one," Rom. 3:12), nevertheless in some sense less than earning God's eternal approval or merit, unbelievers do "do good." Jesus implies this when he says, "If you do good to those *who do good to you,* what credit is that to you? For *even sinners do the same*" (Luke 6:33; cf. 2 Kings 12:2 and 2 Chron. 24:2, where Joash is said to have done good during his reign as king, with 2 Chron. 24:17–25, where he did such evil as to make it apparent that there was not saving faith in his life). Of course, in areas where the gospel has had great influence and the church is strong, it will have a stronger moral influence on society than in places where the gospel has never reached, or where it has little restraining influence (for example, in cannibalistic societies—or even in modern Western society where belief in the gospel and moral absolutes have both been abandoned by the dominant culture).

God also demonstrates his common grace by giving *warnings of final judgment in the operation of the natural world.* God has so ordered the world that living according to

---

[3]Of course, the operation of conscience is never perfect in sinful people in this life (as Paul realizes in Rom. 2:15), so societies will vary in the degree to which they approve differing aspects of God's moral laws. Nevertheless, significant resemblance to the moral laws of Scripture is found in the laws and customs of every human society.

his moral standards very often brings rewards in the natural realm, and violating God's standards often brings destruction to people, in both cases indicating the eventual direction of the final judgment: Honesty, hard work, showing love and kindness to others, and faithfulness in marriage and family will (except in the most corrupt societies) bring much more material and emotional reward in this life than dishonesty, laziness, cruelty, marital infidelity, and other wrongs such as drunkenness, drug abuse, theft, and so forth. These normal consequences of sin or righteousness should serve as a warning of judgment to come, and, in this way, they are also examples of God's common grace.

4. The Creative Realm. God has allowed significant measures of skill in artistic and musical areas, as well as in other spheres in which creativity and skill can be expressed, such as athletics, cooking, writing, and so forth. Moreover, God gives to us an ability to appreciate beauty in many areas of life. And in this area as well as in the physical and intellectual realm, the blessings of common grace are sometimes poured out on unbelievers even more abundantly than on believers. Yet in all cases it is a result of the grace of God.

5. The Societal Realm. God's grace is also evident in the existence of various organizations and structures in human society. We see this first in the human family, evidenced in the fact that Adam and Eve remained husband and wife after the fall and then had children, both sons and daughters (Gen. 5:4). Adam and Eve's children married and formed families for themselves (Gen. 4:17, 19, 26). The human family persists today, not simply as an institution for believers, but for all people.

Human government is also a result of common grace. It was instituted in principle by God after the flood (see Gen. 9:6), and is clearly stated to be given by God in Romans 13:1: "There is no authority except from God, and those that exist have been instituted by God." It is clear that government is a gift from God for mankind generally, for Paul says the ruler is "God's servant for your good" and that he is "the servant of God to execute his wrath on the wrongdoer" (Rom. 13:4). One of the primary means God uses to restrain evil in the world is human government. Human laws and police forces and judicial systems provide a powerful deterrent to evil actions, and these are necessary, for there is much evil in the world that is irrational and that can only be restrained by force, because it will not be deterred by reason or education. Of course, the sinfulness of man can also affect governments themselves, so that they become corrupt and actually encourage evil rather than encourage good. This is just to say that human government, like all the other blessings of common grace that God gives, can be used either for good or for evil purposes.

Other organizations in human society include educational institutions, businesses and corporations, voluntary associations (such as many charitable and public service groups), and countless examples of ordinary human friendship. All of these function to bring some measure of good to human beings, and all are expressions of the common grace of God.

6. The Religious Realm. Even in the realm of human religion, God's common grace brings some blessings to unbelieving people. Jesus tells us, "Love your enemies and *pray for those who persecute you*" (Matt. 5:44), and since there is no restriction in the context simply to pray for their salvation, and since the command to pray for our persecutors is coupled with a command to love them, it seems reasonable to conclude that God intends to answer our prayers even for our persecutors with regard to many areas of life. In fact, Paul specifically commands that we pray "for kings and all who are in high positions" (1 Tim. 2:1–2). When we seek good for unbelievers it is consistent with God's own practice of granting sunshine and rain "on the just and on the unjust" (Matt. 5:45) and also consistent with the practice of Jesus during his earthly ministry when he healed every person who was brought to him (Luke 4:40). There is no indication that he required all of them to believe in him or to agree that he was the Messiah before he granted physical healing to them.

Does God answer the prayers of unbelievers? Although God has not promised to answer the prayers of unbelievers as he has promised to answer the prayers of those who come in Jesus' name, and although he has no obligation to answer the prayers of unbelievers, nonetheless, God may out of his common grace still hear and grant the prayers of unbelievers, thus demonstrating his mercy and goodness in yet another way (cf. Ps. 145:9, 15; Matt. 7:22; Luke 6:35–36). This is apparently the sense of 1 Timothy 4:10, which says that God is "the Savior of all men, especially of those who believe." Here "Savior" cannot be restricted in meaning to "one who forgives sins and gives eternal life," because these things are not given to those who do not believe; "Savior" must have a more general sense here, namely, "one who rescues from distress, one who delivers." In cases of trouble or distress God often does hear the prayers of unbelievers, and graciously delivers them from their trouble. Moreover, even unbelievers often have a sense of gratitude toward God for the goodness of creation, for deliverance from danger, and for the blessings of family, home, friendships, and country. In addition, unbelievers who come in close contact with the church and perhaps associate with it for a time can have some religious experiences that seem very close to the experience of those who are saved (see Heb. 6:4–6; Matt. 7:22–23).[4]

Finally, even the proclamation of the gospel to those who do not ultimately accept it is a clear declaration of the mercy and grace of God, which gives clear witness to the fact that God does not delight in the death or condemnation of any of his creatures (cf. Ezek. 33:11; 1 Tim. 2:4).

7. Common Grace and Special Grace Influence Each Other. Common grace, of course, influences and enriches the church, since apart from God's common grace given to carpenters and other kinds of craftsmen, there would be no church buildings; apart from common grace given to printers and typesetters and bookbinders (and even to those who work in paper mills or cut trees from forests to make paper), there would be no Bibles. In countless ways in everyday activities the church benefits from common grace.

On the other hand, the special grace that God gives to those who are saved brings more of the blessings of common grace to unbelievers living in the realm of the church's influence. Unbelievers benefit from the example of Christian lives that they see in society, from the prayers and the acts of mercy that Christians do for the community, from the knowledge of the teachings of Scripture and its wisdom in which they find some intellectual and moral benefit, and from the influence on laws, customs, and beliefs of a society that comes

---

[4]See the extended discussion of Heb. 6:4–6 in chapter 11, Section C.

through the social and political activities of Christians. Historically it has often been the powerful presence of those whose lives were changed by the gospel that has resulted in freedom for slaves (in the British colonies and the United States), rights for women, widespread public education, technological and scientific progress, increased productivity in the economy, a high value placed on work and thrift and honesty, and so forth.

8. Common Grace Does Not Save People. In spite of all of this, we must realize that common grace is different from saving grace. Common grace does not change the human heart or bring people to genuine repentance and faith—it cannot and does not save people (though in the intellectual and moral sphere it can give some preparation to make people more disposed toward accepting the gospel). Common grace restrains sin but does not change anyone's foundational disposition to sin, nor does it in any significant measure purify fallen human nature.[5]

We must also recognize that the actions of unbelievers performed by virtue of common grace do not in themselves merit God's approval or favor. These actions do not spring from faith ("Whatever does not proceed from faith is sin," Rom. 14:23), nor are they motivated by a love for God (Matt. 22:37), but rather love of self in some form or another. Therefore, although we may readily say that the works of unbelievers that externally conform to the laws of God are "good" in some sense, they nonetheless are not good in terms of meriting God's approval nor of making God obligated to the sinner in any way.

Finally, we should recognize that unbelievers often receive more common grace than believers—they may be more skillful, harder working, more intelligent, more creative, or have more of the material benefits of this life to enjoy. This in no way indicates that they are more favored by God in an absolute sense or that they will gain any share in eternal salvation, but only that God distributes the blessings of common grace in various ways, often granting very significant blessings to unbelievers. In all of this, they should, of course, acknowledge God's goodness (Acts 14:17), and should recognize that God's revealed will is that "God's kindness" should eventually lead them "to repentance" (Rom. 2:4).

C. Reasons for Common Grace

Why does God bestow common grace on undeserving sinners who will never come to salvation? We can suggest at least four reasons.

1. To Redeem Those Who Will Be Saved. Peter says that the day of judgment and final execution of punishment is being delayed because there are yet more people who will be saved: "The Lord is not slow about his promise as some count slowness, but is forbearing toward

---

[5]The viewpoint on common grace presented in this chapter is consistent with the Reformed or Calvinistic perspective of the book as a whole, a perspective that has been argued for more specifically in discussing regeneration (chapters 3–5). We should note, however, that an Arminian understanding of common grace would be different at this point; it would say that common grace gives to every person the *ability* to turn to God in faith and repentance, and in fact *influences* the sinner to do this unless he or she specifically resists it. Therefore, on an Arminian understanding, common grace has a function that much more clearly relates to saving grace—in fact, common grace is simply an early expression of the totality of saving grace. This position (that the ability to repent and believe is given to all people) is discussed in chapter 3 on election and chapters 4 and 5 on the gospel call and regeneration.

you, *not wishing that any should perish, but that all should reach repentance.* But the day of the Lord will come like a thief" (2 Peter 3:9–10). In fact, this reason was true from the beginning of human history, for if God wanted to save any people out of the whole mass of sinful humanity, he could not have destroyed all sinners immediately (for then there would be no human race left). He chose rather to allow sinful humans to live for some time, so that they might have an opportunity to repent, and also so that they would bear children and enable subsequent generations to live and then hear the gospel and repent.

2. To Demonstrate God's Goodness and Mercy. God's goodness and mercy are not only seen in the salvation of believers, but also in the blessings he gives to undeserving sinners. When God "is kind to the ungrateful and the selfish" (Luke 6:35), his kindness is revealed in the universe, to his glory. David says, "The LORD is *good to all,* and his compassion is over all that he has made" (Ps. 145:9). In the story of Jesus talking with the rich young ruler, we read, "And Jesus looking upon him *loved him*" (Mark 10:21), even though the man was an unbeliever and would in a moment turn away from Jesus because of his great possessions. Louis Berkhof says that God "showers untold blessings upon all men and also clearly indicates that these are the expressions of a favorable disposition in God, which falls short however of the positive volition to pardon their sin, to lift their sentence, and to grant them salvation."[6]

It is not unjust for God to delay the execution of punishment upon sin and to give temporary blessings to human beings, because the punishment is not forgotten, but just delayed. In delaying punishment, God shows clearly that he has no pleasure in executing final judgment, but rather delights in the salvation of men and women. "As I live, says the LORD God, I have no pleasure in the death of the wicked, but that the wicked turn back from his way and live" (Ezek. 33:11). God "desires all men to be saved and to come to the knowledge of the truth" (1 Tim. 2:4). In all of this the delay of punishment gives clear evidence of God's mercy and goodness and love.

3. To Demonstrate God's Justice. When God repeatedly invites sinners to come to faith and when they repeatedly refuse his invitations, the justice of God in condemning them is seen much more clearly. Paul warns that those who persist in unbelief are simply storing up more wrath for themselves: "By your hard and impenitent heart you are storing up wrath for yourself on the day of wrath when God's righteous judgment will be revealed" (Rom. 2:5). On the day of judgment "every mouth" will be "stopped" (Rom. 3:19) and no one will be able to object that God has been unjust.

4. To Demonstrate God's Glory. Finally, God's glory is shown in many ways by the activities of human beings in all the areas in which common grace is operative. In developing and exercising dominion over the earth, men and women demonstrate and reflect the wisdom of their Creator, demonstrate God-like qualities of skill and moral virtue and authority over the universe, and so forth. Though all of these activities are tainted

---

[6]Louis Berkhof, *Systematic Theology* (Grand Rapids: Eerdmans, 1939, 1941), p. 445.

by sinful motives, they nonetheless reflect the excellence of our Creator and therefore bring glory to God, not fully or perfectly, but nonetheless significantly.

D. Our Response to the Doctrine of Common Grace

In thinking about the varying kinds of goodness seen in the lives of unbelievers because of God's abundant common grace, we should keep three points in mind:

1. Common Grace Does Not Mean That Those Who Receive It Will Be Saved. Even exceptionally large amounts of common grace do not imply that those who receive it will be saved. Even the most skilled, most intelligent, most wealthy and powerful people in the world still need the gospel of Jesus Christ or they will be condemned for eternity! Even the most moral and kind of our neighbors still need the gospel of Jesus Christ or they will be condemned for eternity! They may appear outwardly to have no needs, but Scripture still says that unbelievers are "enemies" of God (Rom. 5:10; cf. Col. 1:21; James 4:4) and are "against" Christ (Matt. 12:30). They "live as enemies of the cross of Christ" and have their "minds set on earthly things" (Phil. 3:18–19) and are "by nature children of wrath, like the rest of mankind" (Eph. 2:3).

2. We Must Be Careful Not to Reject the Good Things That Unbelievers Do as Totally Evil. By common grace, unbelievers do *some* good, and we should see God's hand in it and be thankful for common grace as it operates in every friendship, every act of kindness, every way in which it brings blessing to others. All of this—though the unbeliever does not know it—is ultimately from God and he deserves the glory for it.

3. The Doctrine of Common Grace Should Stir Our Hearts to Much Greater Thankfulness to God. When we walk down a street and see houses and gardens and families dwelling in security, or when we do business in the marketplace and see the abundant results of technological progress, or when we walk through the woods and see the beauty of nature, or when we are protected by government,[7] or when we are educated from the vast storehouse of human knowledge, we should realize not only that God in his sovereignty is ultimately responsible for all of these blessings, but also that God has granted them all to sinners who are *totally undeserving* of any of them! These blessings in the world are not only evidence of God's power and wisdom, they are also continually a manifestation of his abundant *grace*. The realization of this fact should cause our hearts to swell with thanksgiving to God in every activity of life.

---

[7]Paul explicitly directs us to offer to God "thanksgivings" for "kings and all who are in high positions" (1 Tim. 2:1–2).

QUESTIONS FOR PERSONAL APPLICATION

1. Before you read this chapter, did you have a different viewpoint on whether unbelievers deserved the ordinary benefits of the world around them? How has your perspective changed, if at all?

2. Do you know of examples where God has answered the prayers of unbelievers who were in difficulty, or answered your prayers for the needs of an unbelieving friend? Has it provided an opening for sharing the gospel? Did the unbeliever eventually come to salvation in Christ? Do you think that God often uses the blessings of common grace as a means to prepare people to receive the gospel?

3. In what ways will this doctrine change the way you relate to an unbelieving neighbor or friend? Will it tend to make you thankful for the good that you see in their lives? How do you think this might affect your relationship with that person in a more general sense?

4. As you look around the place where you are at this moment, can you name at least twenty different examples of common grace that you can see? How does that make you feel?

5. Has this chapter changed the way you view creative activities such as music, art, architecture, or poetry, or (something that is very similar) the creativity expressed in athletic activities?

6. If you are kind to an unbeliever and he or she never comes to accept Christ, has it done any good in God's sight (see Matt. 5:44–45; Luke 6:32–36)? What good has it done? Why do you think that God is good even to those who will never be saved—in what way does it further his purposes for the universe? Do you think we have any obligation to give more effort to showing good to believers than to unbelievers? Can you name any passages of Scripture that help in answering this question?

SPECIAL TERMS

common grace
special grace

BIBLIOGRAPHY

Hoekema, Anthony A. "The Restraint of Sin." In *Created In God's Image.* Grand Rapids: Eerdmans, and Exeter: Paternoster, 1986, pp. 187–202.
Hughes, P. E. "Grace." In *EDT,* pp. 479–82.
Kearsley, R. "Grace." In *NDT,* pp. 280–81.

Van Til, Cornelius. *Common Grace and the Gospel.* Nutley, N.J.: Presbyterian and Reformed, 1972.

Van Til, Cornelius. *In Defense of the Faith,* vol. 5: *An Introduction to Systematic Theology.* n.p.: Presbyterian and Reformed Publishing Co., 1976, pp. 75–99, 253–62.

SCRIPTURE MEMORY PASSAGE

Luke 6:35–36: *But love your enemies, and do good, and lend, expecting nothing in return; and your reward will be great, and you will be sons of the Most High; for he is kind to the ungrateful and the selfish. Be merciful, even as your Father is merciful.*

HYMN

"All People That on Earth Do Dwell"

This very old setting of Psalm 100 is a call to all people on earth to praise God because of his abundant goodness.

> All people that on earth do dwell,
> Sing to the Lord with cheerful voice;
> Him serve with fear, his praise forthtell,
> Come ye before him and rejoice.
>
> The Lord ye know is God indeed;
> Without our aid he did us make;
> We are his folk, he doth us feed,
> And for his sheep he doth us take.
>
> O enter then his gates with praise,
> Approach with joy his courts unto;
> Praise, laud, and bless his name always,
> For it is seemly so to do.
>
> For why? The Lord our God is good,
> His mercy is forever sure;
> His truth at all times firmly stood,
> And shall from age to age endure.

AUTHOR: WILLIAM KETHE, 1561

ELECTION AND REPROBATION

When and why did God choose us?
Are some not chosen?

We all have sinned and deserve eternal punishment from God, and Christ died and *earned* salvation for us. In the rest of this book (chapters 3 – 14) we will look at the way God *applies* that salvation to our lives. We begin in this chapter with God's work of election, that is, his decision to choose us to be saved before the foundation of the world. This act of election is, of course, not (strictly speaking) part of the *application* of salvation to us, since it came before Christ earned our salvation when he died on the cross. But we treat election at this point because it is chronologically the *beginning* of God's dealing with us in a gracious way. Therefore, it is rightly thought of as the first step in the process of God's bringing salvation to us individually.[1]

Other steps in God's work of applying salvation to our lives include our hearing the gospel call, our being regenerated by the Holy Spirit, our responding in faith and repentance, and God forgiving us and giving us membership in his family, as well as granting us growth in the Christian life and keeping us faithful to himself throughout life. At the end of our life we die and go into his presence, then when Christ returns we receive resurrection bodies, and the process of acquiring salvation is complete.

Various theologians have given specific terms to a number of these events, and have often listed them in a specific order in which they believe that they occur in our lives. Such a list of the events in which God applies salvation to us is called the *order of salvation,* and is sometimes referred to by a Latin phrase, *ordo salutis,* which simply means "order of salvation." Before discussing any of these elements in the application of salvation to our lives, we can give a complete list here of the elements that will be treated in the following chapters:

---

[1]This chapter could be placed in chapter 11, as part of the discussion of perseverance, especially related to the question of assurance of salvation, since God's choice of us to be saved gives great assurance that he will fulfill his purposes. But I have chosen to place it here at the beginning of the chapters that discuss God's personal dealing with us in grace. (Note the similar ordering of topics by Paul in Rom. 8:29-30.)

"The Order of Salvation"
1. Election (God's choice of people to be saved)
2. The gospel call (proclaiming the message of the gospel)
3. Regeneration (being born again)
4. Conversion (faith and repentance)
5. Justification (right legal standing)
6. Adoption (membership in God's family)
7. Sanctification (right conduct of life)
8. Perseverance (remaining a Christian)
9. Death (going to be with the Lord)
10. Glorification (receiving a resurrection body)

We should note here that items 2–6 and part of 7 are all involved in "becoming a Christian." Numbers 7 and 8 work themselves out in this life, number 9 occurs at the end of this life, and number 10 occurs when Christ returns.[2]

We begin our discussion of the order of salvation with the first element, election. In connection with this we will also discuss at the end of this chapter the question of "reprobation," the decision of God to pass over those who will not be saved, and to punish them for their sins. As will be explained below, election and reprobation are different in several important respects, and it is important to distinguish these so that we do not think wrongly about God or his activity.

The term *predestination* is also frequently used in this discussion. In this book, and in Reformed theology generally, *predestination* is a broader term and includes the two aspects of election (for believers) and reprobation (for unbelievers). However, the term *double predestination* is not a helpful term because it gives the impression that both election and reprobation are carried out in the same way by God and have no essential differences between them, which is certainly not true. Therefore, the term *double predestination* is not generally used by Reformed theologians, though it is sometimes used to refer to Reformed teaching by those who criticize it. The term *double predestination* will not be used in this book to refer to election and reprobation, since it blurs the distinctions between them and does not give an accurate indication of what is actually being taught.

EXPLANATION AND SCRIPTURAL BASIS

We may define election as follows: *Election is an act of God before creation in which he chooses some people to be saved, not on account of any foreseen merit in them, but only because of his sovereign good pleasure.*

There has been much controversy in the church and much misunderstanding over this doctrine, such as questions regarding man's will and responsibility and regarding the

---

[2]For a discussion of the order of events in this list, see John Murray, *Redemption Accomplished and Applied* (Grand Rapids: Eerdmans, 1955), pp. 79–87. New approaches to a synthesis of Pauline themes in the order of salvation are found in Vern Poythress, "Using Multiple Thematic Centers in Theological Synthesis: Holiness as a Test Case in Developing a Pauline Theology" (unpublished manuscript available from the Campus Bookstore, Westminster Theological Seminary, P.O. Box 27009, Philadelphia, PA, 19118).

justice of God with respect to human choices. We will focus here only on those questions that apply specifically to the question of election.

Our approach in this chapter will be first simply to cite a number of passages from the New Testament that discuss election. Then we will attempt to understand the purpose of God that the New Testament authors see in the doctrine of election. Finally, we will attempt to clarify our understanding of this doctrine and answer some objections, and also to consider the doctrine of reprobation.

A. Does the New Testament Teach Predestination?

Several passages in the New Testament seem to affirm quite clearly that God ordained beforehand those who would be saved. For example, when Paul and Barnabas began to preach to the Gentiles in Antioch in Pisidia, Luke writes, "And when the Gentiles heard this, they were glad and glorified the word of God; and *as many as were ordained to eternal life believed*" (Acts 13:48). It is significant that Luke mentions the fact of election almost in passing. It is as if this were the normal occurrence when the gospel was preached. How many believed? "As many as were ordained to eternal life believed."

In Romans 8:28–30, we read:

> We know that in everything God works for good with those who love him, who are called according to his purpose. *For those whom he foreknew he also predestined to be conformed to the image of his Son,* in order that he might be the first-born among many brethren. *And those whom he predestined he also called; and those whom he called he also justified; and those whom he justified he also glorified.*[3]

In the following chapter, when talking about God's choosing Jacob and not Esau, Paul says it was not because of anything that Jacob or Esau had done, but simply in order that God's purpose of election might continue.

> Though they were not yet born and had done nothing either good or bad, *in order that God's purpose of election might continue,* not because of works but because of his call, she was told, "The elder will serve the younger." As it is written, "Jacob I loved, but Esau I hated." (Rom. 9:11–13)

Regarding the fact that some of the people of Israel were saved, but others were not, Paul says: "Israel failed to obtain what it sought. *The elect* obtained it, but the rest were hardened" (Rom. 11:7). Here again Paul indicates two distinct groups within the people of Israel. Those who were "the elect" obtained the salvation that they sought, while those who were not the elect simply "were hardened."

---

[3]Clark Pinnock says that this text does not speak of predestination to salvation, but rather to a certain privilege, that of being conformed to Jesus Christ: "There is no predestination to salvation or damnation in the Bible. There is only a predestination for those who are already children of God with respect to certain privileges out ahead of them" (*Grace Unlimited* [Minneapolis: Bethany Fellowship, 1975], p. 18). But such a view does not do justice to Rom. 8:29–30, because those who are said to be predestined in this verse are not yet children of God, because Paul here speaks of predestination before calling or justification. Moreover, the privilege of being conformed to the image of Christ is not just for some Christians, but for all.

Paul talks explicitly about God's choice of believers before the foundation of the world in the beginning of Ephesians.

> "*He chose us in him before the foundation of the world,* that we should be holy and blameless before him. *He destined us in love* to be his sons through Jesus Christ, according to the purpose of his will, to the praise of his glorious grace." (Eph. 1:4–6)

Here Paul is writing to believers and he specifically says that God "chose us" in Christ, referring to believers generally. In a similar way, several verses later he says, "We who first hoped in Christ have been *destined and appointed* to live for the praise of his glory" (Eph. 1:12).

He writes to the Thessalonians, "For we know, brethren beloved by God, that *he has chosen you;* for our gospel came to you not only in word, but also in power and in the Holy Spirit and with full conviction" (1 Thess. 1:4–5).

Paul says that the fact that the Thessalonians *believed* the gospel when he preached it ("for our gospel came to you . . . in power . . . and with full conviction") *is the reason he knows that God chose them.* As soon as they came to faith Paul concluded that long ago God had chosen them, and therefore they had believed when he preached. He later writes to the same church, "We are bound to give thanks to God always for you, brethren beloved by the Lord, because *God chose you from the beginning to be saved,* through sanctification by the Spirit and belief in the truth" (2 Thess. 2:13).

Although the next text does not specifically mention the election of human beings, it is interesting at this point also to notice what Paul says about angels. When he gives a solemn command to Timothy, he writes, "In the presence of God and of Christ Jesus and of *the elect angels* I charge you to keep these rules without favor" (1 Tim. 5:21). Paul is aware that there are good angels witnessing his command and witnessing Timothy's response to it, and he is so sure that it is God's act of election that has affected every one of those good angels that he can call them "*elect angels.*"

When Paul talks about the reason why God saved us and called us to himself, he explicitly denies that it was because of our works, but points rather to God's own purpose and his unmerited grace in eternity past. He says God is the one "who saved us and called us with a holy calling, not in virtue of our works but in virtue of *his own purpose* and the *grace which he gave us in Christ Jesus ages ago*" (2 Tim. 1:9).

When Peter writes an epistle to hundreds of Christians in many churches in Asia Minor, he writes, "To *God's elect* . . . scattered throughout Pontus, Galatia, Cappadocia, Asia and Bithynia" (1 Peter 1:1 NIV). He later calls them "a *chosen race*" (1 Peter 2:9).

In John's vision in Revelation, those who do not give in to persecution and begin to worship the beast are persons whose names have been written in the book of life before the foundation of the world: "And authority was given it over every tribe and people and tongue and nation, and all who dwell on earth will worship it, *every one whose name has not been written before the foundation of the world in the book of life* of the Lamb that was slain" (Rev. 13:7–8)[4]

---

[4]Grammatically the phrase "before the foundation of the world" could modify either "whose name has not been writ- ten" (as here, in the RSV; also in the NASB and NIV mg.), or "the lamb that was slain" (so KJV, NIV). But the parallel

In a similar way, we read of the beast from the bottomless pit in Revelation 17: "The dwellers on earth *whose names have not been written in the book of life from the foundation of the world*, will marvel to behold the beast, because it was and is not and is to come" (Rev. 17:8).

B. How Does the New Testament Present the Teaching of Election?

After reading this list of verses on election, it is important to view this doctrine in the way the New Testament itself views it.

1. As a Comfort. The New Testament authors often present the doctrine of election as a comfort to believers. When Paul assures the Romans that "in everything God works for good with those who love him, who are called according to his purpose" (Rom. 8:28), he gives God's work of predestination as a reason why we can be assured of this truth. He explains in the next verse, "*For* those whom he foreknew he also predestined to be conformed to the image of his Son . . . And those whom he predestined he also called . . . justified . . . glorified" (Rom. 8:29–30). Paul's point is to say that God has *always* acted for the good of those whom he called to himself. If Paul looks into the distant past before the creation of the world, he sees that God foreknew and predestined his people to be conformed to the image of Christ.[5] If he looks at the recent past he finds that God called and justified his people whom he had predestined. And if he then looks toward the future when Christ returns, he sees that God has determined to give perfect, glorified bodies to those who believe in Christ. From eternity to eternity God has acted with the good of his people in mind. But if God has *always* acted for our good and will in the future act for our good, Paul reasons, then *will he not also in our present circumstances* work every circumstance together for our good as well? In this way predestination is seen as a comfort for believers in the everyday events of life.

2. As a Reason to Praise God. Paul says, "He destined us in love to be his sons through Jesus Christ, according to the purpose of his will, *to the praise of his glorious grace*" (Eph. 1:5–6). Similarly, he says, "We who first hoped in Christ have been destined and appointed to live *for the praise of his glory*" (Eph. 1:12).

Paul tells the Christians at Thessalonica, "*We give thanks to God* always for you all. . . . *For we know*, brethren beloved by God, *that he has chosen you*" (1 Thess. 1:2, 4). The reason Paul can give thanks to God for the Thessalonian Christians is that he knows God is ultimately responsible for their salvation and has in fact chosen them to be saved. This is

---

expression in Rev. 17:8, "whose names have not been *written in the book of life from the foundation of the world*," seems decisive, and there only one sense is possible (the parallel wording is striking in the Greek text, since the two verses share eleven identical words in talking about people whose names are written in the book of life). Moreover, the RSV/NASB reading makes much better sense in light of the rest of Scripture: the Bible often talks about God choosing us before the foundation of the world, but nowhere else does Scripture say that Christ was slain

from the foundation of the world—a statement that simply is not true in any literal sense, because Christ was not slain until he died on the cross. Therefore, on the NIV/KJV reading, the verse must be interpreted to mean something like, "God *planned* from the foundation of the world that Christ would be slain"—but that is not what the text actually says, on either reading.

[5]See the discussion below (pp. 52–55) on the meaning of "foreknow" here.

made even clearer in 2 Thessalonians 2:13: "But *we are bound to give thanks to God* always for you, brethren beloved by the Lord, *because God chose you* from the beginning to be saved." Paul was obligated to give thanks to God for the Christians at Thessalonica because he knew that their salvation was ultimately due to God's choice of them. Therefore it is appropriate for Paul to thank God for them rather than praising them for their own saving faith.

Understood in this way, the doctrine of election does increase praise given to God for our salvation and seriously diminishes any pride that we might feel if we thought that our salvation was due to something good in us or something for which we should receive credit.

3. As an Encouragement to Evangelism. Paul says, "I endure everything for the sake of the elect, that they also may obtain salvation in Christ Jesus with its eternal glory" (2 Tim. 2:10). He knows that God has chosen some people to be saved, and he sees this as an encouragement to preach the gospel, even if it means enduring great suffering. Election is Paul's guarantee that there will be some success for his evangelism, for he knows that some of the people he speaks to will be the elect, and they will believe the gospel and be saved. It is as if someone invited us to come fishing and said, "I guarantee that you will catch some fish—they are hungry and waiting."

C. Correcting Misunderstandings of the Doctrine of Election

1. Election Is Not Fatalistic or Mechanistic. Sometimes those who object to the doctrine of election say that it is "fatalism" or that it presents a "mechanistic system" for the universe. Two somewhat different objections are involved here. By "fatalism" is meant a system in which human choices and human decisions really do not make any difference. In fatalism, no matter what we do, things are going to turn out as they have been previously ordained. Therefore, it is futile to attempt to influence the outcome of events or the outcome of our lives by putting forth any effort or making any significant choices, because these will not make any difference any way. In a true fatalistic system, of course, our humanity is destroyed for our choices really mean nothing, and the motivation for moral accountability is removed.

In a mechanistic system the picture is one of an impersonal universe in which all things that happen have been inflexibly determined by an impersonal force long ago, and the universe functions in a mechanical way so that human beings are more like machines or robots than genuine persons. Here also genuine human personality would be reduced to the level of a machine that simply functions in accordance with predetermined plans and in response to predetermined causes and influences.

By contrast to the mechanistic picture, the New Testament presents the entire outworking of our salvation as something brought about by a *personal* God in relationship with *personal* creatures. God "destined us *in love* to be his sons through Jesus Christ" (Eph. 1:5). God's act of election was neither impersonal nor mechanistic, but was permeated with personal love for those whom he chose. Moreover, the personal care of God for his creatures, even those who rebel against him, is seen clearly in God's plea through Ezekiel, "As I live, says the Lord God, *I have no pleasure in the death of the wicked, but that the wicked turn from his way and live;* turn back, turn back from your evil ways; for why will you die, O house of Israel?" (Ezek. 33:11).

When talking about our response to the gospel offer, Scripture continually views us not as mechanistic creatures or robots, but as *genuine persons,* personal creatures who make willing choices to accept or reject the gospel. Jesus invites everyone, *"Come to me,* all who labor and are heavy laden, and I will give you rest" (Matt. 11:28). And we read the invitation at the end of Revelation: "The Spirit and the Bride say, 'Come.' And let him who hears say, 'Come.' And let him who is thirsty come, let *him who desires* take the water of life without price" (Rev. 22:17). This invitation and many others like it are addressed to genuine persons who are capable of hearing the invitation and responding to it by a decision of their wills. Regarding those who will not accept him, Jesus clearly emphasizes their hardness of heart and their stubborn refusal to come to him: "Yet you *refuse* to come to me that you may have life" (John 5:40). And Jesus cries out in sorrow to the city that had rejected him, "O Jerusalem, Jerusalem, killing the prophets and stoning those who are sent to you! How often would I have gathered your children together as a hen gathers her brood under her wings, *and you would not!"* (Matt. 23:37).

In contrast to the charge of fatalism, we also see a much different picture in the New Testament. Not only do we make willing choices as real persons, but these choices are also *real choices* because they do affect the course of events in the world. They affect our own lives and they affect the lives and destinies of others. So, *"He who believes in him* is not condemned; *he who does not believe* is condemned already, because he has not believed in the name of the only Son of God" (John 3:18). Our personal decisions to believe or not believe in Christ have eternal consequences in our lives, and Scripture is quite willing to talk about our decision to believe or not believe as the factor that decides our eternal destiny.

The implication of this is that we certainly must preach the gospel, and people's eternal destiny hinges on whether we proclaim the gospel or not. Therefore when the Lord one night told Paul, "Do not be afraid, but speak and do not be silent; for I am with you, and no man shall attack you to harm you; for *I have many people in this city"* (Acts 18:9–10), Paul did not simply conclude that the "many people" who belong to God would be saved whether he stayed there preaching the gospel or not. Rather, *"he stayed a year and six months,* teaching the word of God among them" (Acts 18:11)—this was longer than Paul stayed in any other city except Ephesus during his three missionary journeys. When Paul was told that God had many elect people in Corinth, he stayed a long time and preached, in order that those elect people might be saved! Paul is quite clear about the fact that unless people preach the gospel others will not be saved:

> But how are men to call upon him in whom they have not believed? *And how are they to believe in him of whom they have never heard? And how are they to hear without a preacher?* . . . So faith comes from what is heard, and what is heard comes by the preaching of Christ. (Rom. 10:14, 17)

Did Paul know before he went to a city who was elected by God for salvation and who was not? No, he did not. That is something that God does not show to us ahead of time. But once people come to faith in Christ then we can be confident that God had earlier chosen them for salvation. This is exactly Paul's conclusion regarding the Thessalonians; he says that he knows that God chose them because when he preached to them, the gospel came in power and with full conviction: "For we know, brethren beloved by God, that he has chosen you; *for our gospel came to you* not only in word, but also in *power* and in the *Holy Spirit* and *with full conviction*" (1 Thess. 1:4–5). Far from saying that whatever he did made no difference, and that God's elect would be saved whether he preached or not, Paul endured a life of incredible hardship in order to bring the gospel to those whom God had chosen. At the end of a life filled with suffering he said, "Therefore *I endure everything for the sake of the elect, that they also may obtain salvation* in Christ Jesus with its eternal glory" (2 Tim. 2:10).

2. Election Is Not Based on God's Foreknowledge of Our Faith. Quite commonly people will agree that God predestines some to be saved, but they will say that he does this by looking into the future and seeing who will believe in Christ and who will not. If he sees that a person is going to come to saving faith, then he will predestine that person to be saved, *based on foreknowledge of that person's faith.* If he sees that a person will not come to saving faith, then he does not predestine that person to be saved. In this way, it is thought, the ultimate reason why some are saved and some are not lies *within the people themselves,* not within God. All that God does in his predestining work is to give confirmation to the decision he knows people will make on their own. The verse commonly used to support this view is Romans 8:29: "For those *whom he foreknew* he also predestined to be conformed to the image of his Son."[6]

a. Foreknowledge of Persons, Not Facts: But this verse can hardly be used to demonstrate that God based his predestination on foreknowledge of *the fact that a person would believe.* The passage speaks rather of the fact that God knew *persons* ("*those whom* he foreknew"), not that he knew some *fact about them,* such as the fact that they would believe. It is a personal, relational knowledge that is spoken of here: God, looking into the future, thought of certain people in saving relationship to him, and in that sense he "knew them" long ago. This is the sense in which Paul can talk about God's "knowing" someone, for example, in 1 Corinthians 8:3: "But if one loves God, one is *known by him.*" Similarly, he says, "but now that you have come to know God, or rather *to be known by God . . .*" (Gal. 4:9). When people *know* God in Scripture, or when God *knows* them, it is personal knowledge that involves a saving relationship. Therefore in Romans 8:29, "those whom he *foreknew*" is best understood to mean, "those whom he long ago *thought of in a saving relationship to himself.*" The text actually says nothing about God foreknowing or foreseeing that certain people would believe, nor is that idea mentioned in any other text of Scripture.[7]

Sometimes people say that God elected *groups* of people, but not individuals to salvation. In some Arminian views, God just elected the church as a group, while the Swiss theologian Karl Barth (1886–1968) said that God elected Christ, and all people in Christ. But Romans

---

[6]The idea that predestination is based on God's foreknowledge of those who would believe is argued in Jack W. Cottrell, "Conditional Election," in *Grace Unlimited,* pp. 51–73. Cottrell says, "Through his foreknowledge God sees who will believe upon Jesus Christ as Savior and Lord, and become united with him in Christian baptism; then even before the creation of the world he predestines these believers to share the glory of the risen Christ" (p. 62).

[7]Rom. 11:2 similarly speaks of God's foreknowing *persons,* not facts about people or the fact that they would believe: "God has not rejected his people *whom he foreknew.*"

8:29 talks about certain people whom God foreknew (*"those whom* he foreknew"), not just undefined or unfilled groups. And in Ephesians Paul talks about certain people whom God chose, including himself: "He *chose us* in him before the foundation of the world" (Eph. 1:4). To talk about God choosing a group with no people in it is not biblical election at all. But to talk about God choosing a group of people means that he chose specific individuals who constituted that group.[8]

b. Scripture Never Speaks of Our Faith As the Reason God Chose Us: In addition, when we look beyond these specific passages that speak of foreknowledge and look at verses that talk about the *reason* God chose us, we find that Scripture never speaks of our faith or the fact that we would come to believe in Christ as the reason God chose us. In fact, Paul seems explicitly to exclude the consideration of what people would do in life from his understanding of God's choice of Jacob rather than Esau: he says, "Though they were not yet born and had done nothing either good or bad, *in order that God's purpose of election might continue,* not because of works but because of his call, she was told, 'The elder will serve the younger.' As it is written, 'Jacob I loved, but Esau I hated'" (Rom. 9:11–13). Nothing that Jacob or Esau would do in life influenced God's decision; it was simply in order that his purpose of election might continue.

When discussing the Jewish people who have come to faith in Christ, Paul says, "So too at the present time there is a remnant, *chosen by grace.* But if it is by grace, it is no longer on the basis of works" (Rom. 11:5–6). Here again Paul emphasizes God's grace and the complete absence of human merit in the process of election. Someone might object that faith is not viewed as a "work" in Scripture and therefore faith should be excluded from the quotation above ("It is no longer on the basis of *works*"). Based on this objection, Paul could actually mean, "But if it is by grace, it is no longer on the basis of works, but rather on the basis of whether someone would believe." However, this is unlikely in this context: Paul is not contrasting human faith and human works; he is contrasting God's sovereign choosing of people with *any* human activity, and he points to God's sovereign will as the ultimate basis for God's choice of the Jews who have come to Christ.

Similarly, when Paul talks about election in Ephesians, there is no mention of any foreknowledge of the fact that we would believe, or any idea that there was anything worthy or meritorious in us (such as a tendency to believe) that was the basis for God's choosing us. Rather, Paul says, "He destined us *in love* to be his sons through Jesus Christ, *according to the purpose of his will,* to the praise of his glorious grace *which he freely bestowed on us* in the Beloved" (Eph. 1:5–6). Now if God's grace is to be praised for election, and not human ability to believe or decision to believe, then once again it is consistent for Paul to mention nothing of human faith but only to mention God's predestining activity, his purpose and will, and his freely given grace.

Again in 2 Timothy, Paul says that God "saved us and called us with a holy calling, not in virtue of our works but *in virtue of his own purpose* and the grace which he gave us in Christ Jesus ages ago" (2 Tim. 1:9). Once again God's sovereign purpose is seen as the ultimate rea-

---

[8]In answer to Barth's view that all are chosen in Christ, see the discussion below on reprobation (the fact that some are not chosen).

son for our salvation, and Paul connects this with the fact that God gave us grace in Christ Jesus ages ago—another way of speaking of the truth that God freely gave favor to us when he chose us without reference to any foreseen merit or worthiness on our part.

c. Election Based on Something Good in Us (Our Faith) Would Be the Beginning of Salvation by Merit: Yet another kind of objection can be brought against the idea that God chose us because he foreknew that we would come to faith. If the *ultimate* determining factor in whether we will be saved or not is our own decision to accept Christ, then we shall be more inclined to think that we deserve some credit for the fact that we were saved: in distinction from other people who continue to reject Christ, we were wise enough in our judgment or good enough in our moral tendencies or perceptive enough in our spiritual capacities to decide to believe in Christ. But once we begin to think this way then we seriously diminish the glory that is to be given to God for our salvation. We become uncomfortable speaking like Paul who says that God "destined us . . . *according to the purpose of his will,* to the praise of his glorious *grace*" (Eph. 1:5–6), and we begin to think that God "destined us . . . according to the fact that he knew that we would have enough tendencies toward goodness and faith within us that we would believe." When we think like this we begin to sound very much unlike the New Testament when it talks about election or predestination. By contrast, if election is solely based on God's own good pleasure and his sovereign decision to love us in spite of our lack of goodness or merit, then certainly we have a profound sense of appreciation to him for a salvation that is totally undeserved, and we will forever be willing to praise his "glorious grace" (Eph. 1:6).

In the final analysis, the difference between two views of election can be seen in the way they answer a very simple question. Given the fact that in the final analysis some people will choose to accept Christ and some people will not, the question is, "What makes people differ?" That is, what *ultimately* makes the difference between those who believe and those who do not? If our answer is that it is ultimately based on something God does (namely, his sovereign election of those who would be saved), then we see that salvation at its most foundational level is based on *grace alone.* On the other hand, if we answer that the ultimate difference between those who are saved and those who are not is because of *something in man* (that is, a tendency or disposition to believe or not believe), then salvation ultimately depends on a combination of grace plus human ability.[9]

d. Predestination Based on Foreknowledge Still Does Not Give People Free Choice: The idea that God's predestination of some to believe is based on foreknowledge of their faith encounters still another problem: upon reflection, this system turns out to give no real freedom to man either. For if God can look into the future and see that person A *will* come to faith in Christ, and that person B *will not* come to faith in Christ, then those facts are already

---

[9]The fact that the Arminian position ultimately makes something in man the determining factor in whether people are saved or not is seen clearly in the statement of I. Howard Marshall: "The effect of the call of God is to place man in a position where he can say 'yes' or 'no' (which he could not do before God called him; till then he was in a continuous attitude of 'no')" ("Predestination in the New Testament," in *Grace Unlimited,* p. 140). In this statement of Marshall's we see that the final determinant of whether people are saved or not is whether they say yes or no to God's call, and therefore salvation still ultimately depends on something in man, an ability or tendency within him that persuades him to say yes rather than no.

fixed, they are already *determined.* If we assume that God's knowledge of the future is *true* (which it must be), then it is absolutely certain that person A will believe and person B will not. There is no way that their lives could turn out any differently than this. Therefore it is fair to say that their destinies are still *determined,* for they could not be otherwise. But *by what* are these destinies determined? If they are determined by God himself, then we no longer have election based ultimately on foreknowledge of faith, but rather on God's sovereign will. But if these destinies are not determined by God, then who or what determines them? Certainly no Christian would say that there is some powerful being other than God controlling people's destinies. Therefore it seems that the only other possible solution is to say they are determined by some impersonal force, some kind of fate, operative in the universe, making things turn out as they do. But what kind of benefit is this? We have then sacrificed election in love by a personal God for a kind of determinism by an impersonal force and God is no longer to be given the ultimate credit for our salvation.

e. Conclusion: Election Is Unconditional: It seems best, for the previous four reasons, to reject the idea that election is based on God's foreknowledge of our faith. We conclude instead that the reason for election is simply God's sovereign choice—he "destined us in love to be his sons" (Eph. 1:5). God chose us simply because he decided to bestow his love upon us. It was not because of any foreseen faith or foreseen merit in us.

This understanding of election has traditionally been called "unconditional election."[10] It is "unconditional" because it is not *conditioned upon* anything that God sees in us that makes us worthy of his choosing us.[11]

D. Objections to the Doctrine of Election

It must be said that the doctrine of election as presented here is by no means universally accepted in the Christian church, either in Catholicism or Protestantism. There is a long history of acceptance of the doctrine as here presented, but many others have objected to it as well. Among current evangelicals, those in more Reformed or Calvinistic circles (conservative Presbyterian denominations, for example) will accept this view, as will many

---

[10]Unconditional election is the "U" in the acronym TULIP, which stands for "the five points of Calvinism." The other letters stand for *Total* depravity, *Limited* atonement, *Irresistible* grace (see chapter 5), and *Perseverance* of the saints (see chapter 11).

[11]Regarding the doctrine of election, there has been a dispute in Reformed circles (those who hold to election as presented here) between two positions known as *supralapsarianism* and *infralapsarianism.* The difference concerns what happened in God's mind before the foundation of the world. It does not concern something that happened in time, but rather it concerns the *logical* order of God's thoughts. The question is whether, in logical order, (a) God decided first that he would *save some people* and second that he would *allow sin* into the world so that he could save them from it (the supralapsarian position), or whether it was the other way around, so that (b) God first decided that he would *allow sin* into the world and second decided that

he would *save some people* from it (the infralapsarian position). The word *supralapsarian* means "before the fall," and the word *infralapsarian* means "after the fall." The discussion is complex and highly speculative because there is very little direct biblical data to help us with it. Good arguments have been advanced in support of each view, and there is probably some element of truth in each one. But in the last analysis it seems wiser to say that Scripture does not give us enough data to probe into this mystery, and, moreover, it does not seem very edifying to do so.

I mention the discussion at this point only because the words "supralapsarian" and "infralapsarian" are sometimes used in theological circles as symbols for the most abstract and obscure of theological discussions, and it seemed to me appropriate simply to inform the reader of the nature of this dispute and the meaning of these terms. For those interested, a further discussion is found in Louis Berkhof, *Systematic Theology* (Grand Rapids: Eerdmans, 1939, 1941), pp. 118–25.

Lutherans and Anglicans (Episcopalians) and a large number of Baptists and people in independent churches. On the other hand, it will be rejected quite decisively by nearly all Methodists, as well as by many others in Baptist, Anglican, and independent churches.[12]

1. Election Means That We Do Not Have a Choice in Whether We Accept Christ or Not. According to this objection, the doctrine of election denies all the gospel invitations that appeal to the will of man and ask people to make a choice in whether to respond to Christ's invitation or not. In response to this, we must affirm that the doctrine of election is fully able to accommodate the idea that we have a voluntary choice and we make willing decisions in accepting or rejecting Christ. Our choices are voluntary because they are what we want to do and what we decide to do.[13] This does not mean that our choices are absolutely free, because God can work sovereignly through our desires so that he guarantees that our choices come about as he has ordained, but this can still be understood as a real choice because God has created us and he ordains that such a choice is real. In short, we can say that God causes us to choose Christ voluntarily. The mistaken assumption underlying this objection is that a choice must be absolutely free (that is, not in any way caused by God) in order for it to be a genuine human choice.

2. On This Definition of Election, Our Choices Are Not Real Choices. Continuing the discussion in the previous paragraph, someone might object that if a choice is caused by God, it may appear to us to be voluntary and willed by us, but it is nonetheless not a genuine or real choice, because it is not absolutely free. Once again we must respond by challenging the assumption that a choice must be absolutely free in order to be genuine or valid. If God makes us in a certain way and then tells us that our voluntary choices are real and genuine choices, then we must agree that they are. God is the definition of what is real and genuine in the universe. By contrast, we might ask where Scripture ever says that our choices have to be free from God's influence or control in order to be real or genuine choices. It does not seem that Scripture ever speaks in this way.

3. The Doctrine of Election Makes Us Puppets or Robots, Not Real Persons. According to this objection, if God really causes everything that we choose with regard to salvation, then we are no longer real persons. Once again it must be answered that God has created

---

[12]For a full discussion of objections to election, the reader may refer to two excellent recent collections of essays from what is called an "Arminian" perspective, a perspective that rejects the view of election advocated in this chapter: see Pinnock, *Grace Unlimited,* and Clark H. Pinnock, ed., *The Grace of God, the Will of Man: A Case for Arminianism* (Grand Rapids: Zondervan, 1989). In response to these two books, Tom Schreiner and Bruce Ware have edited a substantial collection of essays from Reformed scholars, published as *Still Sovereign: Contemporary Perspectives on Election, Foreknowledge, and Grace* (Grand Rapids: Baker, 2000).

[13]Grant R. Osborne, "Exegetical Notes on Calvinist Texts," in *Grace Unlimited,* pp. 167–89, several times points out evidence of human volition or human choice involved in the imme-diate context of texts that talk about election or predestination. A representative example is seen on p. 175, where Osborne discusses Acts 13:48, "as many as were ordained to eternal life believed." Osborne responds, "While we agree that the basic thrust is divine election, this does not negate the presence of human volition, as seen in the context" (p. 175). Such a response seems to assume that a Reformed view denies human volition or choice. But it must be answered that the Reformed position as traditionally argued certainly allows for genuine human volition or human will in choices that are made, and simply says that God is so wise and powerful that he *ordains* that we respond *willingly.* Osborne does not directly interact with this position.

us and we must allow him to define what genuine personhood is. The analogy of a "puppet" or a "robot" reduces us to a sub-human category of things that have been created by man. But genuine human beings are far greater than puppets or robots, because we do have a genuine will and we do make voluntary decisions based on our own preferences and wants. In fact, it is this ability to make willing choices that is one thing that distinguishes us from much of the lower creation. We are real people created in God's image, and God has allowed us to make genuine choices that have real effects on our lives.

4. The Doctrine of Election Means That Unbelievers Never Had a Chance to Believe. This objection to election says that if God had decreed from eternity that some people would not believe, then there was no genuine chance for them to believe, and the entire system functions unfairly. Two responses can be made to this objection. First, we must note that the Bible does not allow us to say that unbelievers had no chance to believe. When people rejected Jesus he always put the blame on their willful choice to reject him, not on anything decreed by God the Father. "Why do you not understand what I say? It is because you cannot bear to hear my word. You are of your father the devil, and your *will* is to do your father's desires" (John 8:43–44). He says to Jerusalem, "How often would I have gathered your children together . . . *and you would not!*" (Matt. 23:37). He said to the Jews who rejected him, "You *refuse to come to me* that you may have life" (John 5:40). Romans 1 makes it plain that all people are confronted with a revelation from God of such clarity that they are "without excuse" (Rom. 1:20). This is the consistent pattern in Scripture: people who remain in unbelief do so because they are unwilling to come to God, and the blame for such unbelief always lies with the unbelievers themselves, never with God.

At a second level, the answer to this question must simply be Paul's answer to a similar objection: "But who are you, a man, to answer back to God? Will what is molded say to its molder, 'Why have you made me thus?'" (Rom. 9:20).

5. Election Is Unfair. Sometimes people regard the doctrine of election as unfair, since it teaches that God chooses some to be saved and passes over others, deciding not to save them. How can this be fair?

Two responses may be given at this point. First, we must remember that *it would be perfectly fair for God not to save anyone,* just as he did with the angels: "God did not spare the angels when they sinned, but cast them into hell and committed them to pits of nether gloom to be kept until the judgment" (2 Peter 2:4). What would be perfectly fair for God would be to do with human beings as he did with angels, that is, to save none of those who sinned and rebelled against him. But if he does save *some at all,* then this is a demonstration of grace that goes far beyond the requirements of fairness and justice.

But at a deeper level this objection would say that it is not fair for God to create some people who he knew would sin and be eternally condemned, and whom he would not redeem. Paul raises this objection in Romans 9. After saying that God "has mercy upon whomever he wills, and he hardens the heart of whomever he wills" (Rom. 9:18),[14] Paul then raises this precise objection: "You will say to me then, 'Why does he still find fault? For who can resist his will?'" (Rom. 9:19). Here is the heart of the "unfairness" objection against the doctrine of election. If each person's ultimate destiny is determined by God, not by the person himself or herself (that is, even when people make willing choices that determine whether they will be saved or not, if God is actually behind those choices somehow causing them to occur), then how can this be fair?

Paul's response is not one that appeals to our pride, nor does he attempt to give a philosophical explanation of why this is just. He simply calls on God's rights as the omnipotent Creator:

> But who are you, a man, to answer back to God? Will what is molded say to its molder, "Why have you made me thus?" Has the potter no right over the clay, to make out of the same lump one vessel for beauty and another for menial use? What if God, desiring to show his wrath and to make known his power, has endured with much patience the vessels of wrath made for destruction, in order to make known the riches of his glory for the vessels of mercy, which he has prepared beforehand for glory, even us whom he has called, not from the Jews only but also from the Gentiles? (Rom. 9:20–24)[15]

Paul simply says that there is a point beyond which we cannot answer back to God or question his justice. He has done what he has done according to his sovereign will. He is the Creator; we are the creatures, and we ultimately have no basis from which to accuse him of unfairness or injustice.[16] When we read these words of Paul we are confronted with a decision whether or not to accept what God says here, and what he does, simply because he is God and we are not. It is a question that reaches deep into our understanding of ourselves as creatures and of our relationship to God as our Creator.

This objection of unfairness takes a slightly different form when people say that it is *unfair of God to save some people and not to save all.* This objection is based on an idea of justice among human beings that we sense intuitively. We recognize in human affairs that

---

[14]One Arminian view of this verse is given by Jack Cottrell. He argues that Rom. 9:18, "He has mercy upon whomever he will, and he hardens the heart of whomever he will," refers not to God's choice of people for salvation, but to God's choice of people for certain kinds of service: "He chooses whom he pleases for service, not salvation" ("The Nature of the Divine Sovereignty," in *The Grace of God, the Will of Man,* p. 114). This is not a convincing interpretation, however, because the entire context definitely concerns salvation: Paul says, "I have great sorrow and unceasing anguish in my heart" and "I could wish that I myself were accursed and cut off from Christ for the sake of my brethren, my kinsmen by race" (Rom. 9:2, 3), not because the Jews were not chosen for some particular service, but because they were not saved! He speaks in v. 8 not of those who were chosen for service and those who were not, but of those who are "children of God" and those who are not. And he speaks in v. 22 not of some who missed an opportunity for service, but of "vessels of wrath made for destruction." Salvation is in view in the entire context.

[15]James D. Strauss, "God's Promise and Universal History: The Theology of Romans 9," in *Grace Unlimited,* argues that in Romans 9 "vessels of wrath *made for destruction*" should rather

be translated "fitted themselves" for wrath (p. 200). But he gives no examples of a genuine reflexive use of the verb *katartizō,* which would be required here. BAGD, pp. 417–18, note that the *passive* can be used intransitively (as here if we translate "made for destruction," as the RSV), but they give no example of an active or middle voice of this verb being used without a direct object. Moreover, Strauss' suggestion, "fitted themselves" for wrath, would not really fit the picture of a potter making vessels of various sorts, for pots do not make themselves, but the potter makes them.

Another objection brought by Strauss is to say that the potter and clay imagery in Rom. 9:20–23 is derived from Old Testament passages that emphasize God's call for people freely to choose repentance and faith. He says that this negates the idea of sovereign predestining on God's part (p. 199). But here Strauss simply misunderstands the Reformed position, which never denies human responsibility or human willingness in making choices.

[16]For further discussion, see John Piper, *The Justification of God: An Exegetical and Theological Study of Romans 9:1–23* (Grand Rapids: Baker, 1983).

it is right to treat equal people in an equal way. Therefore it seems intuitively appropriate to us to say that if God is going to save *some* sinners he ought to save *all* sinners. But in answer to this objection it must be said that we really have no right to impose on God our intuitive sense of what is appropriate among human beings. Whenever Scripture begins to treat this area it goes back to God's sovereignty as Creator and says he has a right to do with his creation as he wills (see Rom. 9:19–20, quoted above).[17] If God ultimately decided to create some creatures to be saved and others not to be saved, then that was his sovereign choice, and we have no moral or scriptural basis on which we can insist that it was not fair.

6. The Bible Says That God Wills to Save Everyone. Another objection to the doctrine of election is that it contradicts certain passages of Scripture that say that God wills for all to be saved. Paul writes of God our Savior, "*who desires all men to be saved and to come to the knowledge of the truth*" (1 Tim. 2:4). And Peter says, "The Lord is not slow about his promise as some count slowness, but is forbearing toward you, *not wishing that any should perish,* but that all should reach repentance" (2 Peter 3:9). Do not these passages contradict the idea that God has only chosen certain people to be saved?

One common solution to this question (from the Reformed perspective advocated in this book) is to say that these verses speak of God's *revealed will* (telling us what we should do), not his *hidden will* (his eternal plans for what will happen).[18] The verses simply tell us that God invites and commands every person to repent and come to Christ for salvation, but they do not tell us anything about God's secret decrees regarding who will be saved.

The Arminian theologian Clark Pinnock objects to the idea that God has a secret and a revealed will—he calls it "the exceedingly paradoxical notion of two divine wills regarding salvation."[19] But Pinnock never really answers the question of why all are not saved (from an Arminian perspective). Ultimately Arminians *also* must say that God *wills* something more strongly than he wills the salvation of all people, *for in fact all are not saved.* Arminians claim that the reason why all are not saved is that God wills to preserve the free will of man *more than* he wills to save everyone. But is this not also making a distinction in two aspects of the will of God? On the one hand God wills that all be saved (1 Tim. 2:5–6; 2 Peter 3:9). But on the other hand he wills to preserve man's absolutely free choice. In fact, he wills the second thing *more than* the first. But this means that Arminians also must say that 1 Timothy 2:5–6 and 2 Peter 3:9 do not say that God wills the salvation of everyone in an absolute or unqualified way—they too must say that the verses only refer to one kind or one aspect of God's will.

Here the difference between the Reformed and the Arminian conception of God's will is clearly seen. Both Calvinists and Arminians agree that God's commands in Scripture reveal to us what he wants us to do, and both agree that the commands in Scripture invite us to

---

[17]I. Howard Marshall, "Predestination in the New Testament" (in *Grace Unlimited,* p. 136), specifically says, "I cannot see how it can be just arbitrarily to save one guilty sinner and not another." But that seems to be precisely Paul's point in Rom. 9:18–20: God does save some and decide not to save others, and we have no right, as creatures, to say that this is unjust.

[18]For a discussion of the difference between God's revealed will and his secret will, see John Piper, "Are There Two Wills in God? Divine Election and God's Desire for All to Be Saved," in *Still Sovereign,* ed. Tom Schreiner and Bruce Ware.

[19]Clark Pinnock, "Introduction," in *Grace Unlimited,* p. 13.

repent and trust in Christ for salvation. Therefore, in one sense both agree that God wills that we be saved—it is the will that he reveals to us explicitly in the gospel invitation.

But both sides must also say that there is something else that God deems more important than saving everyone. Reformed theologians say that God deems *his own glory* more important than saving everyone, and that (according to Rom. 9) God's glory is also furthered by the fact that some are not saved. Arminian theologians also say that something else is more important to God than the salvation of all people, namely, the preservation of *man's free will.* So in a Reformed system God's highest value is his own glory, and in an Arminian system God's highest value is the free will of man. These are two distinctly different conceptions of the nature of God, and it seems that the Reformed position has much more explicit biblical support than the Arminian position does on this question.[20]

E. The Doctrine of Reprobation

When we understand election as God's sovereign choice of some persons to be saved, then there is necessarily another aspect of that choice, namely, God's sovereign decision to pass over others and not to save them. This decision of God in eternity past is called reprobation. *Reprobation is the sovereign decision of God before creation to pass over some persons, in sorrow deciding not to save them, and to punish them for their sins, and thereby to manifest his justice.*

In many ways the doctrine of reprobation is the most difficult of all the teachings of Scripture for us to think about and to accept, because it deals with such horrible and eternal consequences for human beings made in the image of God. The love that God gives us for our fellow human beings and the love that he commands us to have toward our neighbor cause us to recoil against this doctrine, and it is right that we feel such dread in contemplating it.[21] It is something that we would not want to believe, and would not believe, unless Scripture clearly taught it.

But are there Scripture passages that speak of such a decision by God? Certainly there are some. Jude speaks of some persons "who *long ago were designated for this condemnation,* ungodly persons who pervert the grace of our God into licentiousness and deny our only Master and Lord, Jesus Christ" (Jude 4).

Moreover, Paul, in the passage referred to above, speaks in the same way of Pharaoh and others:

> For the Scripture says to Pharaoh, "I have raised you up for the very purpose of showing my power in you, so that my name may be proclaimed in all the earth."

[20]An Arminian may object to suggesting that God created us and the whole universe for his own glory and may instead say that God is more glorified when we choose him out of an absolutely free will, but this is simply a doubtful assumption based on intuition or human analogy, and has no specific support from Scripture. Moreover, to be consistent it seems the Arminian would also have to take account of the millions who do not choose God, and would have to say that God is also glori-fied by the free choices of the millions who freely decide against God—otherwise, why would God allow them to persist in this free choice of rebellion?

[21]John Calvin himself says of reprobation, "The decree is dreadful indeed, I confess." Calvin, *Institutes,* 3.23.7 (2:955); but it should be noted that his Latin word *horribilis* does not mean "hateful" but rather "fearful, awe-inspiring."

So then he has mercy upon whomever he wills, and he hardens the heart of whomever he wills. . . . What if God, desiring to show his wrath and to make known his power, has endured with much patience the vessels of wrath made for destruction? (Rom. 9:17–22)

Regarding the results of the fact that God failed to choose all for salvation, Paul says, "The elect obtained it, but the rest were hardened" (Rom. 11:7). And Peter says of those who reject the gospel, "they stumble because they disobey the word, *as they were destined to do*" (1 Peter 2:8).[22]

In spite of the fact that we recoil against this doctrine, we must be careful of our attitude toward God and toward these passages of Scripture. We must never begin to wish that the Bible was written in another way, or that it did not contain these verses. Moreover, if we are convinced that these verses teach reprobation, then we are obligated both to believe it and accept it as fair and just of God, even though it still causes us to tremble in horror as we think of it. In this context it may surprise us to see that Jesus can thank God *both* for hiding the knowledge of salvation from some and for revealing it to others: "Jesus declared, 'I thank you, Father, Lord of heaven and earth, that you have hidden these things from the wise and understanding and revealed them to babes; yea, Father, for such was your gracious will'" (Matt. 11:25–26).

Moreover, we must recognize that somehow, in God's wisdom, the fact of reprobation and the eternal condemnation of some will show God's justice and also result in his glory. Paul says, "What if God, *desiring to show his wrath and to make known his power,* has endured with much patience the vessels of wrath made for destruction" (Rom. 9:22). Paul also notes that the fact of such punishment on the "vessels of wrath" serves to show the greatness of God's mercy toward us: God does this "in order to make known the riches of his glory for the vessels of mercy" (Rom. 9:23).

We also must remember that *there are important differences between election and reprobation as they are presented in the Bible.* Election to salvation is viewed as a cause for rejoicing and praise to God, who is worthy of praise and receives all the credit for our salvation (see Eph. 1:3–6; 1 Peter 1:1–3). God is viewed as actively choosing us for salvation, and doing so in love and with delight. But reprobation is viewed as something that brings God sorrow, not delight (see Ezek. 33:11), and the blame for the condemnation of sinners is always put on the people or angels who rebel, never on God himself (see John 3:18–19; 5:40). So in the presentation of Scripture the cause of election lies in God, and the cause of reprobation lies in the sinner. Another important difference is that the ground of election is God's grace, whereas the ground of reprobation is God's justice. Therefore "double predestination" is not a helpful or accurate phrase, because it neglects these differences between election and reprobation.

The sorrow of God at the death of the wicked ("I have no pleasure in the death of the wicked, but that the wicked turn from his way and live," Ezek. 33:11) helps us understand

---

[22]See discussion of this verse in Wayne Grudem, *1 Peter,* TNTC (Grand Rapids: Eerdmans, 1988), pp. 107–10. The verse does not simply say that God destined the *fact* that those who disobey would stumble, but speaks rather of God destining certain *people* to disobey and stumble: "as they were destined to do." (The Greek verb *etethēsan,* "they were destined," requires a plural subject.)

how appropriate it was that Paul himself felt great sorrow when he thought about the unbelieving Jews who had rejected Christ. Paul says:

> I am speaking the truth in Christ, I am not lying; my conscience bears me witness in the Holy Spirit, that *I have great sorrow and unceasing anguish in my heart.* For I could wish that I myself were accursed and cut off from Christ for the sake of my brethren, my kinsmen by race. They are Israelites. . . . (Rom. 9:1–4)

We ought also to feel this great sorrow as well when we think about the fate of unbelievers.

But it might be objected at this point, if God genuinely feels sorrow at the punishment of the wicked, then why does he allow it or even decree that it will come about? The answer must be that God knows that this will ultimately result in greater glory for himself. It will show his power and wrath and justice and mercy in a way that could not otherwise be demonstrated. Certainly in our own human experience it is possible to do something that causes us great sorrow but which we know will result in long-term greater good. And so, after this faint human analogy, we may somewhat understand that God can decree something that causes him sorrow yet ultimately will further his glory.

F. Practical Application of the Doctrine of Election

In terms of our own relationship with God, the doctrine of election does have significant practical application. When we think of the biblical teaching on both election and reprobation, it is appropriate to apply it to our own lives individually. It is right for each Christian to ask of himself or herself, "Why am I a Christian? What is the final reason why God decided to save me?"

The doctrine of election tells us that I am a Christian simply because God in eternity past decided to set his love on me. But why did he decide to set his love on me? Not for anything good in me, but simply because he decided to love me. There is no more ultimate reason than that.

It humbles us before God to think in this way. It makes us realize that we have no claim on God's grace whatsoever. Our salvation is totally due to grace alone. Our only appropriate response is to give God eternal praise.

QUESTIONS FOR PERSONAL APPLICATION

1. Do you think that God chose you individually to be saved before he created the world? Do you think he did it on the basis of the fact that he knew you would believe in Christ, or was it "unconditional election," not based on anything that he foresaw in you that made you worthy of his love? No matter how you answered the previous question, explain how your answer makes you feel when you think about yourself in relationship to God.

2. Does the doctrine of election give you any comfort or assurance about your future?

3. After reading this chapter, do you honestly feel that you would like to give thanks or praise to God for choosing you to be saved? Do you sense any unfairness in the fact that God did not decide to save everyone?

4. If you agree with the doctrine of election as presented in this chapter, does it diminish your sense of individual personhood or make you feel somewhat like a robot or a puppet in God's hands? Do you think it should make you feel this way?

5. What effect do you think this chapter will have on your motivation for evangelism? Is this a positive or negative effect? Can you think of ways in which the doctrine of election can be used as a positive encouragement to evangelism (see 1 Thess. 1:4–5; 2 Tim. 2:10)?

6. Whether you adopt a Reformed or Arminian perspective on the question of election, can you think of some positive benefits in the Christian life that those who hold the *opposite* position from yours seem more frequently to experience than you do? Even though you do not agree with the other position, can you list some helpful concerns or practical truths about the Christian life that you might learn from that position? Is there anything that Calvinists and Arminians could do to bring about greater understanding and less division on this question?

SPECIAL TERMS

determinism	foreknowledge
election	predestination
fatalism	reprobation

BIBLIOGRAPHY

Basinger, David, and Randall Basinger, eds. *Predestination and Free Will*. Downers Grove, Ill.: InterVarsity Press, 1985.

Berkouwer, G. C. *Divine Election*. Trans. by Hugo Bekker. Grand Rapids: Eerdmans, 1960.

Carson, D. A. *Divine Sovereignty and Human Responsibility: Biblical Perspectives in Tension*. Atlanta: John Knox Press, 1981.

Coppedge, Allan. *John Wesley in Theological Debate*. Wilmore, Ky.: Wesley Heritage Press, 1987.

Feinberg, John S. "God Ordains All Things." In *Predestination and Free Will: Four Views of Divine Sovereignty and Human Freedom*. David Basinger & Randall Basinger, eds. Downers Grove, Ill.: InterVarsity Press, 1986.

Godfrey, William R. "Predestination." In *NDT*, pp. 528–30.

Klein, William W. *The New Chosen People: A Corporate View of Election*. Grand Rapids: Zondervan, 1990.

Klooster, F. H. "Elect, Election." In *EDT*, pp. 348–49.

Nettles, Thomas. *By His Grace and for His Glory: A Historical, Theological and Practical Study of the Doctrines of Grace in Baptist Life.* Grand Rapids: Baker Book House, 1986.

Packer, J. I. "Election." In *IBD*, Vol. 1, pp. 435–38.

Pinnock, Clark H., ed. *Grace Unlimited.* Minneapolis: Bethany, 1975.

_____. *The Grace of God, the Will of Man: A Case for Arminianism.* Grand Rapids: Zondervan, 1989.

Piper, John. *The Justification of God: An Exegetical and Theological Study of Romans 9:1–23.* Grand Rapids: Baker, 1983.

Poythress, Vern. "Using Multiple Thematic Centers in Theological Synthesis: Holiness as a Test Case in Developing a Pauline Theology." Unpublished manuscript available from the Campus Bookstore, Westminster Theological Seminary, P.O. Box 27009, Philadelphia, PA, 19118 (a study on Pauline themes used to describe the application of redemption).

Reid, W. S. "Reprobation." In *EDT*, p. 937.

Schreiner, Thomas, and Bruce Ware, editors. *Still Sovereign: Contemporary Perspectives on Election, Foreknowledge, and Grace.* Grand Rapids: Baker, 2000.

Shank, R. *Elect in the Son: A Study of the Doctrine of Election.* Springfield, Mo.: Westcott, 1970.

Sproul, R. C. *Chosen by God.* Wheaton, Ill.: Tyndale, 1986.

Steele, David N. and Curtis C. Thomas. *The Five Points of Calvinism—Defined, Defended, Documented.* International Library of Philosophy and Theology: Biblical and Theological Studies, ed. J. Marcellus Kik. Phillipsburg, N.J.: Presbyterian and Reformed, 1963.

Storms, C. Samuel. *Chosen for Life: An Introductory Guide to the Doctrine of Divine Election.* Grand Rapids: Baker, 1987.

Warfield, B. B. *The Plan of Salvation.* Grand Rapids: Eerdmans, 1942.

_____. "Predestination." In *Biblical and Theological Studies.* Philadelphia: Presbyterian and Reformed, 1952.

SCRIPTURE MEMORY PASSAGE

Ephesians 1:3–6: *Blessed be the God and Father of our Lord Jesus Christ, who has blessed us in Christ with every spiritual blessing in the heavenly places, even as he chose us in him before the foundation of the world, that we should be holy and blameless before him. He destined us in love to be his sons through Jesus Christ, according to the purpose of his will, to the praise of his glorious grace which he freely bestowed on us in the Beloved.*

HYMN

"When This Passing World Is Done"

This hymn reminds us that when we are once in heaven and look back on our life we will realize how much more we owe to God's mercy and grace than we ever realized in this life.

The last stanza especially emphasizes the fact that our election is not based on anything good in ourselves: "Chosen not for good in me."

> When this passing world is done,
>   When has sunk yon glaring sun,
> When we stand with Christ in glory,
>   Looking o'er life's finished story,
> Then, Lord, shall I fully know,
>   Not till then, how much I owe.
>
> When I hear the wicked call
>   On the rocks and hills to fall,
> When I see them start to shrink
>   On the fiery deluge brink,
> Then, Lord, shall I fully know,
>   Not till then, how much I owe.
>
> When I stand before the throne,
>   Dressed in beauty not my own,
> When I see thee as thou art,
>   Love thee with unsinning heart,
> Then, Lord, shall I fully know,
>   Not till then, how much I owe.
>
> When the praise of heav'n I hear,
>   Loud as thunders to the ear,
> Loud as many waters' noise,
>   Sweet as harp's melodious voice,
> Then, Lord, shall I fully know,
>   Not till then, how much I owe.
>
> Chosen not for good in me,
>   Wakened up from wrath to flee,
> Hidden in the Savior's side,
>   By the Spirit sanctified,
> Teach me, Lord, on earth to show,
>   By my love, how much I owe.

AUTHOR: ROBERT MURRAY MCCHEYNE, 1837

Chapter

THE GOSPEL CALL AND EFFECTIVE CALLING

What is the gospel message?
How does it become effective?

EXPLANATION AND SCRIPTURAL BASIS

When Paul talks about the way that God brings salvation into our lives, he says, "Those whom he *predestined* he also *called;* and those whom he called he also *justified;* and those whom he justified he also *glorified*" (Rom. 8:30). Here Paul points to a definite order in which the blessings of salvation come to us. Although long ago, before the world was made, God "predestined" us to be his children and to be conformed to the image of his Son, Paul points to the fact that in the actual outworking of his purpose in our lives God "called" us (here in this context, God the Father is specifically in view). Then Paul immediately lists justification and glorification, showing that these come after calling. Paul indicates that there is a definite order in God's saving purpose (though not every aspect of our salvation is mentioned here). So we will begin our discussion of the different parts of our experience of salvation with the topic of calling.

A. Effective Calling

When Paul says, "Those whom he predestined *he* also called; and those whom *he* called he also justified" (Rom. 8:30), he indicates that calling is an act of God. In fact, it is specifically an act of God the Father, for he is the one who predestines people "to be conformed to the image of his Son" (Rom. 8:29). Other verses describe more fully what this calling is. When God calls people in this powerful way, he calls them "out of darkness into his marvelous light" (1 Peter 2:9); he calls them "into the fellowship of his Son" (1 Cor. 1:9; cf. Acts 2:39) and "into his own kingdom and glory" (1 Thess. 2:12; cf. 1 Peter 5:10; 2 Peter 1:3). People who have been called by God "belong to Jesus Christ" (Rom. 1:6). They are called to "be saints" (Rom. 1:7; 1 Cor. 1:2), and have come into a realm of peace (1 Cor. 7:15; Col.

3:15), freedom (Gal. 5:13), hope (Eph. 1:18; 4:4), holiness (1 Thess. 4:7), patient endurance of suffering (1 Peter 2:20–21; 3:9), and eternal life (1 Tim. 6:12).

These verses indicate that no powerless, merely human calling is in view. This calling is rather a kind of "summons" from the King of the universe and it has such power that it brings about the response that it asks for in people's hearts. It is an act of God that *guarantees* a response, because Paul specifies in Romans 8:30 that all who were "called" were also "justified."[1] This calling has the capacity to draw us out of the kingdom of darkness and bring us into God's kingdom so we can join in full fellowship with him: "God is faithful, by whom you were *called into the fellowship of his Son,* Jesus Christ our Lord" (1 Cor. 1:9).[2]

This powerful act of God is often referred to as *effective calling,* to distinguish it from the general gospel invitation that goes to all people and which some people reject. This is not to say that human gospel proclamation is not involved. In fact, God's effective calling comes *through* the human preaching of the gospel, because Paul says, "To this he called you *through our gospel,* so that you may obtain the glory of our Lord Jesus Christ" (2 Thess. 2:14). Of course, there are many who hear the general call of the gospel message and do not respond. But in some cases the gospel call is made so effective by the working of the Holy Spirit in people's hearts that they do respond; we can say that they have received "effective calling."[3]

We may define effective calling as follows: *Effective calling is an act of God the Father, speaking through the human proclamation of the gospel, in which he summons people to himself in such a way that they respond in saving faith.*

It is important that we not give the impression that people will be saved by the power of this call *apart from* their own willing response to the gospel (see chapter 6 on the personal faith and repentance that are necessary for conversion). Although it is true that effective calling awakens and brings forth a response from us, we must always insist that this response still has to be a voluntary, willing response in which the individual person puts his or her trust in Christ.

This is why prayer is so important to effective evangelism. Unless God works in peoples' hearts to make the proclamation of the gospel effective, there will be no genuine saving response. Jesus said, "No one can come to me unless the Father who sent me draws him" (John 6:44).

An example of the gospel call working effectively is seen in Paul's first visit to Philippi. When Lydia heard the gospel message, "The Lord *opened her heart* to give heed to what was said by Paul" (Acts 16:14).

In distinction from effective calling, which is entirely an act of God, we may talk about the *gospel call* in general which comes through human speech. This gospel call is offered to all people, even those who do not accept it. Sometimes this gospel call is referred to as *external calling* or *general calling.* By contrast, the effective calling of God that actually brings about a willing response from the person who hears it is sometimes called *internal calling.* The gospel call is general and external and often rejected, while the effective call is particular, internal, and *always* effective. However, this is not to diminish the importance of the gospel call—it is the means God has appointed through which effective calling will come. Without the gospel call, no one could respond and be saved! "How are they to believe in him of whom they have never heard?" (Rom. 10:14). Therefore it is important to understand exactly what the gospel call is.

B. The Elements of the Gospel Call

In human preaching of the gospel, three important elements must be included.

1. Explanation of the Facts Concerning Salvation. Anyone who comes to Christ for salvation must have at least a basic understanding of who Christ is and how he meets our needs for salvation. Therefore an explanation of the facts concerning salvation must include at least the following:

> 1. All people have sinned (Rom. 3:23).
> 2. The penalty for our sin is death (Rom. 6:23).
> 3. Jesus Christ died to pay the penalty for our sins (Rom. 5:8).

But understanding those facts and even agreeing that they are true is not enough for a person to be saved. There must also be an invitation for a personal response on the part of the individual who will repent of his or her sins and trust personally in Christ.

2. Invitation to Respond to Christ Personally in Repentance and Faith. When the New Testament talks about people coming to salvation it speaks in terms of a personal response to an invitation from Christ himself. That invitation is beautifully expressed, for example, in the words of Jesus:

> *Come to me,* all you who are weary and burdened, and I will give you rest. Take my yoke upon you and learn from me, for I am gentle and humble in heart, and you will find rest for your souls. For my yoke is easy and my burden is light. (Matt. 11:28–30 NIV)

It is important to make clear that these are not just words spoken a long time ago by a religious leader in the past. Every non-Christian hearing these words should be encouraged to think of them as words that Jesus Christ is *even now,* at *this very moment,* speaking to him or to her individually. Jesus Christ is a Savior who is now alive in heaven, and each non-Christian should think of Jesus as speaking directly to him or her, saying, "*Come to me . . .* and I will give you rest" (Matt. 11:28). This is a genuine *personal* invitation that seeks a personal response from each one who hears it.

John also talks about the need for personal response when he says, "He came to his own home, and his own people received him not. *But to all who received him,* who believed in his name, he gave power to become children of God" (John 1:11–12). In emphasizing the

---

[1]See the discussion of justification in chapter 7.

[2]1 Thess. 2:12 speaks of God "who *calls you into* his own kingdom and glory," but the sense would even more closely parallel 1 Cor. 1:9 if we adopt the well-attested textual variant *kalesantos* (aorist participle) and translated, "who *has called you into* his own kingdom and glory."

[3]The older term used for "effective calling" was "effectual calling," but the term *effectual* is not as commonly used in English today.

need to "receive" Christ, John, too, points to the necessity of an individual response. To those inside a lukewarm church who do not realize their spiritual blindness the Lord Jesus again issues an invitation that calls for personal response: "Behold, I stand at the door and knock; if any one hears my voice and opens the door, I will come in to him and eat with him, and he with me" (Rev. 3:20).

Finally, just five verses from the end of the entire Bible, there is another invitation from the Holy Spirit and the church to come to Christ: "The Spirit and the Bride say, 'Come.' And let him who hears say, 'Come.' And let him who is thirsty come, let him who desires take the water of life without price" (Rev. 22:17).

But what is involved in coming to Christ? Although this will be explained more fully in chapter 6, it is sufficient to note here that if we come to Christ and trust him to save us from our sin, we cannot any longer cling to sin but must willingly renounce it in genuine repentance. In some cases in Scripture both repentance and faith are mentioned together when referring to someone's initial conversion (Paul said that he spent his time "testifying both to Jews and to Greeks of *repentance* to God and of *faith* in our Lord Jesus Christ," Acts 20:21). But at other times only repentance of sins is named and saving faith is assumed as an accompanying factor ("that *repentance* and forgiveness of sins should be preached in his name to all nations" [Luke 24:47; cf. Acts 2:37–38; 3:19; 5:31; 17:30; Rom. 2:4; 2 Cor. 7:10, et al.]). Therefore, any genuine gospel proclamation must include an invitation to make a conscious decision to forsake one's sins and come to Christ in faith, asking Christ for forgiveness of sins. If either the need to repent of sins or the need to trust in Christ for forgiveness is neglected, there is not a full and true proclamation of the gospel.[4]

But what is promised for those who come to Christ? This is the third element of the gospel call.

3. A Promise of Forgiveness and Eternal Life. Although the words of personal invitation spoken by Christ do have promises of rest, and power to become children of God, and partaking of the water of life, it is helpful to make explicit just what Christ promises to those who come to him in repentance and faith. The primary thing that is promised in the gospel message is the promise of forgiveness of sins and eternal life with God. "For God so loved the world that he gave his only Son, that whoever believes in him *should not perish but have eternal life*" (John 3:16). And in Peter's preaching of the gospel he says, "Repent therefore, and turn again, *that your sins may be blotted out*" (Acts 3:19; cf. 2:38).

Coupled with the promise of forgiveness and eternal life should be an assurance that Christ will accept all who come to him in sincere repentance and faith seeking salvation: "Him who comes to me I will not cast out" (John 6:37).

C. The Importance of the Gospel Call

The doctrine of the gospel call is important, because if there were no gospel call we could not be saved. "How are they to believe in him of whom they have never heard?" (Rom. 10:14).

The gospel call is important also because through it God addresses us in the fullness of our humanity. He does not save us "automatically" without seeking for a response from us as whole persons. Rather, he addresses the gospel call to our intellects, our emotions, and our wills. He speaks to our intellects by explaining the facts of salvation in his Word. He speaks to our emotions by issuing a heartfelt personal invitation to respond. He speaks to our wills by asking us to hear his invitation and respond willingly in repentance and faith—to decide to turn from our sins and receive Christ as Savior and rest our hearts in him for salvation.

QUESTIONS FOR PERSONAL APPLICATION

1. Can you remember the first time you heard the gospel and responded to it? Can you describe what it felt like in your heart? Do you think the Holy Spirit was working to make that gospel call effective in your life? Did you resist it at the time?

2. In your explanation of the gospel call to other people, have some elements been missing? If so, what difference would it make if you added those elements to your explanation of the gospel? Do you think those elements are important to add? What is the one thing most needed to make your proclamation of the gospel more effective?

3. Before reading this chapter, had you thought of Jesus in heaven speaking the words of the gospel invitation personally to people even today? If non-Christians do begin to think of Jesus speaking to them in this way, how do you think it will affect their response to the gospel?

4. Do you understand the elements of the gospel call clearly enough to present them to others? Could you easily turn in the Bible to find four or five appropriate verses that would explain the gospel call clearly to people? (Memorizing the elements of the gospel call and the verses that explain it should be one of the first disciplines of anyone's Christian life.)

SPECIAL TERMS

effective calling	the gospel call
external calling	internal calling

BIBLIOGRAPHY

Aldrich, Joseph C. *Life-Style Evangelism: Crossing Traditional Boundaries to Reach the Unbelieving World.* Portland: Multnomah, 1981.

Alleine, Joseph. *Sure Guide to Heaven.* Carlisle, Pa.: Banner of Truth, 1978. First published in 1672 as *An Alarm to the Unconverted.*

Baxter, Richard. *A Call to the Unconverted to Turn and Live.* Reprint: Grand Rapids: Zondervan, 1953.

Coleman, Robert E. *The Master Plan of Evangelism.* Old Tappan, N.J.: Revell, 1963.

---

[4]See chapter 6, pp. 86–90, for a fuller discussion of the need for both genuine repentance and genuine faith, and a discussion of the question of whether someone can be saved by "accepting Jesus as Savior but not as Lord."

Hoekema, Anthony A. *Saved by Grace.* Grand Rapids: Eerdmans, and Exeter: Paternoster, 1989, pp. 68–92.

Kennedy, D. James. *Evangelism Explosion.* 3d ed. Wheaton, Ill.: Tyndale, 1983.

Kevan, Ernest F. *Salvation.* Phillipsburg, N.J.: Presbyterian and Reformed, 1973.

Little, Paul. *How to Give Away Your Faith.* Revised by Marie Little. Downers Grove, Ill.: InterVarsity Press, 1988.

MacArthur, John F., Jr. *The Gospel According to Jesus.* Grand Rapids: Zondervan, 1988.

Murray, John. "Effectual Calling." In *Redemption Accomplished and Applied.* Grand Rapids: Eerdmans, 1955, pp. 88–94.

Packer, J. I. "Call, Calling." In *EDT*, p. 184.

_____. *Evangelism and the Sovereignty of God.* Downers Grove, Ill.: InterVarsity Press, 1961.

Wells, David F. *God the Evangelist: How the Holy Spirit Works to Bring Men and Women to Faith.* Grand Rapids: Eerdmans, 1987.

SCRIPTURE MEMORY PASSAGE

Matthew 11:28–30: *Come to me, all who labor and are heavy laden, and I will give you rest. Take my yoke upon you, and learn from me; for I am gentle and lowly in heart, and you will find rest for your souls. For my yoke is easy, and my burden is light.*

HYMN

"I Heard the Voice of Jesus Say"

I heard the voice of Jesus say, "Come unto me and rest;
    Lay down, thou weary one, lay down thy head upon my breast."
I came to Jesus as I was, weary and worn and sad,
    I found in him a resting place, and he has made me glad.

I heard the voice of Jesus say, "Behold, I freely give
    The living water; thirsty one, stoop down and drink, and live."
I came to Jesus, and I drank of that life-giving stream;
    My thirst was quenched, my soul revived, and now I live in him.

I heard the voice of Jesus say, "I am this dark world's light;
    Look unto me, thy morn shall rise, and all thy day be bright."
I looked to Jesus, and I found in him my star, my sun;
    And in that light of life I'll walk, till trav'ling days are done.

AUTHOR: HORATIUS BONAR, 1846

Chapter

REGENERATION

What does it mean to be born again?

EXPLANATION AND SCRIPTURAL BASIS

We may define regeneration as follows: *Regeneration is a secret act of God in which he imparts new spiritual life to us.* This is sometimes called "being born again" (using language from John 3:3–8).

A. Regeneration Is Totally a Work of God

In some of the elements of the application of redemption that we discuss in subsequent chapters, we play an active part (this is true, for example, of conversion, sanctification and perseverance). But in the work of regeneration we play no active role at all. It is instead totally a work of God. We see this, for example, when John talks about those to whom Christ gave power to become children of God—they "were born, not of blood nor of the will of the flesh nor of the will of man, but of God" (John 1:13). Here John specifies that children of God are those who are "born . . . of God" and our human will ("the will of man") does not bring about this kind of birth.

The fact that we are passive in regeneration is also evident when Scripture refers to it as being "born" or being "born again" (cf. James 1:18; 1 Peter 1:3; John 3:3–8). We did not choose to be made physically alive and we did not choose to be born—it is something that happened to us; similarly, these analogies in Scripture suggest that we are entirely passive in regeneration.

This sovereign work of God in regeneration was also predicted in the prophecy of Ezekiel. Through him God promised a time in the future when he would give new spiritual life to his people:

> A *new heart* I will give you, and *a new spirit I will put within you;* and I will take out of your flesh the heart of stone and give you a heart of flesh. And I will put my spirit within you, and cause you to walk in my statutes and be careful to observe my ordinances. (Ezek. 36:26–27)

Which member of the Trinity is the one who causes regeneration? When Jesus speaks of being "born of the Spirit" (John 3:8), he indicates that it is especially God the Holy Spirit who produces regeneration. But other verses also indicate the involvement of God the Father in regeneration: Paul specifies that it is God who "made us alive together with Christ" (Eph. 2:5; cf. Col. 2:13). And James says that it is the "Father of lights" who gave us new birth: "Of his own will *he brought us forth* by the word of truth that we should be a kind of first fruits of his creatures" (James 1:17–18).[1] Finally, Peter says that God "according to his abundant mercy *has given us new birth* . . . through the resurrection of Jesus Christ from the dead" (1 Peter 1:3, author's translation). We can conclude that both God the Father and God the Holy Spirit bring about regeneration.

What is the connection between effective calling[2] and regeneration? As we will see later in this chapter, Scripture indicates that regeneration must come before we can respond to effective calling with saving faith. Therefore we can say that regeneration comes before the *result* of effective calling (our faith). But it is more difficult to specify the exact relationship in time between regeneration and the human proclamation of the gospel through which God works in effective calling. At least two passages suggest that God regenerates us at the same time as he speaks to us in effective calling: Peter says, "You have been *born anew,* not of perishable seed but of imperishable, *through the living and abiding word of God. . . .* That word is the good news which was preached to you" (1 Peter 1:23, 25). And James says, "He chose to *give us birth through the word of truth*" (James 1:18 NIV). As the gospel comes to us, God speaks through it to summon us to himself (effective calling) and to give us new spiritual life (regeneration) so that we are enabled to respond in faith. Effective calling is thus God the Father *speaking powerfully to us,* and regeneration is God the Father and God the Holy Spirit *working powerfully in us,* to make us alive. These two things must have happened simultaneously as Peter was preaching the gospel to the household of Cornelius, for while he was still preaching "the Holy Spirit fell on all who heard the word" (Acts 10:44).

Sometimes the term *irresistible grace*[3] is used in this connection. It refers to the fact that God effectively calls people and also gives them regeneration, and both actions guarantee that we will respond in saving faith. The term *irresistible grace* is subject to misunderstanding, however, since it *seems* to imply that people do not make a voluntary, willing choice in responding to the gospel—a wrong idea, and a wrong understanding of the term *irresistible grace.* The term does preserve something valuable, however, because it indicates that God's work reaches into our hearts to bring about a response that is absolutely certain—even though we respond voluntarily.[4]

B. The Exact Nature of Regeneration Is Mysterious to Us

Exactly what happens in regeneration is mysterious to us. We know that somehow we who were spiritually dead (Eph. 2:1) have been made alive to God and in a very real sense we have been "born again" (John 3:3, 7; Eph. 2:5; Col. 2:13). But we don't understand how this happens or what exactly God does to us to give us this new spiritual life.

Jesus says, "The wind blows where it wills, and you hear the sound of it, but you do not know whence it comes or whither it goes; so it is with every one who is born of the Spirit" (John 3:8).

Scripture views regeneration as something that affects us as whole persons. Of course, our "spirits are alive" to God after regeneration (Rom. 8:10), but that is simply because we as *whole persons* are affected by regeneration. It is not just that our spirits were dead before—*we* were dead to God in trespasses and sins (see Eph. 2:1). And it is not correct to say that the only thing that happens in regeneration is that our spirits are made alive (as some would teach),[5] for *every part of us* is affected by regeneration: "If any one is in Christ, *he is a new creation;* the old has passed away, behold, the new has come" (2 Cor. 5:17).

Because regeneration is a work of God within us in which he gives us new life it is right to conclude that it is an *instantaneous event*. It happens only once. At one moment we are spiritually dead, and then at the next moment we have new spiritual life from God. Nevertheless, we do not always know exactly when this instantaneous change occurs. Especially for children growing up in a Christian home, or for people who attend an evangelical church or Bible study over a period of time and grow gradually in their understanding of the gospel, there may not be a dramatic crisis with a radical change of behavior from "hardened sinner" to "holy saint," but there will be an instantaneous change nonetheless, when God through the Holy Spirit, in an unseen, invisible way, awakens spiritual life within. The change will *become evident* over time in patterns of behavior and desires that are pleasing to God.

In other cases (in fact, probably most cases when adults become Christians) regeneration takes place at a clearly recognizable time at which the person realizes that previously he or she was separated from God and spiritually dead, but immediately afterward there was clearly new spiritual life within. The results can usually be seen at once—a heartfelt trusting in Christ for salvation, an assurance of sins forgiven, a desire to read the Bible and pray (and a sense that these are meaningful spiritual activities), a delight in worship, a desire for Christian fellowship, a sincere desire to be obedient to God's Word in Scripture, and a desire to tell others about Christ. People may say something like this: "I don't know exactly what happened, but before that moment I did not trust in Christ for salvation. I was still wondering and questioning in my mind. But after that moment I realized that I did trust in Christ and he was my Savior. Something happened in my heart."[6] Yet even in these cases we are not quite sure exactly what has happened in our hearts. It is just as Jesus said with respect to the wind—we hear its sound and we see the result, but we cannot actually see the wind itself. So it is with the working of the Holy Spirit in our hearts.

---

[1]When James says that God "brought us forth," he uses language that ordinarily applies to physical birth (being brought forth out of our mothers' wombs, and into the world) and applies it to spiritual birth.

[2]See chapter 4, on effective calling.

[3]This is the "I" in the "five points of Calvinism" represented by the acronym TULIP. The other letters stand for *T*otal deprav-ity, *U*nconditional election (see chapter 3), *L*imited atonement, and *P*erseverance of the saints (see chapter 11).

[4]Some people will object here that God cannot *guarantee* a response that is still willing and voluntary on our part. But this objection simply inserts into the discussion a definition of "voluntary" or "willing" that is not itself supported by Scripture.

C. In This Sense of "Regeneration," It Comes Before Saving Faith

Using the verses quoted above, we have defined regeneration to be the act of God awakening spiritual life within us, bringing us from spiritual *death* to spiritual *life.* On this definition, it is natural to understand that regeneration comes before saving faith. It is in fact this work of God that gives us the spiritual *ability* to respond to God in faith. However, when we say that it comes "before" saving faith, it is important to remember that they usually come so close together that it will ordinarily seem to us that they are happening at the same time. As God addresses the effective call of the gospel to us, he regenerates us and we respond in faith and repentance to this call. So *from our perspective* it is hard to tell any difference in time, especially because regeneration is a spiritual work that we cannot perceive with our eyes or even understand with our minds.

Yet there are several passages that tell us that this secret, hidden work of God in our spirits does in fact come before we respond to God in saving faith (though often it may be only seconds before we respond). When talking about regeneration with Nicodemus, Jesus said, "Unless one is born of water and the Spirit, *he cannot enter the kingdom of God*" (John 3:5). Now we enter the kingdom of God when we become Christians at conversion. But Jesus says that we have to be born "of the Spirit" before we can do that.[7] Our inability to come to Christ on our own, without an initial work of God within us, is also emphasized when Jesus says, "No one can come to me unless the Father who sent me draws him" (John 6:44), and "No one can come to me unless it is granted him by the Father" (John 6:65). This inward act of regeneration is described beautifully when Luke says of Lydia, *"The Lord opened her heart* to give heed to what was said by Paul" (Acts 16:14). First the Lord opened her heart, then she was able to give heed to Paul's preaching and to respond in faith.

By contrast, Paul tells us, "The man without the Spirit [literally, the 'natural man'] does not accept the things that come from the Spirit of God, for they are foolishness to him, and he cannot understand them, because they are spiritually discerned" (1 Cor. 2:14 NIV). He also says of people apart from Christ, "no one understands, No one seeks for God" (Rom. 3:11).

The solution to this spiritual deadness and inability to respond only comes when God gives us new life within. "But God, who is rich in mercy, out of the great love with which he loved us, even *when we were dead through our trespasses,* made us alive together with Christ" (Eph. 2:4–5). Paul also says, *"When you were dead in your sins* and in the uncircumcision of your sinful nature, *God made you alive with Christ"* (Col. 2:13 NIV).[8]

The idea that regeneration comes before saving faith is not always understood by evangelicals today. Sometimes people will even say something like, "If you believe in Christ as your Savior, then (after you believe) you will be born again." But Scripture itself never says anything like that. This new birth is viewed by Scripture as something that God does within us in order to enable us to believe.

---

[5]This view of regeneration usually depends on viewing man as trichotomous or consisting of three parts (body, soul, and spirit). But if we reject trichotomy and see "soul" and "spirit" as synonyms in Scripture that speak of the immaterial part of our nature, then such an explanation is not persuasive. Even for those who accept trichotomy, the Scriptures that speak of us as a new creation and that say that *we* have been born again (not just our spirits), should be good reason for seeing more in regeneration than merely making our spirits alive.

The reason that evangelicals often think that regeneration comes after saving faith is that they *see the results* (love for God and his Word, and turning from sin) *after* people come to faith, and they think that regeneration must therefore have come after saving faith. Yet here we must decide on the basis of what Scripture tells us, because regeneration itself is not something we see or know about directly: "The wind blows where it wills, and you hear the sound of it, but you do not know whence it comes or whither it goes; so it is with every one who is born of the Spirit" (John 3:8).

Because Christians often tend to focus on the *results* of regeneration, rather than the hidden spiritual act of God itself, some evangelical statements of faith have contained wording that suggests that regeneration comes after saving faith. So, for example, the statement of faith of the Evangelical Free Church of America (which has been adapted by a number of other evangelical organizations) says,

> We believe that the true Church is composed of all such persons who *through saving faith* in Jesus Christ *have been regenerated* by the Holy Spirit and are united together in the body of Christ of which He is the Head. (paragraph 8)

Here the word "regeneration" apparently means the *outward evidence of regeneration* that is seen in a changed life, evidence that certainly does come after saving faith. Thus "being born again" is thought of not in terms of the initial impartation of new life, but in terms of the *total life change that results* from that impartation. If the term "regeneration" is understood in this way, then it would be true that regeneration comes after saving faith.

Nevertheless, if we are to use language that closely conforms to the actual wording of Scripture, it would be better to restrict the word "regeneration" to the instantaneous, *initial* work of God in which he imparts spiritual life to us. Then we can emphasize that we do not see regeneration itself but only the results of it in our lives, and that faith in Christ for salvation is the first result that we see. In fact, we can never know that we have been

---

[6]C. S. Lewis tells the story of his own conversion: "I know very well when, but hardly how, the final step was taken. I was driven to Whipsnade one sunny morning. When we set out I did not believe that Jesus Christ is the Son of God, and when we reached the zoo I did. Yet I had not exactly spent the journey in thought. Nor in great emotion" (*Surprised by Joy* [New York: Harcourt, Brace and World, 1955], p. 237).

[7]When Jesus talks about being "born of water" here, the most likely interpretation of this is that he is referring to *spiritual cleansing from sin,* which Ezekiel prophesied when he said, "I will sprinkle clean water upon you, and you shall be clean from all your uncleannesses, and from all your idols I will cleanse you. A new heart I will give you, and a new spirit I will put within you" (Ezek. 36:25–26). Here the water symbolizes spiritual cleansing from sin, just as the new heart and new spirit speak of the new spiritual life that God will give. Ezekiel is prophesying that God will give an internal cleansing from the pollution of sin in the heart at the same time as he awakens new spiritual life within his people. The fact that these two ideas are connected so closely in this well-known prophecy from Ezekiel, and the fact that Jesus assumes that Nico-

demus should have understood this truth ("Are you a teacher of Israel, and yet you do not understand this?" [John 3:10]), together with the fact that throughout the conversation Jesus is talking about intensely spiritual concerns, all suggest that this is the most likely understanding of the passage. Another suggestion has been that "born of water" refers to physical birth and the "water" (or amniotic fluid) that accompanies it, but it would hardly be necessary for Jesus to specify that one has to be born in this way when he is talking about spiritual birth, and it is questionable whether first-century Jews would have understood the phrase in this way either. Another interpretation is that Jesus is referring to the water of baptism here, but baptism or any other similar ceremony is not in view in this passage (and it would have been anachronistic for Jesus to speak of Christian baptism here, since that did not begin until Pentecost); moreover, this would make Jesus teach that a physical act of baptism is necessary for salvation, something that would contradict the New Testament emphasis on salvation by faith alone as necessary for salvation, and something which, if it were true, we would certainly expect to find taught much more explicitly in the other New Testament passages that clearly deal with baptism.

regenerated until we come to faith in Christ, for that is the outward evidence of this hidden, inward work of God. Once we do come to saving faith in Christ, we know that we have been born again.

By way of application, we should realize that the explanation of the gospel message in Scripture does not take the form of a command, "Be born again and you will be saved," but rather, "Believe in Jesus Christ and you will be saved."[9] This is the consistent pattern in the preaching of the gospel throughout the book of Acts, and also in the descriptions of the gospel given in the Epistles.

D. Genuine Regeneration Must Bring Results in Life

In an earlier section we saw a beautiful example of the first result of regeneration in a person's life, when Paul spoke the gospel message to Lydia and "the Lord opened her heart to give heed to what was said by Paul" (Acts 16:14; cf. John 6:44, 65; 1 Peter 1:3). Similarly, John says, "Everyone who believes that Jesus is the Christ *is born of God*" (1 John 5:1 NIV).[10] But there are also other results of regeneration, many of which are specified in John's first epistle. For example, John says, "No one who is born of God will continue to sin, because God's seed remains in him; he *cannot go on sinning,* because he has been born of God" (1 John 3:9 NIV). Here John explains that a person who is born again has that spiritual "seed" (that life-generating and growing power) within him, and that this keeps the person living a life free of continual sin. This does not of course mean that the person will have a perfect life, but only that the pattern of life will not be one of continuing indulgence in sin. When people are asked to characterize a regenerated person's life, the adjective that comes to mind should not be "sinner," but rather something like "obedient to Christ" or "obedient to Scripture." We should notice that John says this is true of everyone who is truly born again: "*No one* who is born of God will continue to sin." Another way of looking at this is to say that "every one who does what is right has been born of him" (1 John 2:29).

A genuine, Christlike *love* will be one specific result in life: "Everyone who loves has been born of God and knows God" (1 John 4:7 NIV). Another effect of the new birth is *overcoming the world:* "And his commands are not burdensome, for everyone born of God has overcome the world" (1 John 5:3–4 NIV). Here John explains that regeneration gives the ability to overcome the pressures and temptations of the world that would otherwise keep us from obeying God's commandments and following his paths. John says that we will overcome these pressures and therefore it will not be "burdensome" to obey God's commands but, he implies, it will rather be joyful. He goes on to explain that the process

---

[8]The RSV translates Col. 2:13 with a relative clause: "And you, *who were dead* in trespasses and the uncircumcision of your flesh, God made alive together with him," but the Greek text has no relative pronoun (*hous*), which Paul could easily have used, but rather has a participial phrase with the present participle *ontas,* "being," giving a nuance of continuing activity that occurred *at the same time* that the action of the main verb ("made alive") took place. Thus, the NIV expresses the appropriate sense: at the time when we were continuing in the state of being dead in our sins, God made us alive. No matter whether we translate the participle as concessive, causative, or expressing attendant circumstances, or with any other sense possible to the participle, this temporal nuance of time simultaneous with the main verb would still be present as well. Yet the NIV, in translating it as an explicitly temporal participle ("*when* you were dead") seems to have given the best rendering of the intended sense of the verse.

through which we gain victory over the world is continuing in faith: "This is the victory that has overcome the world, even our faith" (1 John 5:4 NIV).

Finally, John notes that another result of regeneration is *protection from Satan* himself: "We know that anyone born of God does not continue to sin; the one who was born of God [that is, Jesus] keeps him safe, *and the evil one cannot harm him*" (1 John 5:18 NIV). Though there may be attacks from Satan, John reassures his readers that "the one who is in you is greater than the one who is in the world" (1 John 4:4 NIV), and this greater power of the Holy Spirit within us keeps us safe from ultimate spiritual harm by the evil one.

We should realize that John emphasizes these as *necessary* results in the lives of those who are born again. If there is genuine regeneration in a person's life, he or she *will* believe that Jesus is the Christ, and *will* refrain from a life pattern of continual sin, and *will* love his brother, and *will* overcome the temptations of the world, and *will* be kept safe from ultimate harm by the evil one. These passages show that it is impossible for a person to be regenerated and not become truly converted.[11]

Other results of regeneration are listed by Paul where he speaks of the "*fruit of the Spirit,*" that is, the result in life that is produced by the power of the Holy Spirit working within every believer: "But the fruit of the Spirit is love, joy, peace, patience, kindness, goodness, faithfulness, gentleness, self-control" (Gal. 5:22–23). If there is true regeneration then these elements of the fruit of the Spirit will be more and more evident in that person's life. But by contrast, those who are unbelievers, including those who are pretending to be believers but are not, will clearly lack of these character traits in their lives. Jesus told his disciples:

> Beware of false prophets, who come to you in sheep's clothing but inwardly are ravenous wolves. *You will know them by their fruits.* Are grapes gathered from thorns, or figs from thistles? So, every sound tree bears good fruit, but the bad tree bears evil fruit. A sound tree cannot bear evil fruit, nor can a bad tree bear good fruit. Every tree that does not bear good fruit is cut down and thrown into the fire. Thus you will know them by their fruits. (Matt. 7:15–20)

Neither Jesus nor Paul nor John point to activity in the church or miracles as evidence of regeneration. They rather point to character traits in life. In fact, immediately after the verses quoted above Jesus warns that on the day of judgment many will say to him, "Lord, Lord, did we not prophesy in your name, and cast out demons in your name, and do many mighty works in your name?" But he will declare to them, "I *never knew you;* depart from me, you evildoers" (Matt. 7:22–23). Prophecy, exorcism, and many miracles and mighty works in Jesus' name (to say nothing of other kinds of intensive church activity in the strength of the flesh over perhaps decades of a person's life) do not provide convincing evi-

---

[9]It is true that Jesus tells Nicodemus that he needs to be born again (John 3:7: "Do not marvel that I said to you, 'You must be born anew'"), but this is not a command to Nicodemus to do something that no one can ever do (that is, give himself new spiritual life). It is an indicative sentence, not an imperative sentence. It is a statement of fact designed to point out to Nicodemus his total spiritual need and lack of ability on his own to enter the kingdom of God. A little later, when Jesus begins to speak about the response that is expected from Nicodemus, he speaks about the personal response of faith as the thing necessary: "So must the Son of man be lifted up, that *whoever believes in him* may have eternal life" (John 3:14–15).

[10]The perfect participle translated here "is born" could more explicitly be translated "has been born and continues in the new life that resulted from that event."

dence that a person is truly born again. Apparently all these can be produced in the natural man or woman's own strength, or even with the help of the evil one. But genuine love for God and his people, heartfelt obedience to his commands, and the Christlike character traits that Paul calls the fruit of the Spirit, demonstrated consistently over a period of time in a person's life, simply *cannot* be produced by Satan or by the natural man or woman working in his or her own strength. These can only come about by the Spirit of God working within and giving us new life.

QUESTIONS FOR PERSONAL APPLICATION

1. Have you been born again? Is there evidence of the new birth in your life? Do you remember a specific time when regeneration occurred in your life? Can you describe how you knew that something had happened?

2. If you (or friends who come to you) are not sure whether you have been born again, what would Scripture encourage you to do in order to gain greater assurance (or to be truly born again for the first time)? (Note: further discussion of repentance and saving faith is given in the next chapter.)

3. Have you thought before that regeneration is prior to saving faith? Are you convinced of it now, or is there still some question in your mind?

4. What do you think about the fact that your regeneration was totally a work of God, and that you contributed nothing to it? How does it make you feel toward yourself? How does it make you feel toward God? By way of analogy, how do you feel about the fact that when you were born physically you had no choice in the matter?

5. Are there areas where the results of regeneration are not very clearly seen in your own life? Do you think it is possible for a person to be regenerated and then stagnate spiritually so that there is little or no growth? What circumstances might a person live in that would lead to such spiritual stagnation and lack of growth (if that is possible), even though the person was truly born again? To what degree does the kind of church one attends, the teaching one receives, the kind of Christian fellowship one has, and the regularity of one's personal time of Bible reading and prayer, affect one's own spiritual life and growth?

6. If regeneration is entirely a work of God and human beings can do nothing to bring it about, then what good does it do to preach the gospel to people at all? Is it somewhat absurd or even cruel to preach the gospel and ask for a response from people who cannot respond because they are spiritually dead? How do you resolve this question?

---

[11]Since we indicated above that a person is first regenerated, and then subsequently comes to saving faith, there will be a brief time in which someone is regenerated and the results (faith, love, etc.) are not yet seen. But John is saying that the results *will* follow; they are inevitable once someone is born again.

SPECIAL TERMS

born again   irresistible grace
born of the Spirit   regeneration
born of water

BIBLIOGRAPHY

Hoekema, Anthony A. "Regeneration." In *Saved by Grace*. Grand Rapids: Eerdmans, and
    Exeter: Paternoster, 1989, pp. 93–112.
Kevan, E. F. *Salvation*. Phillipsburg, N.J.: Presbyterian and Reformed, 1973.
Packer, J. I. "Regeneration." In *EDT*, pp. 924–26.
Toon, Peter. *Born Again: A Biblical and Theological Study of Regeneration*. Grand Rapids:
    Baker, 1987.

SCRIPTURE MEMORY PASSAGE

John 3:5–8: *Jesus answered, "Truly, truly, I say to you, unless one is born of water and the Spirit, he cannot enter the kingdom of God. That which is born of the flesh is flesh, and that which is born of the Spirit is spirit. Do not marvel that I said to you, 'You must be born anew.' The wind blows where it wills, and you hear the sound of it, but you do not know whence it comes or whither it goes; so it is with every one who is born of the Spirit."*

HYMN

"I Sought the Lord, and Afterward I Knew"

This hymn beautifully expresses thanks to God for the fact that, though we did not know it, he sought us, worked in our hearts in a mysterious way, and enabled us to believe, before we came to trust in him.

I sought the Lord, and afterward I knew
He moved my soul to seek him, seeking me;
It was not I that found, O Savior true,
No, I was found of thee.

Thou didst reach forth thy hand and mine enfold;
I walked and sank not on the storm-vexed sea,
'Twas not so much that I on thee took hold,
As thou, dear Lord, on me.

I find, I walk, I love, but, O the whole
Of love is but my answer, Lord, to thee;
For thou wert long beforehand with my soul,
Always thou lovedst me.

ANON., C. 1904

Chapter

CONVERSION (FAITH AND REPENTANCE)

What is true repentance? What is saving faith?
Can people accept Jesus as Savior and not as Lord?

EXPLANATION AND SCRIPTURAL BASIS

The last two chapters have explained how God himself (through the human preaching of the Word) issues the gospel call to us and, by the work of the Holy Spirit, regenerates us, imparting new spiritual life within. In this chapter we examine our response to the gospel call. We may define conversion as follows: *Conversion is our willing response to the gospel call, in which we sincerely repent of sins and place our trust in Christ for salvation.*

The word *conversion* itself means "turning"—here it represents a spiritual turn, a turning *from* sin *to* Christ. The turning from sin is called *repentance,* and the turning to Christ is called *faith.* We can look at each of these elements of conversion, and in one sense it does not matter which one we discuss first, for neither one can occur without the other, and they must occur together when true conversion takes place. For the purposes of this chapter, we shall examine saving faith first, and then repentance.

A. True Saving Faith Includes Knowledge, Approval, and Personal Trust

1. Knowledge Alone Is Not Enough. Personal saving faith, in the way Scripture understands it, involves more than mere knowledge. Of course *it is necessary that we have some knowledge of who Christ is and what he has done,* for "how are they to believe in him of whom they have never heard?" (Rom. 10:14). But knowledge about the *facts* of Jesus' life, death, and resurrection for us is not enough, for people can know facts but rebel against them or dislike them. For example, Paul tells us that many people know God's laws but dislike them: "Though they *know* God's decree that those who do such things deserve to die, they not only do them but approve those who practice them" (Rom. 1:32). Even the demons know who God is and know the facts about Jesus' life and saving works, for James says, "You believe that God is one; you do well. Even the demons believe—and shudder" (James 2:19). But that knowledge certainly does not mean that the demons are saved.

2. Knowledge and Approval Are Not Enough. Moreover, merely knowing the facts and *approving* of them or *agreeing* that they are true is not enough. Nicodemus knew that Jesus had come from God, for he said, "Rabbi, we know that you are a teacher come from God; for no one can do these signs that you do, unless God is with him" (John 3:2). Nicodemus had evaluated the facts of the situation, including Jesus' teaching and his remarkable miracles, and had drawn a correct conclusion from those facts: Jesus was a teacher come from God. But this alone did not mean that Nicodemus had saving faith, for he still had to put his trust in Christ for salvation; he still had to "believe in him." King Agrippa provides another example of knowledge and approval without saving faith. Paul realized that King Agrippa knew and apparently viewed with approval the Jewish Scriptures (what we now call the Old Testament). When Paul was on trial before Agrippa, he said, "King Agrippa, do you believe the prophets? I know that *you believe*" (Acts 26:27). Yet Agrippa did not have saving faith, for he said to Paul, "In a short time you think to make me a Christian!" (Acts 26:28).

3. I Must Decide to Depend on Jesus to Save Me Personally. In addition to knowledge of the facts of the gospel and approval of those facts, in order to be saved, I must decide to depend on Jesus to save me. In doing this I move from being an interested observer of the facts of salvation and the teachings of the Bible to being someone who enters into a new relationship with Jesus Christ as a living person. We may therefore define saving faith in the following way: *Saving faith is trust in Jesus Christ as a living person for forgiveness of sins and for eternal life with God.*

This definition emphasizes that saving faith is not just a belief in facts but *personal trust in Jesus* to save *me.* As we will explain in the following chapters, much more is involved in salvation than simply forgiveness of sins and eternal life, but someone who initially comes to Christ seldom realizes the extent of the blessings of salvation that will come. Moreover, we may rightly summarize the two major concerns of a person who trusts in Christ as "forgiveness of sins" and "eternal life with God." Of course, eternal life with God involves such matters as a declaration of righteousness before God (part of justification, as explained in the next chapter), adoption, sanctification, and glorification, but these things may be understood in detail later. The main thing that concerns an unbeliever who comes to Christ is the fact that sin has separated him or her from the fellowship with God for which we were made. The unbeliever comes to Christ seeking to have sin and guilt removed and to enter into a genuine relationship with God that will last forever.

The definition emphasizes *personal trust* in Christ, not just belief in facts about Christ. Because saving faith in Scripture involves this personal trust, the word "trust" is a better word to use in contemporary culture than the word "faith" or "belief." The reason is that we can "believe" something to be true with no personal commitment or dependence involved in it. I can *believe* that Canberra is the capital of Australia, or that 7 times 6 is 42, but have no personal commitment or dependence on anyone when I simply believe those facts. The word *faith,* on the other hand, is sometimes used today to refer to an almost irrational commitment to something in spite of strong evidence to the contrary, a sort of irrational decision to believe something that we are quite sure is *not* true! (If your favorite football team continues to lose games, someone might encourage you to "have faith" even though all the facts point the opposite direction.) In these two popular senses, the word "belief" and the word "faith" have a meaning contrary to the biblical sense.[1]

The word *trust* is closer to the biblical idea, since we are familiar with trusting persons in everyday life. The more we come to know a person, and the more we see in that person a pattern of life that warrants trust, the more we find ourselves able to place trust in that person to do what he or she promises, or to act in ways that we can rely on. This fuller sense of personal trust is indicated in several passages of Scripture in which initial saving faith is spoken of in very personal terms, often using analogies drawn from personal relationships. John says, "To all who *received him,* who believed in his name, he gave power to become children of God" (John 1:12). Much as we would receive a guest into our homes, John speaks of receiving Christ.

John 3:16 tells us that "whoever *believes in him* should not perish but have eternal life." Here John uses a surprising phrase when he does not simply say, "whoever *believes him*" (that is, believes that what he says is true and able to be trusted), but rather, "whoever *believes in him.*" The Greek phrase *pisteuō eis auton* could also be translated "believe *into* him" with the sense of trust or confidence that goes *into* and rests *in* Jesus as a person. Leon Morris can say, "Faith, for John, is an activity which takes men right out of themselves and makes them one with Christ." He understands the Greek phrase *pisteuō eis* to be a significant indication that New Testament faith is not just intellectual assent but includes a "moral element of personal trust."[2] Such an expression was rare or perhaps nonexistent in the secular Greek found outside the New Testament, but it was well suited to express the personal trust in Christ that is involved in saving faith.

Jesus speaks of "coming to him" in several places. He says, "All that the Father gives me will *come to me;* and him who comes to me I will not cast out" (John 6:37). He also says, "If any one thirst, let him *come to me* and drink" (John 7:37). In a similar way, he says, "*Come to me,* all who labor and are heavy laden, and I will give you rest. Take my yoke upon you, and learn from me; for I am gentle and lowly in heart, and you will find rest for your souls. For my yoke is easy, and my burden is light" (Matt. 11:28–30). In these passages we have the idea of coming to Christ and asking for acceptance, for living water to drink, and for rest and instruction. All of these give an intensely personal picture of what is involved in saving faith. The author of Hebrews also asks us to think of Jesus as now alive in heaven, ready to receive us: "He is able for all time to save those who draw near to God through him, since *he always lives* to make intercession for them" (Heb. 7:25). Jesus is pictured here (as many times in the New Testament) as one who is now alive in heaven, always able to help those who come to him.

Reformed theologian J. I. Packer quotes the following paragraphs from the British Puritan writer John Owen, describing the invitation of Christ to respond in personal faith:

> This is somewhat of the word which he now speaks unto you: Why will ye die?
> why will ye perish? why will ye not have compassion on your own souls? Can your

hearts endure, or can your hands be strong, in the day of wrath that is approaching? . . . Look unto me, and be saved; come unto me, and I will ease you of all sins, sorrows, fears, burdens, and give rest to your souls. Come, I entreat you; lay aside all procrastinations, all delays; put me off no more; eternity lies at the door . . . do not so hate me as that you will rather perish than accept of deliverance by me.

These and the like things doth the Lord Christ continually declare, proclaim, plead and urge upon the souls of sinners. . . . He doth it in the preaching of the word, as if he were present with you, stood amongst you, and spake personally to every one of you. . . . He hath appointed the ministers of the gospel to appear before you, and to deal with you in his stead, avowing as his own the invitations which are given you in his name. (2 Cor. 5:19–20)[3]

With this understanding of true New Testament faith, we may now appreciate that when a person comes to trust in Christ, all three elements must be present. There must be some basic knowledge or *understanding* of the facts of the gospel. There must also be *approval* of, or agreement with, these facts. Such agreement includes a conviction that the facts spoken of the gospel are true, especially the fact that I am a sinner in need of salvation and that Christ alone has paid the penalty for my sin and offers salvation to me. It also includes an awareness that I need to trust in Christ for salvation and that he is the only way to God, and the only means provided for my salvation. This approval of the facts of the gospel will also involve a desire to be saved through Christ. But all this still does not add up to true saving faith. That comes only when I make a decision of my will to depend on, or put my *trust* in, Christ as *my* Savior. This personal decision to place my trust in Christ is something done with my heart, the central faculty of my entire being that makes commitments for me as a whole person.

4. Faith Should Increase as Our Knowledge Increases. Contrary to the current secular understanding of "faith," true New Testament faith is not something that is made stronger by ignorance or by believing against the evidence. Rather, saving faith is consistent with knowledge and true understanding of facts. Paul says, "Faith comes from hearing, and hearing by the word of Christ" (Rom. 10:17 NASB). When people have true information about Christ, they are better able to put their trust in him. Moreover, the more we know about him and about the character of God that is completely revealed in him, the more fully we are able to put our trust in him. Thus faith is not weakened by knowledge but should increase with more true knowledge.

In the case of saving faith in Christ, our knowledge of him comes by believing a reliable testimony about him. Here, the reliable testimony that we believe is the words of Scripture. Since they are God's very words, they are completely reliable, and we gain true knowledge

---

[1]Of course, the words *believe/belief* and *faith* occur frequently in the Bible, and we should not completely give up using them in a proper biblical sense just because our culture sometimes gives them an incorrect sense. My point is simply that when explaining the gospel to an unbeliever, the word *trust* seems to be most likely to convey the biblical sense today.

[2]Leon Morris, *The Gospel According to John* (Grand Rapids:

Eerdmans, 1971), p. 336, with reference to the longer discussion by C. H. Dodd, *The Interpretation of the Fourth Gospel* (Cambridge: Cambridge University Press, 1953), pp. 179–86, and a note that Dodd finds no parallel to the use of *pisteuō* followed by the preposition *eis,* to refer to trust in a person, in secular Greek. The expression rather is a literal translation of the expression "to believe in" from the Hebrew Old Testament.

of Christ through them. This is why "Faith comes from hearing, and hearing by the word of Christ" (Rom. 10:17 NASB). In everyday life, we come to believe many things when we hear testimony from a person we consider to be reliable or trustworthy. This kind of decision is even more justified here, when the actual words of God provide that testimony and we believe it.

B. Faith and Repentance Must Come Together

We may define repentance as follows: *Repentance is a heartfelt sorrow for sin, a renouncing of it, and a sincere commitment to forsake it and walk in obedience to Christ.*

This definition indicates that repentance is something that can occur at a specific point in time, and is not equivalent to a demonstration of change in a person's pattern of life. Repentance, like faith, is an intellectual *understanding* (that sin is wrong), an emotional *approval* of the teachings of Scripture regarding sin (a sorrow for sin and a hatred of it), and a *personal decision* to turn from it (a renouncing of sin and a decision of the will to forsake it and lead a life of obedience to Christ instead). We cannot say that someone has to actually *live* that changed life over a period of time before repentance can be genuine, or else repentance would be turned into a kind of obedience that we could *do* to merit salvation for ourselves. Of course, genuine repentance will result in a changed life. In fact, a truly repentant person will begin at once to live a changed life, and we can call that changed life the fruit of repentance. But we should never attempt to require that there be a period of time in which a person actually lives a changed life before we give assurance of forgiveness. Repentance is something that occurs in the heart and involves the whole person in a decision to turn from sin.

It is important to realize that mere sorrow for one's actions, or even deep remorse over one's actions, does not constitute genuine repentance unless it is accompanied by a sincere decision to forsake sin that is being committed against God. Paul preached about "repentance *to God* and of faith in our Lord Jesus Christ" (Acts 20:21). He says that he rejoiced over the Corinthians, "not because you were grieved, but because you were *grieved into repenting. . . . For godly grief produces a repentance that leads to salvation and brings no regret, but worldly grief produces death*" (2 Cor. 7:9–10). A worldly sort of grief may involve great sorrow for one's actions and probably also fear of punishment but no genuine renouncing of sin or commitment to forsake it in one's life. Hebrews 12:17 tells us that Esau wept over the consequences of his actions but did not truly repent. Moreover, as 2 Corinthians 7:9–10 indicates, even true godly grief is just one factor that leads to genuine repentance, but such grief is not itself the sincere decision of the heart in the presence of God that makes genuine repentance.

Scripture puts repentance and faith together as different aspects of the one act of coming to Christ for salvation. It is not that a person first turns from sin and next trusts in Christ, or first trusts in Christ and then turns from sin, but rather that both occur at the same time. When we turn to Christ *for* salvation from our sins, we are simultaneously turning *away*

---

[3]J. I. Packer, *Evangelism and the Sovereignty of God*
(Downers Grove, Ill.: InterVarsity Press, 1961), p. 104.

from the sins that we are asking Christ to save us from. If that were not true our turning to Christ for salvation from sin could hardly be a genuine turning to him or trusting in him.

The fact that repentance and faith are simply two different sides of the same coin, or two different aspects of the one event of conversion, may be seen in figure 6.1.

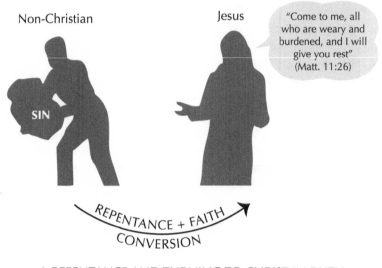

A REPENTANCE AND TURNING TO CHRIST IN FAITH
Figure 6.1

In this diagram, the person who genuinely turns to Christ for salvation must at the same time release the sin to which he or she has been clinging and turn away from that sin in order to turn to Christ. Thus, neither repentance nor faith comes first; they must come together. John Murray speaks of "penitent faith" and "believing repentance."[4]

Therefore, it is clearly contrary to the New Testament evidence to speak about the possibility of having true saving faith without having any repentance for sin. It is also contrary to the New Testament to speak about the possibility of someone accepting Christ "as Savior" but not "as Lord," if that means simply depending on him for salvation but not committing oneself to forsake sin and to be obedient to Christ from that point on.

Some prominent voices within evangelicalism have differed with this point, arguing that a gospel presentation that requires *repentance* as well as faith is really preaching salvation by works. They argue that the view advocated in this chapter, that repentance and faith must go together, is a false gospel of "lordship salvation." They would say that saving faith *only* involves trusting Christ as Savior, and that submitting to him as Lord is an optional later step that is unnecessary for salvation. For many who teach this view, saving faith only requires an intellectual agreement with the facts of the gospel.[5]

When Jesus invites sinners, "Come to me, all who labor and are heavy laden, and I will give you rest," he immediately adds, "*Take my yoke upon you, and learn from me*" (Matt.

11:28–29). To come to him includes taking his yoke upon us, being subject to his direction and guidance, learning from him and being obedient to him. If we are unwilling to make such a commitment, then we have not truly placed our trust in him.

When Scripture speaks of trusting in God or in Christ, it frequently connects such trust with genuine repentance. For example, Isaiah gives an eloquent testimony that is typical of the message of many of the Old Testament prophets:

> Seek the LORD while he may be found,
>> call upon him while he is near;
> let the wicked *forsake his way,*
>> and the unrighteous man his thoughts;
> let him *return to the LORD,* that he may have mercy on him,
>> and to our God, for he will abundantly pardon. (Isa. 55:6–7)

Here both repentance from sin and coming to God for pardon are mentioned. In the New Testament, Paul summarizes his gospel ministry as one of "testifying both to Jews and to Greeks of *repentance* to God and of *faith* in our Lord Jesus Christ" (Acts 20:21). The author of Hebrews includes as the first two elements in a list of elementary doctrines "*repentance* from dead works" and "*faith* toward God" (Heb. 6:1).

Of course sometimes faith alone is named as the thing necessary for coming to Christ for salvation (see John 3:16; Acts 16:31; Rom. 10:9; Eph. 2:8–9, et al.). These are familiar passages and we emphasize them often when explaining the gospel to others. But what we do not often realize is the fact that there are many other passages where *only repentance* is named, for it is simply assumed that true repentance will also involve faith in Christ for forgiveness of sins. The New Testament authors understood so well that genuine repentance and genuine faith had to go together that they often simply mentioned repentance alone with the understanding that faith would also be included, because turning *from* sins in a genuine way is impossible apart from a genuine turning *to* God. Therefore, just before Jesus ascended into heaven, he told his disciples, "Thus it is written, that the Christ should suffer and on the third day rise from the dead, and that *repentance* and forgiveness of sins should be preached in his name to all nations" (Luke 24:46–47). Saving faith is implied in the phrase "forgiveness of sins," but it is not explicitly named.

The preaching recorded in the book of Acts shows the same pattern. After Peter's sermon at Pentecost, the crowd asked, "Brethren, what shall we do?" Peter replied, "*Repent,* and be baptized every one of you in the name of Jesus Christ for the forgiveness of your sins" (Acts 2:37–38). In his second sermon Peter spoke to his hearers in a similar way, saying, "*Repent* therefore, and turn again, that your sins may be blotted out, that times of refreshing may come from the presence of the Lord" (Acts 3:19). Later, when the apostles were on trial before the Sanhedrin, Peter spoke of Christ, saying, "God exalted him at his right hand as Leader and Savior, to give *repentance* to Israel and forgiveness of sins" (Acts 5:31). And when Paul was preaching on the Areopagus in Athens to an assembly of Greek philosophers, he said, "The times of ignorance God overlooked, but now *he commands*

---

[4]John Murray, *Redemption Accomplished and Applied* (Grand Rapids: Eerdmans, 1955), p. 113.

all men everywhere to repent" (Acts 17:30). He also says in his epistles, "Do you not know that God's kindness is meant to lead you to repentance?" (Rom. 2:4), and he speaks of "a *repentance* that leads to salvation" (2 Cor. 7:10).

We also see that when Jesus encounters people personally he requires them to turn from their sin before they come to follow him. Whether it be speaking to the rich young ruler and asking that he give up his possessions (Luke 18:18–30), coming to the house of Zacchaeus and declaring that salvation had come to him that day because he had given half his goods to the poor and had repaid fourfold anything that he had stolen (Luke 19:1–10), speaking to the woman at the well and asking her to call her husband (John 4:16), or speaking to Nicodemus and rebuking his rabbinic unbelief and pride in his own knowledge (John 3:1–21), Jesus consistently puts his finger on the area of sin most influential in that person's life. In fact, we may ask whether anyone in the gospels ever came to sincere faith in Christ without repenting of his or her sins.

When we realize that genuine saving faith must be accompanied by genuine repentance for sin, it helps us to understand why some preaching of the gospel has such inadequate results today. If there is no mention of the need for repentance, sometimes the gospel message becomes only, "Believe in Jesus Christ and be saved" without any

---

[5]The source of this view of the gospel is apparently Lewis Sperry Chafer, especially in his *Systematic Theology,* vol. 3 (Dallas: Dallas Seminary Press, 1947–48), where he says, "The New Testament does not impose repentance upon the unsaved as a condition of salvation" (p. 376). Chafer recognizes that many verses call upon people to repent, but he simply defines repentance away as a "change of mind" that does not include sorrow for sin or turning from sin (pp. 372–75). Thus he can say, "Repentance, which is a change of mind, is included in believing" (p. 375). He argues that "the added demand that the unsaved must dedicate themselves to do God's will in their daily life, as well as to believe upon Christ" is a "confusing intrusion into the doctrine that salvation is conditioned alone upon believing" (p. 384). Chafer provides a basis for the view that people must first accept Christ as Savior, and later as Lord, when he says that the preacher has the obligation "of preaching the Lordship of Christ to Christians exclusively, and the Saviorhood of Christ to those who are unsaved" (p. 387). The most vocal contemporary proponent of this view has been Dallas Seminary professor Zane C. Hodges: see his book *The Gospel Under Siege* (Dallas: Redención Viva, 1981).

But not all at Dallas Seminary or all within Dispensational theology would hold this view. A controversy over this point erupted in American evangelicalism when John MacArthur, himself a Dispensationalist, published *The Gospel According to Jesus* (Grand Rapids: Zondervan, 1988, rev. ed. 1994). This excellent book (with enthusiastic forewords by J. I. Packer and James Montgomery Boice) strongly criticized the views of writers like Chafer and Hodges on evangelism and the nature of saving faith. MacArthur argued very convincingly from many New Testament passages that one cannot truly accept Christ as Savior without also accepting him as Lord, or, in other words, that there can be no true saving faith without genuine repentance as

well. He said that any other view preaches a cheap gospel that offers unconverted people false security, telling them they are saved simply because they agreed that the facts of the gospel were true or prayed a prayer, but they had no true repentance and no real change of life. MacArthur argued that such unbiblical evangelism has never been the teaching of the church through history, and that the weakened gospel heard so often today has resulted in a whole generation of professing Christians whose lives are no different from the surrounding culture and who are really not saved at all. Hodges quickly responded to MacArthur with another book, *Absolutely Free! A Biblical Reply to Lordship Salvation* (Dallas: Redención Viva, and Grand Rapids: Zondervan, 1989).

As I have argued in this chapter, it seems to me clear that MacArthur is certainly right to maintain that true saving faith in New Testament terms is more than mere intellectual assent to facts; it must include a heartfelt coming to Christ in personal dependence on him for salvation, combined with a heartfelt repentance from sin. It is misleading to brand this teaching "Lordship salvation" as if it were some new doctrine, or as if there were any other kind of salvation—MacArthur is teaching what has been the historic position of Christian orthodoxy on this matter, as he demonstrates in an appendix to his book (pp. 221–37). This position is not salvation by works, but simply states the gospel of *free* grace, and salvation by grace through faith in all its biblical fullness. The change of life that will result from genuine conversion does not save us, but it will certainly result if our faith is genuine, for "faith by itself, if it has no works, is dead" (James 2:17).

The Sandemanians were a small group of evangelical churches who taught a view similar to Zane Hodges in England and the United States from 1725 until they died out around 1900; see R. E. D. Clark, "Sandemanians," in *NIDCC*, p. 877.

mention of repentance at all.[6] But this watered-down version of the gospel does not ask for a wholehearted commitment to Christ—commitment *to* Christ, if genuine, must include a commitment to turn *from* sin. Preaching the need for faith without repentance is preaching only half of the gospel. It will result in many people being deceived, thinking that they have heard the Christian gospel and tried it, but nothing has happened. They might even say something like, "I accepted Christ as Savior over and over again and it never worked." Yet they never really did receive Christ as their Savior, for he comes to us in his majesty and invites us to receive him as he is—the one who deserves to be, and demands to be, absolute Lord of our lives as well.

Finally, what shall we say about the common practice of asking people to *pray* to receive Christ as their personal Savior and Lord? Since personal faith in Christ must involve an actual decision of the will, it is often very helpful to *express* that decision in spoken words, and this could very naturally take the form of a prayer to Christ in which we tell him of our sorrow for sin, our commitment to forsake it, and our decision actually to put our trust in him. Such a spoken prayer does not in itself save us, but the attitude of heart that it represents does constitute true conversion, and the decision to speak that prayer can often be the point at which a person truly comes to faith in Christ.

C. Both Faith and Repentance Continue Throughout Life

Although we have been considering initial faith and repentance as the two aspects of conversion at the beginning of the Christian life, it is important to realize that faith and repentance are not confined to the beginning of the Christian life. They are rather attitudes of heart that continue throughout our lives as Christians. Jesus tells his disciples to pray daily, "And forgive us our sins as we also have forgiven those who sin against us" (Matt. 6:12, author's translation), a prayer that, if genuine, will certainly involve daily sorrow for sin and genuine repentance. And the risen Christ says to the church in Laodicea, "Those whom I love, I reprove and chasten; so be zealous *and repent*" (Rev. 3:19; cf. 2 Cor. 7:10).

With regard to faith, Paul tells us, "So faith, hope, love abide, these three; but the greatest of these is love" (1 Cor. 13:13). He certainly means that these three abide throughout the course of this life, but he probably also means that they abide for all eternity: if faith is trusting God to provide all our needs, then this attitude will never cease, not even in the age to come. But in any case, the point is clearly made that faith continues throughout this life. Paul also says, "The life I now live in the flesh I live *by faith in the Son of God*, who loved me and gave himself for me" (Gal. 2:20).

Therefore, although it is true that *initial* saving faith and *initial* repentance occur only once in our lives, and when they occur they constitute true conversion, nonetheless, the heart attitudes of repentance and faith only begin at conversion. These same attitudes should continue throughout the course of our Christian lives. Each day there should be heartfelt repentance for sins that we have committed, and faith in Christ to provide for our needs and to empower us to live the Christian life.

QUESTIONS FOR PERSONAL APPLICATION

1. Have you come to trust in Christ personally, or are you still at the point of intellectual knowledge and emotional approval of the facts of salvation without having personally put your trust in Christ? If you have not put your trust in Christ yet, what do you think it is that is making you hesitate?

2. Did this chapter help you think of faith in Christ in more personal terms? If so, how might that increase your own level of faith? Do you think that it might be easier for young children than for adults to think of trust in Christ as trust in a real *person* who is alive today? Why or why not? What does this tell you about the way Christian parents should teach their children about Jesus?

3. If your knowledge about God has increased through reading this book, has your faith in God increased along with that knowledge? Why or why not? If your faith has not increased along with your knowledge, what can you do to encourage your faith to grow more than it has?

4. In terms of human relationships, do you trust a person more when you do not know that person very well or after you have come to know him or her quite well (assuming that the person is essentially a trustworthy and reliable person)? What does that fact tell you about how your trust in God might increase? What things might you do during the day to come to know God better, and to come to know Jesus and the Holy Spirit better?

5. Did you feel a sincere sorrow for sin when you first came to Christ? Can you describe what it felt like? Did it lead you to a genuine commitment to forsake sin? How long was it before you noticed a change in your pattern of life?

6. Have you ever truly repented of sin, or do you think you have been taught a watered-down gospel that did not include repentance? Do you think it is possible for someone genuinely to trust in Christ for forgiveness of sins without also sincerely repenting for sins? Do you think that genuine repentance usually involves only a sincere feeling of sorrow for sin in general, or does it involve genuine sorrow for specific sins, and turning from those specific sins?

7. Have faith and repentance remained a continuing part of your Christian life, or have those attitudes of heart grown somewhat weak in your life? What has been the result in your Christian life?

---

[6]It is true that Paul tells the Philippian jailer in Acts 16:31, "Believe in the Lord Jesus, and you will be saved, you and your household." However, even that sentence includes an acknowledgment that Jesus is "Lord," and, moreover, the next sentence makes it clear that Paul said much more to the man than this brief sentence, for we read, "And they spoke the word of the Lord to him and to all that were in his house" (Acts 16:32).

SPECIAL TERMS

faith
repentance
trust

BIBLIOGRAPHY

Berkouwer, G. C. *Faith and Justification*. Trans. by Lewis B. Smedes. Grand Rapids: Eerdmans, 1954.

Boice, James Montgomery. *Christ's Call to Discipleship*. Chicago: Moody, 1986.

Chantry, Walter. *Today's Gospel: Authentic or Synthetic?* Carlisle, Pa.: Banner of Truth, 1970.

Hodges, Zane C. *Absolutely Free! A Biblical Reply to Lordship Salvation*. Dallas: Redención Viva, and Grand Rapids: Zondervan, 1989.

_____. *The Gospel Under Siege: A Study on Faith and Works*. Dallas: Redención Viva, 1981.

Hoekema, Anthony A. *Saved by Grace*. Grand Rapids: Eerdmans, and Exeter: Paternoster, 1989, pp. 113–51.

Kromminga, C. G. "Repentance." In *EDT*, pp. 936–37.

MacArthur, John F., Jr. *The Gospel According to Jesus*. Grand Rapids: Zondervan, 1988.

Machen, J. Gresham. *What Is Faith?* Grand Rapids: Eerdmans, 1925.

Morris, Leon. "Faith." In *IBD*. Vol. 1, pp. 496–98.

Murray, John. "Faith and Repentance." In *Redemption Accomplished and Applied*. Grand Rapids: Eerdmans, 1955, pp. 106–16.

_____. "Repentance." In *The New Bible Dictionary*. Ed. by J. D. Douglas. London: Tyndale Press, and Grand Rapids: Eerdmans, 1962, pp. 1083–84.

Packer, J. I. "Evangelicals and the Way of Salvation: New Challenges to the Gospel—Universalism and Justification by Faith." In *Evangelical Affirmations*. Ed. by Kenneth S. Kantzer and Carl F. H. Henry. Grand Rapids: Zondervan, 1990, pp. 107–36.

_____. *Evangelism and the Sovereignty of God*. London: Inter-Varsity Press, 1961.

_____. "Faith." In *EDT*, pp. 399–402.

Ryrie, Charles C. *So Great Salvation: What It Means to Believe in Jesus Christ*. Wheaton, Ill.: Scripture Press, 1989.

Watson, Thomas. *The Doctrine of Repentance*. Carlisle, Pa.: Banner of Truth, 1987.

SCRIPTURE MEMORY PASSAGE

John 3:16: *For God so loved the world that he gave his only Son, that whoever believes in him should not perish but have eternal life.*

HYMN

"Just As I Am"

Just as I am, without one plea
  But that thy blood was shed for me,
And that thou bidd'st me come to thee,
  O Lamb of God, I come, I come.

Just as I am, and waiting not
  To rid my soul of one dark blot,
To thee, whose blood can cleanse each spot,
  O Lamb of God, I come, I come.

Just as I am, though tossed about
  With many a conflict, many a doubt,
Fightings and fears within, without,
  O Lamb of God, I come, I come.

Just as I am, poor, wretched, blind;
  Sight, riches, healing of the mind,
Yea, all I need, in thee to find,
  O Lamb of God, I come, I come.

Just as I am! Thou wilt receive,
  Wilt welcome, pardon, cleanse, relieve;
Because thy promise I believe,
  O Lamb of God, I come, I come.

Just as I am! Thy love unknown
  Has broken ev'ry barrier down;
Now, to be thine, yea, thine alone,
  O Lamb of God, I come, I come.

AUTHOR: CHARLOTTE ELLIOT, 1836

Chapter

JUSTIFICATION (RIGHT LEGAL STANDING BEFORE GOD)

How and when do we gain right legal standing before God?

EXPLANATION AND SCRIPTURAL BASIS

In the previous chapters we talked about the gospel call (in which God calls us to trust in Christ for salvation), regeneration (in which God imparts new spiritual life to us), and conversion (in which we respond to the gospel call in repentance for sin and faith in Christ for salvation). But *what about the guilt of our sin?* The gospel call invited us to trust in Christ for forgiveness of sins. Regeneration made it possible for us to respond to that invitation. In conversion we did respond, trusting in Christ for forgiveness of sins. Now the next step in the process of applying redemption to us is that God must respond to our faith and do what he promised, that is, actually declare our sins to be forgiven. This must be a *legal declaration* concerning our relationship to God's laws, stating that we are completely forgiven and no longer liable to punishment.

A right understanding of justification is absolutely crucial to the whole Christian faith. Once Martin Luther realized the truth of justification by faith alone, he became a Christian and overflowed with the new-found joy of the gospel. The primary issue in the Protestant Reformation was a dispute with the Roman Catholic Church over justification. If we are to safeguard the truth of the gospel for future generations, we must understand the truth of justification. Even today, a true view of justification is the dividing line between the biblical gospel of salvation by faith alone and all false gospels of salvation based on good works.

When Paul gives an overview of the process by which God applies salvation to us, he mentions justification explicitly: "Those whom he predestined he also called; and those whom he called he also *justified;* and those whom he justified he also glorified" (Rom. 8:30). As we explained in a previous chapter, the word *called* here refers to the effective calling of the gospel, which includes regeneration and brings forth the response of repentance and faith (or conversion) on our part. After effective calling and the response that it initiates on our part, the next step in the application of redemption is "justification." Here Paul mentions that this is something that God himself does: "Those whom he called *he also justified.*"

Moreover, Paul quite clearly teaches that this justification comes *after* our faith and *as God's response to* our faith. He says that God "justifies him who *has faith* in Jesus" (Rom. 3:26), and that "a man is justified *by faith* apart from works of law" (Rom. 3:28). He says, "Since we are justified *by faith,* we have peace with God through our Lord Jesus Christ" (Rom. 5:1). Moreover, "a man is not justified by works of the law but *through faith* in Jesus Christ" (Gal. 2:16).

Just what is justification? We may define it as follows: *Justification is an instantaneous legal act of God in which he (1) thinks of our sins as forgiven and Christ's righteousness as belonging to us, and (2) declares us to be righteous in his sight.*

In explaining the elements of this definition, we will look first at the second half of it, the aspect of justification in which God "declares us to be righteous in his sight." The reason for treating these items in reverse order is that the emphasis of the New Testament in the use of the word *justification* and related terms is on the second half of the definition, the legal declaration by God. But there are also passages that show that this declaration is based on the fact that God first thinks of righteousness as belonging to us. So

both aspects must be treated, even though the New Testament terms for justification focus on the legal declaration by God.

A. Justification Includes a Legal Declaration By God

The use of the word *justify* in the Bible indicates that justification is a legal declaration by God. The verb *justify* in the New Testament (Gk. *dikaioō*) has a range of meanings, but a very common sense is "to declare righteous." For example, we read, "When they heard this all the people and the tax collectors *justified* God, having been baptized with the baptism of John" (Luke 7:29). Of course the people and the tax collectors did not *make* God to be righteous—that would be impossible for anyone to do. Rather they *declared* God to be righteous. This is also the sense of the term in passages where the New Testament talks about us being declared righteous by God (Rom. 3:20, 26, 28; 5:1; 8:30; 10:4, 10; Gal. 2:16; 3:24). This sense is particularly evident, for example, in Romans 4:5: "And to one who does not work but trusts him who *justifies the ungodly,* his faith is reckoned as righteousness." Here Paul cannot mean that God "makes the ungodly to be righteous" (by changing them internally and making them morally perfect), for then they would have merit or works of their own to depend on. Rather, he means that God declares the ungodly to be righteous in his sight, not on the basis of their good works, but in response to their faith.

The idea that justification is a legal declaration is quite evident also when justification is contrasted with condemnation. Paul says, "Who shall bring any charge against God's elect? It is God who *justifies;* who is to condemn?" (Rom. 8:33–34). To "condemn" someone is to declare that person guilty. The opposite of condemnation is justification, which, in this context, must mean "to declare someone not guilty." This is also evident from the fact that God's act of justifying is given as Paul's answer to the possibility of someone bringing an accusation or "charge" against God's people: such a declaration of guilt cannot stand in the face of God's declaration of righteousness.

Some Old Testament examples of the word *justify* (Gk. *dikaioō* in the Septuagint, when translating the hiphil of *tsādak,* "to justify") add support to this understanding. For example, we read of judges who "*justify the righteous* and condemn the wicked" (Deut. 25:1 NASB). Now in this case "justify" must mean "declare to be righteous or not guilty," just as "condemn" means "declare to be guilty." It would make no sense to say that "justify" here means "to make someone to be good internally," for judges simply do not and cannot make people to be good on the inside. Nor does a judge's act of condemning the wicked make that person to be evil on the inside; it simply declares that the person is guilty with respect to the particular crime that has been brought before the court (cf. Ex. 23:7; 1 Kings 8:32; 2 Chron. 6:23). Similarly, Job refuses to say that his comforters were right in what they said: "Far be it from me that I should *declare you right*" (Job 27:5 NASB, using the same Hebrew and Greek terms for "justify"). The same idea is found in Proverbs: "He who *justifies* the wicked and he who condemns the righteous are both alike an abomination to the LORD" (Prov. 17:15). Here the idea of legal declaration is especially strong. Certainly it would not be an abomination to the Lord if "justify" meant "to *make* someone good or righteous inside." In that case, to "justify the wicked" would be a very good thing in God's sight. But if "justify" means "declare to be righteous," then it is perfectly clear why "he who justifies the wicked" is "an abomination to the LORD." Similarly, Isaiah condemns those "who *justify* the wicked for a bribe" (Isa. 5:23 NASB); again, "justify" must mean "declare to be righteous" (here used in the context of a legal declaration).

In this sense of "*declare* to be righteous" or "*declare* to be not guilty" Paul frequently uses the word to speak of God's justification of us, his declaration that we, though guilty sinners, are nonetheless righteous in his sight. It is important to emphasize that this legal declaration in itself does not change our internal nature or character at all. In this sense of "justify," God issues a legal declaration about us. This is why theologians have also said that justification is *forensic,* where the word *forensic* means "having to do with legal proceedings."

John Murray makes an important distinction between regeneration and justification:

> Regeneration is an act of God in us; justification is a judgment of God with respect to us. The distinction is like that of the distinction between the act of a surgeon and the act of a judge. The surgeon, when he removes an inward cancer, does something in us. That is not what a judge does — he gives a verdict regarding our judicial status. If we are innocent he declares accordingly.
>
> The purity of the gospel is bound up with the recognition of this distinction. If justification is confused with regeneration or sanctification, then the door is opened for the perversion of the gospel at its center. Justification is still the article of the standing or falling of the Church.[1]

B. God Declares Us to Be Just in His Sight

In God's legal declaration of justification, he specifically declares that we are just *in his sight.* This declaration involves two aspects. First, it means that he declares that we have no penalty to pay for sin, including past, present, and future sins. After a long discussion of justification by faith alone (Rom. 4:1–5:21), and a parenthetical discussion on remaining sin in the Christian life, Paul returns to his main argument in the book of Romans and tells what is true of those who have been justified by faith: "There is therefore now *no condemnation* for those who are in Christ Jesus" (Rom. 8:1). In this sense those who are justified have no penalty to pay for sin. This means that we are not subject to any charge of guilt or condemnation: "Who shall bring any charge against God's elect? It is God who *justifies;* who is to condemn?" (Rom. 8:33–34).

The idea of full forgiveness of sins is prominent when Paul discusses justification by faith alone in Romans 4. Paul quotes David as pronouncing a blessing on one "to whom God reckons righteousness apart from works." He then recalls how David said, "Blessed are those *whose iniquities are forgiven,* and whose sins are covered; blessed is the man against whom the Lord will not reckon his sin" (Rom. 4:6–8). This justification therefore clearly involves the forgiveness of sins. David spoke similarly in Psalm 103:12, "As far as the east is from the west, so far does he remove our transgressions from us" (cf. v. 3).

But if God merely declared us to be *forgiven from our sins,* that would not solve our problems entirely, for it would only make us morally neutral before God. We would be in the state that Adam was in before he had done anything right or wrong in God's sight—he was not guilty before God, but neither had he earned a record of righteousness before God. This first aspect of justification, in which God declares that our sins are forgiven, may be represented as in figure 7.1, in which the minus signs represent sins on our account that are completely forgiven in justification.

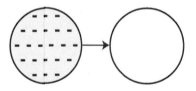

FORGIVENESS OF PAST SINS IS ONE PART OF JUSTIFICATION
Figure 7.1

However, such a movement is not enough to earn us favor with God. We must rather move from a point of moral neutrality to a point of having positive righteousness before God, the righteousness of a life of perfect obedience to him. Our need may therefore be represented as in figure 7.2, in which the plus signs indicate a record of righteousness before God.

[1]John Murray, *Redemption Accomplished and Applied* (Grand Rapids: Eerdmans, 1955), p. 121.

Therefore the second aspect of justification is that God must declare us not to be merely *neutral* in his sight but actually to be *righteous* in his sight. In fact, he must declare us to have the merits of perfect righteousness before him. The Old Testament sometimes spoke of God as giving such righteousness to his people even though they had not earned it themselves. Isaiah says, "He has clothed me with the garments of salvation, *he has covered me with the robe of righteousness*" (Isa. 61:10). But Paul speaks more specifically about this in the New Testament. As a solution to our need for righteousness, Paul tells us that "the righteousness of God has been manifested apart from law, although the law and the prophets bear witness to it, *the righteousness of God through faith in Jesus Christ* for all who believe" (Rom. 3:21–22). He says, "Abraham believed God, and *it was reckoned to him as righteousness*" (Rom. 4:3, quoting Gen. 15:6). This came about through the obedience of Christ, for Paul says at the end of this extensive discussion of justification by faith that "by one man's obedience many will be *made righteous*" (Rom. 5:19). The second aspect of God's declaration in justification, then, is that we have the merits of perfect righteousness before him.

But questions arise: How can God declare that we have no penalty to pay for sin, and that we have the merits of perfect righteousness, if we are in fact guilty sinners? How can God declare us to be not guilty but righteous when in fact *we are unrighteous?* These questions lead to our next point.

C. God Can Declare Us to Be Just Because He Imputes Christ's Righteousness to Us

When we say that God *imputes* Christ's righteousness to us it means that God *thinks of* Christ's righteousness as belonging to us, or regards it *as belonging to* us. He "reckons" it to our account. We read, "Abraham believed God, and *it was reckoned to him as righteousness*" (Rom. 4:3, quoting Gen. 15:6). Paul explains, "To one who does not work but trusts him who justifies the ungodly, his faith *is reckoned* as righteousness. So also David pronounces a blessing upon the man to whom *God reckons righteousness* apart from works" (Rom. 4:6). In this way, Christ's righteousness became ours. Paul says that we are those who received "the free gift of righteousness" (Rom. 5:17).

Three times in Scripture we encounter the idea of *imputing* guilt or righteousness to someone else. First, when Adam sinned, his guilt was imputed to us; God the Father viewed it as belonging to us, and therefore it did. Second, when Christ suffered and died for our sins, our sin was *imputed* to Christ; God thought of it as belonging to him, and he paid the penalty for it.[2] Now in the doctrine of justification we see imputation for the third time. Christ's righteousness is *imputed* to us, and therefore God *thinks of it* as belonging to us. It is not our own righteousness but Christ's righteousness that is freely given to us. So Paul can say that God made Christ to be "our wisdom, *our righteousness* and sanctification and redemption" (1 Cor. 1:30). And Paul says that his goal is to be found in Christ, "not having a righteousness of my own, based on law, but that which is through faith in Christ, *the righteousness from God* that depends on faith" (Phil. 3:9). Paul knows that the righteousness he has before God is not anything of his own doing; it is the righteousness of God that comes through Jesus Christ (cf. Rom. 3:21–22).[3]

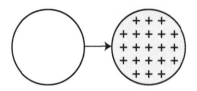

IMPUTATION OF CHRIST'S RIGHTEOUSNESS TO US
IS THE OTHER PART OF JUSTIFICATION
Figure 7.2

It is essential to the heart of the gospel to insist that God declares us to be just or righteous not on the basis of our actual condition of righteousness or holiness, but rather on the basis of Christ's perfect righteousness, which he thinks of as belonging to us. This was the heart of the difference between Protestantism and Roman Catholicism at the Reformation. Protestantism since the time of Martin Luther has insisted that justification does *not* change us internally and it is *not* a declaration based in any way on any goodness that we have in ourselves. If justification changed us internally and then declared us to be righteous based on how good we actually were, then (1) we could never be declared perfectly righteous in this life, because there is always sin that remains in our lives, and (2) there would be no provision for forgiveness of past sins (committed before we were changed internally), and therefore we could never have confidence that we are right before God. We would lose the confidence that Paul has when he says, "Therefore, *since we are justified by faith,* we have peace with God through our Lord Jesus Christ" (Rom. 5:1).[4] If we thought of justification as based on something that we are internally we would never have the confidence to say with Paul, "There is therefore now *no condemnation* for those who are in Christ Jesus" (Rom. 8:1). We would have no assurance of forgiveness with God, no confidence to draw near to him "with a true heart in full assurance of faith" (Heb. 10:22). We would not be able to speak of "the *free gift* of righteousness" (Rom. 5:17), or say that "the *free gift* of God is eternal life in Christ Jesus our Lord" (Rom. 6:23).

The traditional Roman Catholic understanding of justification is very different from this. The Roman Catholic Church understands justification as something that changes us internally and makes us more holy within. "According to the teaching of the Council of Trent, justification is 'sanctifying and renewing of the inner man.'"[5] In order for justification to begin, one must first be baptized and then (as an adult) continue to have faith: "The instrumental cause . . . of the first justification is the Sacrament of Baptism."[6] But "the justification of an adult is not possible without Faith. . . . As far as the content of justifying faith is concerned, the so-called fiducial faith does not suffice. What is demanded is theological or dogmatic faith (confessional faith) which consists in the firm acceptance of the Divine truths of Revelation."[7] Thus baptism is the means by which justification is first obtained, and then faith is necessary if an adult is to receive justification or to continue in the state of justification. Ott explains that "the so-called fiduciary faith" is not enough—meaning that the faith that simply trusts in Christ for forgiveness of sins is not enough. It must be a faith that accepts the content of the teaching of the Catholic Church, "theological or dogmatic faith."

The Roman Catholic view may be said to understand justification as based not on *imputed* righteousness but on *infused* righteousness—that is, righteousness that God actually *puts into us* and that changes us internally and in terms of our actual moral character. Then he gives us varying measures of justification according to the measure of righteousness that has been infused or placed within us.

The result of this Roman Catholic view of justification is that people cannot be sure if they are in a "state of grace" where they experience God's complete acceptance and favor. The Catholic Church teaches that people cannot be certain that they are in this "state of grace" unless they receive a special revelation from God to this effect. The Council of Trent declared,

> If one considers his own weakness and his defective disposition, he may well be fearful and anxious as to the state of grace, as nobody knows with the certainty of faith, which permits of no error, that he has achieved the grace of God.

To this statement Ott adds the comment,

> The reason for the uncertainty of the state of grace lies in this, that without a special revelation nobody can with certainty of faith know whether or not he has fulfilled all the conditions which are necessary for the achieving of justification. The impossibility of the certainty of faith, however, by no means excludes a high moral certainty supported by the testimony of conscience.[8]

Moreover, since the Roman Catholic Church views justification as including something that God does within us, it follows that people can experience varying degrees of justification. We read, "The degree of justifying grace is not identical in all the just" and "grace can be increased by good works."[9] Ott explains how this Catholic view differs from that of the Protestant Reformers: "As the Reformers wrongly regarded justification as a merely

---

[2]Paul says, "God made him who had no sin to be sin for us, so that in him we might become the righteousness of God" (2 Cor. 5:21 NIV).

[3]One sometimes hears the popular explanation that *justified* means "just-as-if-I'd-never-sinned." The definition is a clever play on words and contains an element of truth (for the justified person, like the person who has never sinned, has no penalty to pay for sin). But the definition is misleading in two other ways because (1) it mentions nothing about the fact that Christ's righteousness is reckoned to my account when I am justified; to do this it would have to say also "just-as-if-I'd-lived-a-life-of-perfect-righteousness." (2) But more significantly, it cannot adequately represent the fact that I will *never* be in a state that is "just-as-if-I'd-never-sinned," because I will *always* be conscious of the fact that I *have* sinned and that I am not an innocent person but a guilty person who has been forgiven. This is very different from "just as if I had never sinned"! Moreover, it is different from "just as if I had lived a life of perfect

righteousness," because I will forever know that I *have not* lived a life of perfect righteousness, but that Christ's righteousness is given to me by God's grace.

Therefore both in the forgiveness of sins and in the imputation of Christ's righteousness, my situation is far different from what it would be if I had never sinned and had lived a perfectly righteous life. For all eternity I will remember that I am a forgiven *sinner,* and that my righteousness is not based on my own merit, but on the grace of God in the saving work of Jesus Christ. None of that rich teaching at the heart of the gospel will be understood by those who are encouraged to go through their lives thinking "justified" means "just-as-if-I'd-never-sinned."

[4]The aorist passive participle *dikaōthentes* placed before the main verb conveys the sense of a completed event prior to the present tense main verb, "We have peace," giving the sense, "Since we *have been justified* by faith, we have peace."

external imputation of Christ's justice, they were obliged also to hold that justification is identical in all men. The Council of Trent, however, declared that the measure of the grace of justification received varies in the individual person who is justified, according to the measure of God's free distribution and to the disposition and the co-operation of the recipient himself."[10]

Finally, the logical consequence of this view of justification is that our eternal life with God is not based on God's grace alone, but partially on our merit as well: "For the justified eternal life is both a gift of grace promised by God and a reward for his own good works and merits. . . . Salutary works are, at the same time, gifts of God and meritorious acts of man."[11]

To support this view of justification from Scripture, Ott repeatedly mingles passages from the New Testament that talk not only of justification, but also of many other aspects of the Christian life, such as regeneration (which God works in us), sanctification (which is a process in the Christian life and which of course does vary from individual to individual), the possession and use of various spiritual gifts in the Christian life (which differ from individual to individual), and eternal reward (which also varies according to the individual). To classify all of these passages under the category of "justification" only blurs the issue and ultimately makes forgiveness of sins and right legal standing before God a matter of our own merit, not a free gift from God. Therefore, this blurring of distinctions ultimately destroys the heart of the gospel.

That is what Martin Luther so clearly saw and that is what gave such motivation to the Reformation. When the good news of the gospel truly became the good news of totally free salvation in Jesus Christ, then it spread like wildfire throughout the civilized world. But this was simply a recovery of the original gospel, which declares, "The wages of sin is death, but the *free gift of God* is eternal life in Christ Jesus our Lord" (Rom. 6:23), and insists that "There is therefore now *no condemnation* for those who are in Christ Jesus" (Rom. 8:1).

D. Justification Comes to Us Entirely by God's Grace, Not on Account of Any Merit in Ourselves

After Paul explains in Romans 1:18–3:20 that no one will ever be able to make himself righteous before God ("For no human being will be justified in his sight by works of the law," Rom. 3:20), then Paul goes on to explain that "since all have sinned and fall short of the glory of God, they are justified *by his grace as a gift,* through the redemption which is in Christ Jesus" (Rom. 3:23–24). God's "grace" means his "unmerited favor." Because we are completely unable to earn favor with God, the only way we could be declared righteous is if God freely provides salvation for us by grace, totally apart from our work. Paul explains, "For *by grace* you have been saved through faith; and this is not your own doing, it is the gift of God—not because of works, lest any man should boast" (Eph. 2:8–9; cf.

---

[5]Ludwig Ott, *Fundamentals of Catholic Dogma*, trans. Patrick Lynch (Rockford, Ill.: TAN Books, 1960), p. 257; also quoted with approval on p. 250. It should be noted that Ott represents more traditional, pre-Vatican II Roman Catholicism, and that many contemporary Roman Catholics have sought an understanding of justification that is closer to a Protestant view.

[6]Ibid., p. 251.

[7]Ibid., pp. 252–53.

[8]Ibid., pp. 261–62.

Titus 3:7). Grace is clearly put in contrast to works or merit as the reason why God is willing to justify us. God did not have any obligation to impute our sin to Christ or to impute Christ's righteousness to us; it was only because of his unmerited favor that he did this.

In distinction from the Roman Catholic teaching that we are justified by God's grace *plus some merit of our own,* as we make ourselves fit to receive the grace of justification and as we grow in this state of grace through our good works, Luther and the other Reformers insisted that justification comes by grace *alone,* not by grace plus some merit on our part.

E. God Justifies Us Through Our Faith in Christ

When we began this chapter we noted that justification comes after saving faith. Paul makes this sequence clear when he says, "We have believed in Christ Jesus, *in order to be justified* by faith in Christ, and not by works of the law, because by works of the law shall no one be justified" (Gal. 2:16). Here Paul indicates that faith comes first and it is for the purpose of being justified. He also says that Christ is "to be received by faith" and that God "justifies him who has *faith* in Jesus" (Rom. 3:25, 26). The entire chapter of Romans 4 is a defense of the fact that we are justified by faith, not by works, just as Abraham and David themselves were. Paul says, "We are justified *by faith*" (Rom. 5:1).

Scripture never says that we are justified because of the inherent goodness of our faith, as if our faith has merit before God. It never allows us to think that our faith in itself earns favor with God. Rather, Scripture says that we are justified "by means of" our faith, understanding faith to be the instrument through which justification is given to us, but not at all an activity that earns us merit or favor with God. Rather, we are justified solely because of the merits of Christ's work (Rom. 5:17–19).[12]

But we may ask why God chose *faith* to be the attitude of heart by which we would obtain justification. Why could God not have decided to give justification to all those who sincerely show love? Or who show joy? Or contentment? Or humility? Or wisdom? Why did God choose *faith* as the means by which we receive justification?

It is apparently because *faith* is the one attitude of heart that is the exact opposite of depending on ourselves. When we come to Christ in faith we essentially say, "I give up! I will not depend on myself or my own good works any longer. I know that I can never make myself righteous before God. Therefore, Jesus, I trust you and depend on you completely to give me a righteous standing before God." In this way, faith is the exact opposite of trusting in ourselves, and therefore it is the attitude that perfectly fits salvation that depends not at all on our own merit but entirely on God's free gift of grace. Paul explains this when he says, "That is why it depends *on faith, in order that the promise may rest on grace* and be guaranteed to all his descendants" (Rom. 4:16). This is why the Reformers from Martin Luther on were so firm in their insistence that justification comes not through faith plus some merit or good work on our part, but only *through faith alone.* "For by grace you have been saved *through faith;* and this[13] is not your own doing, it is the gift of God—not because of works, lest any man should boast" (Eph. 2:8–9). Paul repeatedly says that "no human being will

---

[9]Ibid., p. 262.

[10]Ibid., p. 262.

[11]Ibid., p. 264.

be justified in his sight by works of law" (Rom. 3:20); the same idea is repeated in Galatians 2:16; 3:11; 5:4.

But is this consistent with the epistle of James? What can James mean when he says, "You see that a man is *justified by works* and not by faith alone" (James 2:24)? Here we must realize that James is using the word *justified* in a different sense from the way Paul uses it. In the beginning of this chapter we noted that the word *justify* has a range of meanings, and that one significant sense was "declare to be righteous," but we should also notice that the Greek word *dikaioō* can also mean "demonstrate or show to be righteous." For instance, Jesus said to the Pharisees, "You are those who *justify* yourselves before men, but God knows your hearts" (Luke 16:15). The point here was not that the Pharisees went around making legal declarations that they were "not guilty" before God, but rather that they were always attempting to *show others* that they were righteous by their outward deeds. Jesus knew that the truth was otherwise: "But God knows your hearts" (Luke 16:15). Similarly, the lawyer who put Jesus to a test by asking what he should do to inherit eternal life answered Jesus' first question well. But when Jesus told him, "Do this, and you will live," he was not satisfied. Luke tells us, "But he, *desiring to justify himself,* said to Jesus, 'And who is my neighbor?'" (Luke 10:28–29). Now he was not desiring to give a legal pronouncement about himself that he was not guilty in God's sight; rather, he was desiring to "show himself righteous" before others who were listening. Other examples of the word *justify* meaning "show to be righteous" can be found in Matthew 11:19; Luke 7:35; Romans 3:4.

Our interpretation of James 2 depends not only on the fact that "show to be righteous" is an acceptable sense for the word *justified,* but also on the consideration that this sense fits well in the context of James 2. When James says, "Was not Abraham our father *justified by works,* when he offered his son Isaac upon the altar?" (v. 21) he is referring to something later in Abraham's life, the story of the sacrifice of Isaac, which occurred in Genesis 22. This is long after the time recorded in Genesis 15:6 where Abraham believed God "and he reckoned it to him as righteousness." Yet this earlier incident at the beginning of Abraham's covenantal relationship with God is the one that Paul quotes and repeatedly refers to in Romans 4. Paul is talking about the time God justified Abraham once for all, reckoning righteousness to him as a result of his faith in God. But James is talking about something far later, after Abraham had waited many years for the birth of Isaac, and then after Isaac had grown old enough to carry wood up the mountain for a sacrifice. At that point Abraham was "shown to be righteous" by his works, and in that sense James says that Abraham was "justified by works, when he offered his son Isaac upon the altar" (James 2:21).[14]

The larger concern of James in this section also fits this understanding. James is concerned to show that mere intellectual agreement with the gospel is a "faith" that is really no faith at all. He is concerned to argue against those who say they have faith but show no

---

[12]One example from ordinary life might be seen in receiving a paycheck for work that has been done for an employer. The "means" or "instrument" that I use to get this paycheck is the act of reaching out my hand and taking an envelope from my mail box, then opening it and pulling out the check. But my employer does not pay me for doing any of those actions. The pay is entirely for work that I did prior to that. Actually taking the check did not earn me one cent of the money I received—it was simply the *instrument* or *means* I used to take the payment into my possession. Similarly, faith is the *instrument* we use to receive justification from God, but in itself gains us no merit with God. (The analogy is helpful but it is not perfect, because I had previously worked to earn the money, whereas justification is based on the work of Christ. The analogy would be closer if I had worked and then died, and my wife then picked up the paycheck from my mail box.)

change in their lives. He says, "Show me your faith apart from your works, and I by my works will show you my faith" (James 2:18). "For as the body apart from the spirit is dead, so faith apart from works is dead" (James 2:26). James is simply saying here that "faith" that has no results or "works" is not real faith at all; it is "dead" faith. He is not denying Paul's clear teaching that justification (in the sense of a declaration of right legal standing before God) is by faith alone apart from works of the law; he is simply affirming a different truth, namely, that "justification" in the sense of an outward showing that one is righteous only occurs as we see evidence in a person's life. To paraphrase, James is saying that a person is "*shown to be righteous* by his works, and not by his faith alone." This is something with which Paul also would certainly agree (2 Cor. 13:5; Gal. 5:19–24).

The practical implications of the doctrine of justification by faith alone are very significant. First, this doctrine enables us to offer genuine *hope* to unbelievers who know they could never make themselves righteous before God: if salvation is a free gift to be received through faith *alone,* then anyone who hears the gospel may hope that eternal life is freely offered and may be obtained.

Second, this doctrine gives us confidence that God will never make us pay the penalty for sins that have been forgiven on Christ's merits. Of course, we may continue to suffer the ordinary *consequences* of sin (an alcoholic who quits drinking may still have physical weakness for the rest of his or her life, and a thief who is justified may still have to go to jail to pay the penalty for his or her crime). Moreover, God may *discipline* us if we continue to act in ways that are disobedient to him (see Heb. 12:5–11), doing this out of love and for our own good. But God can never nor will ever *take vengeance* on us for past sins or *make us pay the penalty* that is due for them or *punish us out of wrath* and *for the purpose of doing us harm.* "There is therefore now no condemnation for those that are in Christ Jesus" (Rom. 8:1). This fact should give us a great sense of joy and confidence before God that we are accepted by him and that we stand before him as "not guilty" and "righteous" forever.

QUESTIONS FOR PERSONAL APPLICATION

1. Are you confident that God has declared you "not guilty" forever in his sight? Do you know when that happened in your own life? Did you do or think anything that resulted in God's justifying of you? Did you do anything to deserve justification? If you are not sure that God has justified you fully and for all time, is there something you need to do before that will happen? What would persuade you that God has certainly justified you?

2. If you think of yourself standing before God on the day of judgment, would you think that it is enough simply to have your sins all forgiven, or would you also feel a need to have the righteousness of Christ reckoned to your account?

---

[13]The word translated "this" is the neuter pronoun *touto,* which refers not to "faith" or to "grace" specifically in the previous clause (for they are both feminine nouns in Greek, and would require feminine pronouns), but to the entire idea expressed in the preceding phrase, the idea that you have been saved by grace through faith.

3. Do you think the difference between the Roman Catholic and Protestant understanding of justification is an important one? Describe how you would feel about your relationship to God if you held the Roman Catholic view of justification. Do modern Roman Catholics you know seem to hold to this traditional Roman Catholic view of justification, or do they have another view?

4. Have you ever wondered if God is still continuing to punish you from time to time for sins you have done in the past, even long ago? How does the doctrine of justification help you deal with those feelings?

SPECIAL TERMS

forensic   infused righteousness

impute   justification

BIBLIOGRAPHY

Berkouwer, G. C. *Faith and Justification*. Trans. by Lewis B. Smedes. Grand Rapids: Eerdmans, 1954.

Carson, D. A., ed. *Right With God: Justification in the Bible and the World*. Grand Rapids: Baker, 1992.

Hoekema, Anthony A. "Justification." In *Saved by Grace*. Grand Rapids: Eerdmans, and Exeter: Paternoster, 1989, pp. 152–91.

McGrath, Alister E. *Iustitia Dei: A History of the Christian Doctrine of Justification*. 2 vols. Cambridge: Cambridge University Press, 1986.

_____. *Justification by Faith: An Introduction*. Grand Rapids: Zondervan, 1988.

Morris, Leon. *The Apostolic Preaching of the Cross*. 3d ed. Grand Rapids: Eerdmans, 1965, pp. 251–98.

Murray, John. "Justification." In *Redemption Accomplished and Applied*. Grand Rapids: Eerdmans, 1955, pp. 117–31.

Packer, J. I. et al. *Here We Stand: Justification by Faith Today*. London: Hodder and Stoughton, 1986.

_____. "Justification." In *EDT*, pp. 593–97.

Pink, A. W. *The Doctrines of Election and Justification*. Grand Rapids: Baker, 1974.

Wright, N. T. "Justification." In *NDT*, pp. 359–61.

Ziesler, J.A. *The Meaning of Righteous in Paul*. Cambridge: Cambridge University, 1972.

---

[14]James does quote the text, "Abraham believed God, and it was reckoned to him as righteousness" in v. 23, but he says that Scripture "was fulfilled" when Abraham offered his son, apparently meaning that the earlier declaration of righteousness was then worked out and its results were seen to be true in Abraham's life when he offered Isaac on the altar.

SCRIPTURE MEMORY PASSAGE

Romans 3:27–28: *Then what becomes of our boasting? It is excluded. On what principle? On the principle of works? No, but on the principle of faith. For we hold that a man is justified by faith apart from works of law.*

HYMN

"Jesus, Thy Blood and Righteousness"

Jesus, thy blood and righteousness
　　My beauty are, my glorious dress;
'Midst flaming worlds, in these arrayed,
　　With joy shall I lift up my head.

Bold shall I stand in thy great day;
　　For who aught to my charge shall lay?
Fully absolved through these I am
　　From sin and fear, from guilt and shame.

When from the dust of death I rise
　　To claim my mansion in the skies,
Ev'n then this shall be all my plea,
　　Jesus hath lived, hath died, for me.

Jesus, be endless praise to thee,
　　Whose boundless mercy hath for me —
For me a full atonement made,
　　An everlasting ransom paid.

O let the dead now hear thy voice;
　　Now bid thy banished ones rejoice;
Their beauty this, their glorious dress,
　　Jesus, thy blood and righteousness.

AUTHOR: COUNT NIKOLAUS LUDWIG VON ZINZENDORF, 1739

(TRANS. JOHN WESLEY, 1740, ALT.)

Chapter

ADOPTION (MEMBERSHIP IN GOD'S FAMILY)

What are benefits of being a member of God's family?

EXPLANATION AND SCRIPTURAL BASIS

In regeneration God gives us new spiritual life within. In justification God gives us right legal standing before him. But in adoption God makes us members of his family. Therefore, the biblical teaching on adoption focuses much more on the personal relationships that salvation gives us with God and with his people.

A. Scriptural Evidence for Adoption

We may define adoption as follows: *Adoption is an act of God whereby he makes us members of his family.*

John mentions adoption at the beginning of his gospel, where he says, "But to all who received him, who believed in his name, he gave power *to become children of God*" (John 1:12). By contrast, those who do not believe in Christ are not children of God or adopted into his family, but are "children of wrath" (Eph. 2:3) and "sons of disobedience" (Eph. 2:2; 5:6). Although those Jews who rejected Christ tried to claim that God was their father (John 8:41), Jesus told them, "If God were your Father, you would love me. . . . You are of your father the devil, and your will is to do your father's desires" (John 8:42–44).

The New Testament epistles bear repeated testimony to the fact that we are now God's children in a special sense, members of his family. Paul says:

> For all who are led by the Spirit of God are *sons of God*. For you did not receive the spirit of slavery to fall back into fear, but you have received the *spirit of sonship*. When we cry, "Abba! Father!" it is the Spirit himself bearing witness with

our spirit that we are *children of God,* and if children, then heirs, heirs of God and fellow heirs with Christ, provided we suffer with him in order that we may also be glorified with him. (Rom. 8:14–17)

But if we are God's children, are we then related to one another as family members? Certainly so. In fact, this adoption into God's family makes us partakers together in *one family* even with the believing Jews of the Old Testament, for Paul says that we are Abraham's children as well: "Not all are children of Abraham because they are his descendants; but 'Through Isaac shall your descendants be named.' This means that it is not the children of the flesh who are the children of God, but the children of the promise are reckoned as descendants" (Rom. 9:7–8). He further explains in Galatians, "Now we, brethren, like Isaac, are children of promise . . . we are not children of the slave but of the free woman" (Gal. 4:28, 31; cf. 1 Peter 3:6, where Peter sees believing women as daughters of Sarah in the new covenant).

Paul explains that this status of adoption as God's children was not fully realized in the old covenant. He says that "before faith came, we were confined under the law . . . the law was our custodian until Christ came, that we might be justified by faith. But now that faith has come, we are no longer under a custodian; for *in Christ Jesus you are all sons of God, through faith*" (Gal. 3:23–26). This is not to say that the Old Testament completely omitted talk of God as our Father, for God did call himself the Father of the children of Israel and called them his children in several places (Ps. 103:13; Isa. 43:6–7; Mal. 1:6; 2:10). But even though there was a consciousness of God as Father to the people of Israel, the full benefits and privileges of membership in God's family, and the full realization of that membership, did not come until Christ came and the Spirit of the Son of God was poured into our hearts, bearing witness with our spirit that we were God's children.

What evidence do we see in our lives that we are God's children? Paul sees clear evidence in the fact that the Holy Spirit bears witness in our hearts that we are God's children: "But when the time had fully come, God sent forth his Son, born of woman, born under the law, to redeem those who were under the law, so that we might receive *adoption as sons.* And because *you are sons,* God has sent the Spirit of his Son into our hearts, crying, 'Abba! Father!' So through God you are no longer a slave *but a son,* and *if a son then an heir*" (Gal. 4:4–7).

John's first epistle places much emphasis on our status as children of God: "See what love the Father has given us, that we should be called *children of God;* and so we are. . . . Beloved, we are God's children now" (1 John 3:1–2; John frequently calls his readers "children" or "little children").[1]

Although Jesus does call us his "brothers" (Heb. 2:12 NIV) and he is therefore in one sense our older brother in God's family (cf. Heb. 2:14), and can be called "the firstborn among many brethren" (Rom. 8:29), he is nevertheless careful to make a clear distinction between the way in which God is our heavenly Father and the way in which he relates to God the Father. He says to Mary Magdalene, "I am ascending *to my Father and your Father,* to my God and your God" (John 20:17), thus making a clear distinction between the far greater and eternal sense in which God is his Father, and the sense in which God is our Father.

Although the New Testament says that we are *now* God's children (1 John 3:2), we should also note that there is another sense in which our adoption is still future because we will not receive the full benefits and privileges of adoption until Christ returns and we have new resurrection bodies. Paul speaks of this later, fuller sense of adoption when he says, "Not only the creation, but we ourselves, who have the first fruits of the Spirit, groan inwardly as we wait for adoption as sons, *the redemption of our bodies*" (Rom. 8:23). Here Paul sees the receiving of new resurrection bodies as the fulfillment of our privileges of adoption, so much so that he can refer to it as our "adoption as sons."

B. Adoption Follows Conversion and Is an Outcome of Saving Faith

We might initially think that we would become God's children by regeneration, since the imagery of being "born again" in regeneration makes us think of children being born into a human family. But the New Testament never connects adoption with regeneration: indeed, the idea of *adoption* is opposite to the idea of being born into a family!

Rather, the New Testament connects adoption with saving faith, and says that in response to our trusting in Christ, God has adopted us into his family. Paul says, "In Christ Jesus you are all *sons of God, through faith*" (Gal. 3:23–26). And John writes, "But to all who received him, who *believed in his name*, he gave power *to become children of God*" (John 1:12).[2] These two verses make it clear that adoption follows conversion and is God's response to our faith.

One objection to this might be brought from Paul's statement, "*Because you are sons,* God has sent the Spirit of his Son into our hearts, crying, 'Abba! Father!'" (Gal. 4:6). Someone might understand this verse to mean that first God adopted us as sons and second he gave us the Holy Spirit to bring regeneration to our hearts. But a few verses earlier Paul had said that we have become sons of God "through faith" (Gal. 3:26). Therefore Paul's statement in Galatians 4:6 is best understood not to refer to the giving of the Holy Spirit in regeneration, but rather to an additional activity of the Holy Spirit in which he begins to bear witness with our spirit and to assure us that we are members of God's family. This work of the Holy Spirit gives us *assurance* of our adoption, and it is in this sense that Paul says that, after we have become sons, God causes his Holy Spirit within our hearts to cry, "Abba! Father!" (cf. Rom. 8:15–16).

C. Adoption Is Distinct From Justification

Although adoption is a privilege that comes to us at the time we become Christians (John 1:12; Gal. 3:26; 1 John 3:1–2), nevertheless, it is a privilege that is distinct from justification and distinct from regeneration. In regeneration we are made spiritually alive, able to relate to God in prayer and worship and able to hear his Word with receptive hearts. But it is possible that God could have creatures who are spiritually alive and yet are not members of his family and do not share the special privileges of family members—angels, for example, apparently fall into that category.[3] Therefore, it would

---

[1]There are several other passages that speak about our status as God's children or our membership in his family (see Matt. 5:48; 7:11; 2 Cor. 6:18; Eph. 5:1; Phil. 2:15; Heb. 2:13–14; 12:5–11; 1 Peter 1:14; 1 John 3:10).

have been possible for God to decide to give us regeneration without the great privileges of adoption into his family.

Moreover, God could have given us justification without the privileges of adoption into his family, for he could have forgiven our sins and given us right legal standing before him without making us his children. It is important to realize this because it helps us to recognize how great are our privileges in adoption. Regeneration has to do with our spiritual life within. Justification has to do with our standing before God's law. But adoption has to do with our *relationship* with God as our Father, and in adoption we are given many of the greatest blessings that we will know for all eternity. When we begin to realize the excellence of these blessings, and when we appreciate that God has no obligation to give us any of them, then we will be able to exclaim with the apostle John, "See *what love* the Father has given us, that we should be called children of God; and so we are" (1 John 3:1).

D. The Privileges of Adoption

The benefits or privileges that accompany adoption are seen, first, in the way God relates to us, and then also in the way we relate to one another as brothers and sisters in God's family.

One of the greatest privileges of our adoption is being able to speak to God and *relate to him as a* good and loving *Father*. We are to pray, "Our Father who art in heaven" (Matt. 6:9), and we are to realize that we are "no longer slaves, but sons" (Gal. 4:7). Therefore, we now relate to God not as a slave relates to a slave master, but as a child relates to his or her father. In fact, God gives us an *internal witness from the Holy Spirit* that causes us instinctively to call God our Father. "When we cry, 'Abba! Father!' it is the Spirit himself bearing witness with our spirit that we are children of God" (Rom. 8:15–16). This relationship to God as our Father is the foundation of many other blessings of the Christian life, and it becomes the primary way in which we relate to God. Certainly it is true that God is our Creator, our judge, our Lord and Master, our teacher, our provider and protector, and the one who by his providential care sustains our existence. But the role that is most intimate, and the role that conveys the highest privileges of fellowship with God for eternity, is his role as our heavenly Father.

The fact that God relates to us as Father shows very clearly that he *loves us* (1 John 3:1), that he *understands us* ("As a father has compassion on his children, so the LORD has compassion on those who fear him; for he knows how we are formed, he remembers that we are dust" [Ps. 103:13–14 NIV]), and that he *takes care of our needs* ("For the Gentiles seek all these things; and your heavenly Father knows that you need them all," Matt. 6:32). Moreover, in his role as our Father, God *gives us many good gifts:* "If you then, who are evil, know how to give good gifts to your children, how much more will your Father who is in heaven give good things to those who ask him!" (Matt. 7:11). He especially *gives us* the gift of *the Holy Spirit* to comfort us and to empower us for ministry and for living the Christian life

---

[2]It is true that in John 1:13 he specifies that these were people who were born "of God," but this is simply giving additional information about them (namely, that they had been regenerated by God). That does not negate the fact that it was to those who "believed in his name" that Christ gave power to become children of God.

(Luke 11:13).[4] In fact, it is not only gifts in this life that God gives to us, but he also gives us a great *inheritance in heaven,* because we have become joint heirs with Christ. Paul says, "You are no longer a slave, but a son, and if a son then an heir" (Gal. 4:7); we are in fact "heirs of God and fellow heirs with Christ" (Rom. 8:17). As heirs we have the rights to a great eternal "inheritance which is imperishable, undefiled, and unfading, kept in heaven for you" (1 Peter 1:4). All the great privileges and blessings of heaven are laid up for us and put at our disposal because we are children of the King, members of the royal family, princes and princesses who will reign with Christ over the new heavens and new earth (Rev. 2:26–27; 3:21). As a foretaste of this great privilege, angels are even now sent to minister to us and serve us (Heb. 1:14).

It is in the context of this relationship with God as our heavenly Father that we are to understand the prayer that Jesus told his disciples to pray daily, "*Our Father* who art in heaven . . . *forgive us our sins,* as we also have forgiven those who sin against us" (Matt. 6:9–12, author's translation). This daily prayer for forgiveness of sins is not a prayer that God would give us justification again and again throughout our lives, for justification is a one-time event that occurs immediately after we trust in Christ with saving faith. Rather, the prayer for forgiveness of sins each day is a prayer that God's fatherly relationship with us, which has been disrupted by sin that displeased him, be restored, and that he relate to us once again as a Father who delights in his children whom he loves. The prayer, "Forgive us our sins," therefore, is one in which we are relating not to God as eternal judge of the universe, but to God as a Father. It is a prayer in which we wish to restore the open fellowship with our Father that has been broken because of sin (see also 1 John 1:9; 3:19–22).

The privilege of being *led by the Holy Spirit* is also a benefit of adoption. Paul indicates that this is a moral benefit whereby the Holy Spirit puts in us desires to obey God and live according to his will. He says, "All who are *led by the Spirit of God* are *sons of God*" (Rom. 8:14), and he gives this as the *reason* Christians should "put to death the deeds of the body" by means of the Holy Spirit working within them (v. 13; note "for" at the beginning of v. 14). He sees the Holy Spirit as leading and guiding God's children in paths of obedience to God.

Another privilege of adoption into God's family, though we do not always recognize it as a privilege, is the fact that God *disciplines us* as his children. "My son, do not regard lightly the discipline of the Lord, nor lose courage when you are punished by him. For the Lord disciplines him whom he loves, and chastises every son whom he receives" (Heb. 12:5–6, quoting Prov. 3:11–12). The author of Hebrews explains, "God is treating you as sons; for what son is there whom his father does not discipline? . . . he disciplines us for our good, that we may share his holiness" (Heb. 12:7, 10). Just as earthly children grow in obedience and righteousness when they are disciplined properly by their earthly fathers, so we grow in righteousness and holiness when we are disciplined by our heavenly Father.

---

[3]Although both good and evil angels are in one place in Scripture called "the sons of God" (Job 1:6), this is apparently a reference to the status of sonship that comes by the fact that God created them. It does not seem to indicate that angels generally (especially evil angels) share in any of the family privileges that we receive as God's children. In fact, Heb. 2:14–16 makes a clear distinction between our status as God's children and the status of angels. Moreover, angels are nowhere else referred to as members of God's family or said to have the family privileges that belong to us as God's children. (It is unlikely that Gen. 6:2–4 refers to angels; see Wayne Grudem, *1 Peter,* TNTC [Grand Rapids: Eerdmans, 1988], pp. 211–15.)

Related to the fatherly discipline of God is the fact that, as children of God and joint heirs with Christ, we have the *privilege of sharing both in his sufferings and in his subsequent glory.* Just as it was "necessary that the Christ should suffer these things and enter into his glory" (Luke 24:26), so God gives us the privilege of walking the same path that Christ walked, enduring sufferings in this life that we may also receive great glory in the life to come: "if children, then heirs, heirs of God and fellow heirs with Christ, *provided we suffer with him* in order that we may also be *glorified with him*" (Rom. 8:17).

In addition to these great privileges that concern our relationship to God and fellowship with him, we also have privileges of adoption that affect the way that we relate to each other and affect our own personal conduct. Because we are God's children, our relationship with each other is far deeper and more intimate than the relationship that angels, for example, have to one another, for we are all *members of one family.* Many times the New Testament refers to Christians as "brothers" and "sisters" in Christ (Rom. 1:13; 8:12; 1 Cor. 1:10; 6:8; James 1:2; Matt. 12:50; Rom. 16:1; 1 Cor. 7:15; Philem. 1:2; James 2:15). In addition to this, the many verses in which entire churches are referred to as "brothers" should not be understood to refer to the men in the congregation only, but are rather generic references to the whole church, and, except where the context explicitly indicates otherwise, should be taken to mean "brothers and sisters in the Lord." The designation "brother" is so common in the epistles that it seems to be the predominant way in which the New Testament authors refer to the other Christians to whom they are writing. This indicates the strong consciousness they had of the nature of the church as the family of God. In fact, Paul tells Timothy to relate to the church at Ephesus, and to the individuals within the church, as he would relate to members of a large family: "Do not rebuke an older man but exhort him as you would a *father;* treat younger men like *brothers,* older women like *mothers,* younger women like *sisters,* in all purity" (1 Tim. 5:1–2).[5]

This concept of the church as God's family should give us a new perspective on the work of the church; it is "family work," and the various members of the family never should compete with each other or hinder one another in their efforts, but should encourage one another and be thankful for whatever good or whatever progress comes to any member of the family, for all are contributing to the good of the family and the honor of God our Father. In fact, just as members of an earthly family often have times of joy and fellowship when they work together on a single project, so our times of working together in building up the church ought to be times of great joy and fellowship with one another. Moreover, just as members of an earthly family honor their parents and fulfill the purpose of a family most when they eagerly welcome any brothers or sisters who are newly adopted into that family, so we ought to welcome new members of the family of Christ eagerly and with love.

Another aspect of our membership in God's family is that we, as God's children, are to *imitate our Father* in heaven in all our conduct. Paul says, "be imitators of God, as beloved children" (Eph. 5:1). Peter echoes this theme when he says, "As obedient children, do not be conformed to the passions of your former ignorance, but as he who called you is holy,

---

[4]In this verse Jesus says, "If you then, who are evil, know how to give good gifts to your children, how much more will the heavenly Father give the Holy Spirit to those who ask him!" Here he seems to mean not the gift of the Holy Spirit dwelling within as he comes at regeneration, but the gift of further empowering for ministry, for gifts to be used in ministry, or for Christian living.

be holy yourselves in all your conduct; since it is written, 'You shall be holy, for I am holy'" (1 Peter 1:14–16). Both Peter and Paul realize that it is natural for children to imitate their earthly fathers. They appeal to this natural sense that children have in order to remind us that we are to imitate our heavenly Father—indeed, this should be something we naturally want to do and delight in. If God our Father in heaven is holy, we should be holy as obedient children.

When we walk in paths of righteous conduct we *honor our heavenly Father* and bring glory to him. When we act in a way that is pleasing to God, we are to do so that others "may see your good works and give glory to your Father who is in heaven" (Matt. 5:16). Paul encourages the Philippians to maintain pure conduct before unbelievers "that you may be blameless and innocent, *children of God* without blemish in the midst of a crooked and perverse generation, among whom you shine as lights in the world" (Phil. 2:15). Indeed, a consistent pattern of moral conduct is also evidence that we are truly children of God. John says, "By this it may be seen who are the children of God, and who are the children of the devil: whoever does not do right is not of God, nor he who does not love his brother" (1 John 3:10).

QUESTIONS FOR PERSONAL APPLICATION

1. Look back over the list of privileges that come with our adoption as God's children. Had you previously thought of these as automatically yours because you had been born again? Can you describe what our eternal life would be like if we had regeneration and justification and many of the other privileges that come with salvation, but no adoption into God's family? Now how do you feel about the fact that God has adopted you into his family compared with the way you felt before reading this chapter?

2. Has your relationship with your own human family become better or more difficult as a result of your becoming a Christian? If your relationship with your earthly family has become more difficult, how have you found Mark 10:29–30 to be true in your life as a Christian?

3. Sometimes people who have had unloving or cruel earthly fathers have found that their background creates difficulty in their thinking about God and relating to him as a heavenly Father. How can Hebrews 12:10; Matthew 7:11; and Luke 11:13, which contrast sinful earthly fathers with our perfect Father in heaven, be of help in that situation? Might 1 Peter 1:18 be helpful in this situation as well? What can a person who has had a cruel and unloving earthly father do to gain a better and better appreciation of who God is and what kind of Father he is? Do you think that any of the people who became Christians in the first century had cruel and unloving fathers,

---

[5]An extensive analysis of the New Testament teaching on the church as a family is found in Vern S. Poythress, "The Church as a Family: Why Male Leadership in the Family Requires Male Leadership in the Church as Well," in W. Grudem and J. Piper, eds., *Recovering Biblical Manhood and Womanhood* (Wheaton, Ill.: Crossway, 1991), pp. 233–47.

or no living fathers at all? What teachings of the Old Testament would have helped them at this point? Do you think that people who have had evil earthly fathers have a God-given inward sense of what a good father would be like?

4. Think of the people who are members of your church. Has this chapter helped you to think of them more as your brothers and sisters (or if they are older, as those who are like "fathers" and "mothers" to you)? How do you think an added appreciation of this idea of the church as a family would be helpful to your church? How could you encourage a greater appreciation of this idea?

5. Does your church have any sense of competition with other churches that might be overcome by greater appreciation of the doctrine of adoption?

6. In the human family, when one of the children commits a crime and is publicly punished for it, the entire family suffers shame. On the other hand, when a family member is honored for an outstanding achievement, the entire family is proud and rejoices. How does this analogy of events in a human family make you feel about your own personal level of holiness in life, and the way it reflects on the other members of your spiritual family? How does it make you feel about the need for personal holiness among your brothers and sisters in the church? Do you personally have a strong inward desire to imitate your heavenly Father in your conduct (Eph. 5:1; 1 Peter 1:14–16)?

7. Do you sense the Holy Spirit within you bearing witness with your spirit that you are a child of God (Rom. 8:15–16; Gal. 4:6)? Can you describe what that sense is like?

8. Do you sense any discrimination against Christians of other races or other social or economic positions? Can you understand how the doctrine of adoption should obliterate such distinctions in the church (see Gal. 3:26–28)? Can you also see how the doctrine of adoption means that neither men nor women should think of the other sex as more important or less important in the church (see Gal. 3:28)?

SPECIAL TERM

adoption

BIBLIOGRAPHY

Davids, P. H. "Adoption." In *EDT,* p. 13.
Murray, John. "Adoption." In *Redemption Accomplished and Applied.* Grand Rapids: Eerdmans, 1955, pp. 132–40.

SCRIPTURE MEMORY PASSAGE

Romans 8:14–17: *For all who are led by the Spirit of God are sons of God. For you did not receive the spirit of slavery to fall back into fear, but you have received the spirit of sonship.*

When we cry, "Abba! Father!" it is the Spirit himself bearing witness with our spirit that we are children of God, and if children, then heirs, heirs of God and fellow heirs with Christ, provided we suffer with him in order that we may also be glorified with him.

HYMN

"Children of the Heavenly Father"

Children of the heav'nly Father
    Safely in his bosom gather;
Nestling bird nor star in heaven
    Such a refuge e'er was given.

God his own doth tend and nourish,
    In his holy courts they flourish;
From all evil things he spares them,
    In his mighty arms he bears them.

Neither life nor death shall ever
    From the Lord his children sever;
Unto them his grace he showeth,
    And their sorrows all he knoweth.

Praise the Lord in joyful numbers,
    Your Protector never slumbers;
At the will of your Defender
    Every foeman must surrender.

Though he giveth or he taketh,
    God his children ne'er forsaketh;
His the loving purpose solely
    To preserve them pure and holy.

AUTHOR: CAROLINE V. SANDELL BERG, C. 1855
(TRANS. ERNST W. OLSON, 1925)

Chapter

SANCTIFICATION (GROWTH IN LIKENESS TO CHRIST)

How do we grow in Christian maturity?
What are the blessings of Christian growth?

EXPLANATION AND SCRIPTURAL BASIS

The previous chapters have discussed several acts of God that occur at the beginning of our Christian lives: the gospel call (which God addresses to us), regeneration (by which God imparts new life to us), justification (by which God gives us right legal standing before him), and adoption (in which God makes us members of his family). We have also discussed conversion (in which we repent of sins and trust in Christ for salvation). These events all occur at the beginning of our Christian lives.[1]

But now we come to a part of the application of redemption that is a *progressive* work that continues throughout our earthly lives. It is also a work in which *God and man cooperate,* each playing distinct roles. This part of the application of redemption is called sanctification: *Sanctification is a progressive work of God and man that makes us more and more free from sin and like Christ in our actual lives.*

A. Differences Between Justification and Sanctification

The following table specifies several differences between justification and sanctification:

Justification	Sanctification
Legal standing	Internal condition
Once for all time	Continuous throughout life
Entirely God's work	We cooperate

Perfect in this life	Not perfect in this life
The same in all Christians	Greater in some than in others

As this chart indicates, sanctification is something that continues throughout our Christian life. The ordinary course of a Christian's life will involve continual growth in sanctification, and it is something that the New Testament encourages us to give effort and attention to.

B. Three Stages of Sanctification

1. Sanctification Has a Definite Beginning at Regeneration. A definite moral change occurs in our lives at the point of regeneration, for Paul talks about the "washing of regeneration and renewal in the Holy Spirit" (Titus 3:5). Once we have been born again we cannot continue to sin as a habit or a pattern of life (1 John 3:9), because the power of new spiritual life within us keeps us from yielding to a life of sin.

This initial moral change is the first stage in sanctification. In this sense, there is some overlap between regeneration and sanctification, for this moral change is actually a part of regeneration. But when we view it from the standpoint of moral change within us, we can also see it as the first stage in sanctification. Paul looks back on a completed event when he says to the Corinthians, "But you were washed, *you were sanctified,* you were justified in the name of the Lord Jesus Christ and in the Spirit of

our God" (1 Cor. 6:11). Similarly, in Acts 20:32 Paul can refer to Christians as "all those who are sanctified."[2]

This initial step in sanctification involves a definite break from the ruling power and love of sin, so that the believer is no longer ruled or dominated by sin and no longer loves to sin. Paul says, "So you also must *consider yourselves dead to sin* and alive to God in Christ Jesus. . . . For *sin will have no dominion over you*" (Rom. 6:11, 14). Paul says that Christians have been "set free from sin" (Rom. 6:18). In this context, to be dead to sin or to be set free from sin involves the power to overcome acts or patterns of sinful behavior in one's life. Paul tells the Romans not to let sin "reign in your mortal bodies," and he also says, "Do not yield your members to sin as instruments of wickedness, but yield yourselves to God" (Rom. 6:12–13). To be dead to the ruling power of sin means that we as Christians, by virtue of the power of the Holy Spirit and the resurrection life of Christ working within us, have power to overcome the temptations and enticements of sin. Sin will no longer be our master, as once it was before we became Christians.

In practical terms, this means that we must affirm two things to be true. On the one hand, we will never be able to say, "I am completely free from sin," because our sanctification will never be completed (see below). But on the other hand, a Christian should never say

---

[1]Although the initial saving faith by which we are justified occurs only at the time of conversion, faith and repentance do continue throughout our lives as well (see chapter 6). Similarly, although regeneration, justification, and adoption are instantaneous one-time events that occur at the beginning of the Christian life, the results of all of these continue throughout life: we continue to have the spiritual life we receive from regeneration, the legal standing we receive from justification, and the membership in God's family we receive from adoption.

(for example), "This sin has defeated me. I give up. I have had a bad temper for thirty-seven years, and I will have one until the day I die, and people are just going to have to put up with me the way I am!" To say this is to say that sin has gained dominion. It is to allow sin to reign in our bodies. It is to admit defeat. It is to deny the truth of Scripture, which tells us, "You also must consider yourselves dead to sin and alive to God in Christ Jesus" (Rom. 6:11). It is to deny the truth of Scripture that tells us that "sin will have no dominion over you" (Rom. 6:14).

This initial break with sin, then, involves a reorientation of our desires so that we no longer have a dominant love for sin in our lives. Paul knows that his readers were formerly slaves to sin (as all unbelievers are), but he says that they are enslaved no longer. "You who were once slaves of sin have become obedient from the heart to the standard of teaching to which you were committed, and, having been set free from sin, have become slaves of righteousness" (Rom. 6:17–18). This change of one's primary love and primary desires occurs at the beginning of sanctification.[3]

2. Sanctification Increases Throughout Life. Even though the New Testament speaks about a definite beginning to sanctification, it also sees it as a process that continues throughout our Christian lives. This is the primary sense in which sanctification is used in systematic theology and in Christian conversation generally today.[4] Although Paul says that his readers have been set free from sin (Rom. 6:18) and that they are "dead to sin and alive to God" (Rom. 6:11), he nonetheless recognizes that sin remains in their lives, so he tells them not to let it reign and not to yield to it (Rom. 6:12–13). Their task, therefore, as Christians is to grow more and more in sanctification, just as they previously grew more and more in sin: "Just as you once yielded your members to impurity and to greater and greater iniquity, so now yield your members to righteousness for sanctification" (Rom. 6:19; the words "just as . . . so now" [Gk. *hōsper . . . houtōs*] indicate that Paul wants them to do this in the same way: "just as" they previously yielded to more and more sin, "in just the same way" they are now to yield themselves to more and more righteousness for sanctification).

Paul says that throughout the Christian life "we all . . . are being changed into his likeness from one degree of glory to another" (2 Cor. 3:18). We are progressively becoming more and more like Christ as we go on in the Christian life. Therefore he says, "Forgetting what lies behind and straining forward to what lies ahead, *I press on* toward the goal for the prize of the upward call of God in Christ Jesus" (Phil. 3:13–14)—this is in the context of saying that he is not already perfect but he presses on to achieve all of the purposes for which Christ has saved him (vv. 9–12).

Paul tells the Colossians that they should not lie to one another, since they have "put on the new nature, which is *being renewed* in knowledge after the image of its creator" (Col. 3:10), thus showing that sanctification even involves increasing likeness to God in our thoughts as well as our words and deeds. The author of Hebrews tells his readers to "lay aside every weight, and sin which clings so closely" (Heb. 12:1), and to *"strive for . . . the*

---

[2]The Greek expression is *tois hēgiasmenois*, a substantival perfect passive participle that expresses both a completed past activity (they were sanctified) and a continuing result (they continue to experience the sanctifying influence of that past action).

holiness without which no one will see the Lord" (Heb. 12:14). James encourages his hearers, "Be doers of the word, and not hearers only" (James 1:22), and Peter tells his readers, "Be holy yourselves in all your conduct" (1 Peter 1:15).

It is not necessary to list multiple additional quotations, because much of the New Testament is taken up with instructing believers in various churches on how they should grow in likeness to Christ. All of the moral exhortations and commands in the New Testament epistles apply here, because they all exhort believers to one aspect or another of greater sanctification in their lives. It is the expectation of all the New Testament authors that our sanctification will increase throughout our Christian lives.

3. Sanctification Is Completed at Death (for Our Souls) and When the Lord Returns (for Our Bodies). Because there is sin that still remains in our hearts even though we have become Christians (Rom. 6:12–13; 1 John 1:8), our sanctification will never be completed in this life (see below). But once we die and go to be with the Lord, then our sanctification is completed in one sense, for our souls are set free from indwelling sin and are made perfect. The author of Hebrews says that when we come into the presence of God to worship we come "to the spirits of just men *made perfect*" (Heb. 12:23). This is only appropriate because it is in anticipation of the fact that "nothing unclean shall enter" into the presence of God, the heavenly city (Rev. 21:27).

However, when we appreciate that sanctification involves the whole person, including our bodies (see 2 Cor. 7:1; 1 Thess. 5:23), then we realize that sanctification will not be entirely completed until the Lord returns and we receive new resurrection bodies. We await the coming of our Lord Jesus Christ from heaven, and he "will change our lowly body to be like his glorious body" (Phil. 3:21). It is "at his coming" (1 Cor. 15:23) that we will be made alive with a resurrection body and then we shall fully "bear the image of the Man of heaven" (1 Cor. 15:49).[5]

---

[3]Some may wish to add to this section one or more passages from Hebrews that speak about our sanctification as having been completed in the past. For example, the author says that by the will of God "we have been sanctified through the offering of the body of Jesus Christ once for all" (Heb. 10:10). The Greek expression is a periphrastic perfect passive participle, *hēgiasmenoi esmen*, which speaks of a continuing present situation that results from a completed past action: "We are continually in the state of 'having been sanctified' (and we continue to feel the results of that previous act of sanctification)."

But in Hebrews the term *sanctify* (Gk. *hagiazō*) is related more to the Old Testament background of ceremonial purity or holiness as necessary for access to God's presence, and therefore "sanctified" in Hebrews means "made holy and righteous in God's sight and therefore fit to draw near to God in worship." As such, "sanctified" in Hebrews is roughly equivalent to "justified" in Paul's vocabulary. This sense of "sanctified" can be seen in Heb. 9:13; 10:10; 13:12. These passages speak of a ceremonial kind of purification that allows access to God, and, as such, "sanctification" here applies to the beginning of the

Christian life. Nevertheless, the focus is more on access to God in worship, while the Pauline emphasis is on justification from the penalty of sin that was due under God's law.

[4]There is a different usage of the word *sanctified* in the Wesleyan/Holiness tradition within Protestantism. In these circles the experience of sanctification is sometimes viewed as a single event subsequent to conversion in which a Christian attains a higher level of holiness, a level sometimes known as "entire sanctification" or "sinless perfection." Within this tradition, sanctification is seen as an experience one seeks for in the Christian life and is sometimes able to attain. Therefore, while most Protestants would say, "I am being sanctified," some within the Wesleyan/Holiness tradition would say, "I *have been* sanctified," referring not to the initial break with sin that comes with conversion, but to a subsequent experience in which they began to know freedom from conscious sin in their lives. The difficulties with this position are outlined in section 4 below, "Sanctification Is Never Completed in This Life."

[5]See chapter 13 on glorification (that is, receiving a resurrection body when Christ returns).

We may diagram the process of sanctification as in figure 9.1, showing that we are slaves to sin prior to conversion, (1) that there is a definite beginning to sanctification at the point of conversion, (2) that sanctification should increase throughout the Christian life, and (3) that sanctification is made perfect at death. (The completion of sanctification when we receive resurrection bodies is omitted from this chart for the sake of simplicity.)

I have shown the progress of sanctification as a jagged line on this chart, indicating that growth in sanctification is not always one-directional in this life, but that progress in sanctification occurs at some times, while at other times we realize that we are regressing somewhat. In the extreme case, a believer who makes very little use of the means of sanctification, but rather has bad teaching, lacks good Christian fellowship, and pays little attention to God's Word and prayer, may actually go for many years with very little progress in sanctification at all—but this is certainly not the normal or expected pattern of the Christian life. It is in fact highly abnormal.

4. Sanctification Is Never Completed in This Life. There have always been some in the history of the church who have taken commands such as Matthew 5:48 ("You, therefore, *must be perfect,* as your heavenly Father is perfect") or 2 Corinthians 7:1 ("let us cleanse ourselves from every defilement of body and spirit, and *make holiness perfect* in the fear of God") and reasoned that since God gives us these commands, he must also give us the ability to obey them perfectly. Therefore, they have concluded, it is possible for us to attain a state of sinless perfection in this life. Moreover, they point to Paul's prayer for the Thessalonians, "May the God of peace himself sanctify you wholly" (1 Thess. 5:23), and infer that Paul's prayer may well have been fulfilled for some of the Thessalonian Christians. In fact, John even says, "No one who abides in him sins" (1 John 3:6)! Do these verses not point to the possibility of sinless perfection in the life of some Christians? In this discussion, I will use the term *perfectionism* to refer to this view that sinless perfection is possible in this life.

On closer inspection, these passages do not support the perfectionist position. First, it is simply not taught in Scripture that when God gives a command, he also gives the ability to obey it in every case. God commands all people everywhere to obey all of his moral laws and holds them accountable for failing to obey them, even though unredeemed people are sinners and, as such, dead in trespasses and sins, and thus unable to obey God's commands. When Jesus commands us to be perfect as our Father in heaven is perfect (Matt. 5:48), this simply shows that God's own absolute moral purity is the standard toward which we are to aim and the standard for which God holds us accountable. The fact that we are unable to attain that standard does not mean that it will be lowered; rather, it means that we need God's grace and forgiveness to overcome our remaining sin. Similarly, when Paul commands the Corinthians to make holiness perfect in the fear of the Lord (2 Cor. 7:1), or prays that God would sanctify the Thessalonians wholly (1 Thess. 5:23), he is pointing to the goal that he desires them to reach. He does not imply

---

[6]1 John 5:18 is to be understood in a similar way.

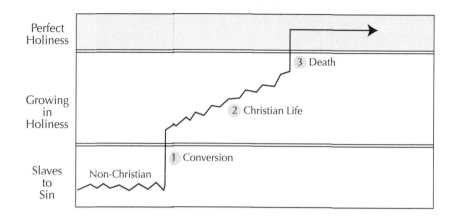

THE PROCESS OF SANCTIFICATION
Figure 9.1

that any reach it, but only that this is the high moral standard toward which God wants all believers to aspire.

John's statement that "No one who abides in him sins" (1 John 3:6) does not teach that some of us attain perfection, because the present-tense Greek verbs are better translated as indicating continual or habitual activity: "No one who lives in him *keeps on sinning.* No one who *continues to sin* has either seen him or known him" (1 John 3:6 NIV). This is similar to John's statement a few verses later, "No one who is born of God will continue to sin, because God's seed remains in him; he cannot go on sinning, because he has been born of God" (1 John 3:9 NIV). If these verses were taken to prove sinless perfection, they would have to prove it for all Christians, because they talk about what is true of everyone born of God, and everyone who has seen Christ and known him.[6]

Therefore, there do not seem to be any convincing verses in Scripture that teach that it is possible for anyone to be completely free of sin in this life. On the other hand, there are passages in both the Old and New Testaments that clearly teach that we cannot be morally perfect in this life. In Solomon's prayer at the dedication of the temple, he says, "If they sin against you—for *there is no man who does not sin*" (1 Kings 8:46). Similarly, we read a rhetorical question with an implied negative answer in Proverbs 20:9: "Who can say, 'I have made my heart clean; I am pure from my sin'?" And we read the explicit statement in Ecclesiastes 7:20, *"Surely there is not a righteous man on earth who does good and never sins."*

In the New Testament, we find Jesus commanding his disciples to pray, "Give us this day our daily bread; and *forgive us our sins,* as we also have forgiven those who sin against us" (Matt. 6:11–12, author's translation). Just as the prayer for daily bread provides a model for a prayer that should be repeated each day, so the prayer for the forgiveness of sins is included in the type of prayer that should be made each day in a believer's life.

As we noted above, when Paul talks about the new power over sin that is given to a Christian, he does not say that there will be no sin in the Christian's life, but simply tells the believers not to let sin "reign" in their bodies nor to "yield" their members to sin (Rom. 6:12–13). He does not say that they will not sin, but says that sin will not dominate or "have

. . . dominion" over them (Rom. 6:14). The very fact that he issues these directions shows his realization that sin will continue to be present in the lives of believers throughout their time on earth. Even James the brother of our Lord could say, *"We all make many mistakes"* (James 3:2), and if James himself can say this, then we certainly should be willing to say it as well. Finally, in the same letter in which John declares so frequently that a child of God will not continue in a pattern of sinful behavior, he also says clearly, "If we say we have no sin, we deceive ourselves, and the truth is not in us" (1 John 1:8). Here John explicitly excludes the possibility of being completely free from sin in our lives. In fact, he says that anyone who claims to be free from sin is simply deceiving himself, and the truth is not in him.

But once we have concluded that sanctification will never be completed in this life, we must exercise pastoral wisdom and caution in the way we use this truth. Some may take this fact and use it as an excuse not to strive for holiness or grow in sanctification—a procedure exactly contrary to dozens of New Testament commands. Others may think about the fact that we cannot be perfect in this life and lose hope of making any progress in the Christian life—an attitude that is also contrary to the clear teaching of Romans 6 and other passages about the resurrection power of Christ in our lives enabling us to overcome sin. Therefore, although sanctification will never be completed in this life, we must also emphasize that it should never stop increasing in this life.

Moreover, as Christians grow in maturity, the kinds of sin that remain in their lives are often not so much sins of words or deeds that are outwardly noticeable to others, but inward sins of attitudes and motives of the heart—desires such as pride and selfishness, lack of courage or faith, lack of zeal in loving God with our whole hearts and our neighbors as ourselves, and failure to fully trust God for all that he promises in every situation. These are real sins! They show how far short we fall of the moral perfection of Christ.

However, recognizing the nature of these sins that will persist even in more mature Christians also helps to guard against misunderstanding when we say that no one will be perfect and free from sin in this life. It is certainly possible that many mature Christians at many times during the day are free from conscious or willful acts of disobedience to God in their words or their deeds. In fact, if Christian leaders are to "set the believers an *example* in speech and conduct, in love, in faith, in purity" (1 Tim. 4:12), then it will frequently be true that their lives will be free from words or deeds that others will count as blameworthy. But this is far removed from attaining total freedom from sin in our motives and in the thoughts and intents of our hearts.

John Murray notes that when Isaiah the prophet came into the presence of God he could only cry out, "Woe is me! For I am lost; for I am a man of unclean lips, and I dwell in the midst of a people of unclean lips; for my eyes have seen the King, the LORD of hosts!" (Isa. 6:5). And when Job, whose righteousness was earlier commended in the story about his life, came into the presence of almighty God, he could only say, "I had heard of you by the hearing of the ear, but now my eye sees you; therefore I despise myself, and repent in dust and ashes" (Job 42:5–6). Murray concludes from these examples and from the testimony of other saints through the history of the church:

---

[7]John Murray, *Redemption Accomplished and Applied* (Grand   Rapids: Eerdmans, 1955), p. 145.

Indeed, the more sanctified the person is, the more conformed he is to the image of his Savior, the more he must recoil against every lack of conformity to the holiness of God. The deeper his apprehension of the majesty of God, the greater the intensity of his love to God, the more persistent his yearning for the attainment of the prize of the high calling of God in Christ Jesus, the more conscious will he be of the gravity of the sin that remains and the more poignant will be his detestation of it. . . . Was this not the effect in all the people of God as they came into closer proximity to the revelation of God's holiness?[7]

C. God and Man Cooperate in Sanctification

Some (such as John Murray)[8] object to saying that God and man "cooperate" in sanctification, because they want to insist that God's work is primary and our work in sanctification is only a secondary one (see Phil. 2:12–13). However, if we explain the nature of God's role and our role in sanctification clearly, it does not seem inappropriate to say that God and man cooperate in sanctification. God works in our sanctification and we work as well, and we work for the same purpose. We are not saying that we have equal roles in sanctification or that we both work in the same way, but simply that we cooperate with God in ways that are appropriate to our status as God's creatures. And the fact that Scripture emphasizes the role that we play in sanctification (with all the moral commands of the New Testament), makes it appropriate to teach that God calls us to cooperate with him in this activity.[9]

1. God's Role in Sanctification. Since sanctification is primarily a work of God, it is appropriate that Paul prays, "May the God of peace himself sanctify you wholly" (1 Thess. 5:23). One specific role of God the Father in this sanctification is his process of disciplining us as his children (see Heb. 12:5–11). Paul tells the Philippians, *"God is at work in you,* both to will and to work for his good pleasure" (Phil. 2:13), thus indicating something of the way in which God sanctifies them—both by causing them to want his will and by giving them power to do it. The author of Hebrews speaks of the role of the Father and the role of the Son in a familiar benediction: "Now may the God of peace . . . equip you with everything good that you may do his will, working in you that which is pleasing in his sight, through Jesus Christ; to whom be glory for ever and ever" (Heb. 13:20–21).

The role of God the Son, Jesus Christ, in sanctification is, first, that he *earned* our sanctification for us. Therefore Paul could say that God made Christ to be "our wisdom, our righteousness and sanctification and redemption" (1 Cor. 1:30). Moreover, in the process of sanctification, Jesus is also our *example,* for we are to run the race of life "looking to Jesus the pioneer and perfecter of our faith" (Heb. 12:2). Peter tells his readers, "Christ also suffered for you, leaving you an example, that you should follow in his steps" (1 Peter 2:21). And John says, "He who says he abides in him ought to walk in the same way in which he walked" (1 John 2:6).

But it is specifically God the Holy Spirit who works within us to change us and sanctify us, giving us greater holiness of life. Peter speaks of the "sanctification of the Spirit" (1 Peter 1:2, author's translation), and Paul speaks of "sanctification by the Spirit" (2 Thess. 2:13). It is the Holy Spirit who produces in us the "fruit of the Spirit" (Gal. 5:22–23), those character traits that are part of greater and greater sanctification. If we grow in sanctification we "walk by the Spirit" and are "led by the Spirit" (Gal. 5:16–18; cf. Rom. 8:14), that is, we are more and more responsive to the desires and promptings of the Holy Spirit in our life and character. The Holy Spirit is the spirit of holiness, and he produces holiness within us.

2. Our Role in Sanctification. The role that we play in sanctification is both a *passive* one in which we depend on God to sanctify us, and an *active* one in which we strive to obey God and take steps that will increase our sanctification. We can now consider both of these aspects of our role in sanctification.

First, what may be called the "passive" role that we play in sanctification is seen in texts that encourage us to trust God or to pray and ask that he sanctify us. Paul tells his readers, "*Yield yourselves to God* as men who have been brought from death to life" (Rom. 6:13; cf. v. 19), and he tells the Roman Christians, "Present your bodies as a living sacrifice, holy and acceptable to God" (Rom. 12:1). Paul realizes that we are dependent on the Holy Spirit's work to grow in sanctification, because he says, "If *by the Spirit* you put to death the deeds of the body you will live" (Rom. 8:13).

Unfortunately today, this "passive" role in sanctification, this idea of yielding to God and trusting him to work in us "to will and to work for his good pleasure" (Phil. 2:13), is sometimes so strongly emphasized that it is the only thing people are told about the path of sanctification. Sometimes the popular phrase "let go and let God" is given as a summary of how to live the Christian life. But this is a tragic distortion of the doctrine of sanctification, for it only speaks of one half of the part we must play, and, by itself, will lead Christians to become lazy and to neglect the active role that Scripture commands them to play in their own sanctification.

That active role which we are to play is indicated by Romans 8:13, where Paul says, "If by the Spirit *you* put to death the deeds of the body you will live." Here Paul acknowledges that it is "by the Spirit" that we are able to do this. But he also says we must do it! It is not the Holy Spirit who is commanded to put to death the deeds of the flesh, but Christians! Similarly, Paul tells the Philippians, "Therefore, my beloved, as you have always obeyed, so now, not only as in my presence but much more in my absence, *work out your own salvation* with fear and trembling; for God is at work in you, both to will and to work for his good pleasure" (Phil. 2:12–13). Paul encourages them to obey even more than they did when he was present. He says that obedience is the way in which they "work out [their] own salvation," meaning that they will "work out" the further realization of the benefits of salvation in their Christian life.[10] The Philippians are to work at this growth in sanctification, and to do it solemnly and with reverence ("with fear and trembling"), for they are doing it in the presence of God himself. But there is more: the reason why they are to work and to expect that their work will yield positive results is that "God is at work in you"—the prior and

[8]Ibid., pp. 148–49.

[9]On the other hand, if we wish to say that sanctification is entirely God's work, and that we use the means of sanctification in order to contribute to it (or some similar expression), the meaning is the same. I am simply concerned that if we say sanctification is entirely God's work, we can be misunderstood and encourage an excessively passive role on the part of Christians, who may be led to think that they need to do nothing in the process of sanctification in their lives.

[10]This verse does not use the word "salvation" to refer to initial justification, but to the ongoing process of experiencing more

foundational work of God in sanctification means that their own work is empowered by God; therefore it will be worthwhile and will bear positive results.

There are many aspects to this active role that we are to play in sanctification. We are to *"Strive . . . for* the *holiness* without which no one will see the Lord" (Heb. 12:14); we are to *"abstain from immorality"* and so obey the will of God, which is our "sanctification" (1 Thess. 4:3). John says that those who hope to be like Christ when he appears will actively work at purification in this life: "And every one who thus hopes in him *purifies himself* as he is pure" (1 John 3:3). Paul tells the Corinthians to *"shun immorality"* (1 Cor. 6:18), and not to have partnership with unbelievers (2 Cor. 6:14). He then says, "Let us *cleanse ourselves* from every defilement of body and spirit, and make holiness perfect in the fear of God" (2 Cor. 7:1). This kind of striving for obedience to God and for holiness may involve great effort on our part, for Peter tells his readers to *"make every effort"* to grow in character traits that accord with godliness (2 Peter 1:5). Many specific passages of the New Testament encourage detailed attention to various aspects of holiness and godliness in life (see Rom. 12:1 – 13:14; Eph. 4:17 – 6:20; Phil. 4:4 – 9; Col. 3:5 – 4:6; 1 Peter 2:11 – 5:11, et al.). We are continually to build up patterns and habits of holiness, for one measure of maturity is that mature Christians "have their faculties trained by practice to distinguish good from evil" (Heb. 5:14).

The New Testament does not suggest any short-cuts by which we can grow in sanctification, but simply encourages us repeatedly to give ourselves to the old-fashioned, time-honored means of Bible reading and meditation (Ps. 1:2; Matt. 4:4; John 17:17), prayer (Eph. 6:18; Phil. 4:6), worship (Eph. 5:18 – 20), witnessing (Matt. 28:19 – 20), Christian fellowship (Heb. 10:24 – 25), and self-discipline or self-control (Gal. 5:23; Titus 1:8).

It is important that we continue to grow both in our passive trust in God to sanctify us and in our active striving for holiness and greater obedience in our lives. If we neglect active striving to obey God, we become passive, lazy Christians. If we neglect the passive role of trusting God and yielding to him, we become proud and overly confident in ourselves. In either case, our sanctification will be greatly deficient. We must maintain faith and diligence to obey at the same time. The old hymn wisely says, *"Trust and obey,* for there's no other way, to be happy in Jesus, but to trust and obey."[11]

One more point must be added to this discussion of our role in sanctification: sanctification is usually a corporate process in the New Testament. It is something that happens in community. We are admonished, "Let us consider how to *stir up one another to love and good works,* not neglecting to meet together, as is the habit of some, but encouraging one another, and all the more as you see the Day drawing near" (Heb. 10:24 – 25). Together Christians are "built into a spiritual house, to be a holy priesthood" (1 Peter 2:5); together they are "a holy nation" (1 Peter 2:9); together they are to "encourage one another and build one another up" (1 Thess. 5:11). Paul says that "to lead a life worthy of the calling to which you have been called" (Eph. 4:1) is to live in a special way in community — "with all lowliness and meekness, with patience, forbearing one another in love, eager to maintain

and more of the blessings of salvation; here, "salvation" is roughly equivalent to "sanctification."

[11]Comparing our life to a tree with two large roots, John Livingstone said, "Satan strikes . . . either at the root of faith or at the

the unity of the Spirit in the bond of peace" (Eph. 4:2–3). When that happens, the body of Christ functions as a unified whole, with each part "working properly," so that corporate sanctification occurs as it "makes bodily growth and upbuilds itself in love" (Eph. 4:16; cf. 1 Cor. 12:12–26; Gal. 6:1–2). It is significant that the fruit of the Spirit includes many things that build community ("love, joy, peace, patience, kindness, goodness, faithfulness, gentleness, self-control," Gal. 5:22–23), whereas "the works of the flesh" destroy community ("fornication, impurity, licentiousness, idolatry, sorcery, enmity, strife, jealousy, anger, selfishness, dissension, party spirit, envy, drunkenness, carousing, and the like," Gal. 5:19–21).

D. Sanctification Affects the Whole Person

We see that sanctification affects our *intellect* and our knowledge when Paul says that we have put on the new nature "which is being renewed in *knowledge* after the image of its creator" (Col. 3:10). He prays that the Philippians may see their love "abound more and more, with knowledge and all discernment" (Phil. 1:9). And he urges the Roman Christians to be "transformed by the renewal of your mind" (Rom. 12:2). Although our knowledge of God is more than intellectual knowledge, there is certainly an intellectual component to it, and Paul says that this knowledge of God should keep increasing throughout our lives: a life "worthy of the Lord, fully pleasing to him" is one that is continually "increasing in the knowledge of God" (Col. 1:10). The sanctification of our intellects will involve growth in wisdom and knowledge as we increasingly "take every thought captive to obey Christ" (2 Cor. 10:5) and find that our thoughts are more and more the thoughts that God himself imparts to us in his Word.

Moreover, growth in sanctification will affect our *emotions*. We will see increasingly in our lives emotions such as "love, joy, peace, patience" (Gal. 5:22). We will be able increasingly to obey Peter's command "to abstain from the passions of the flesh that wage war against your soul" (1 Peter 2:11). We will find it increasingly true that we do not "love the world or things in the world" (1 John 2:15), but that we, like our Savior, delight to do God's will. In ever-increasing measure we will become "obedient from the heart" (Rom. 6:17), and we will "put away" the negative emotions involved in "bitterness and wrath and anger and clamor and slander" (Eph. 4:31).

Moreover, sanctification will have an effect on our *will*, our decision-making faculty, because God is at work in us, "to *will* and to work for his good pleasure" (Phil. 2:13). As we grow in sanctification, our will will be more and more conformed to the will of our heavenly Father.

Sanctification will also affect our *spirit*, the nonphysical part of our beings. We are to "cleanse ourselves from every defilement of body and *spirit*, and make holiness perfect in the fear of God" (2 Cor. 7:1), and Paul says that a concern about the affairs of the Lord will mean taking thought for "how to be holy in body and *spirit*" (1 Cor. 7:34).

root of diligence" (quoted in D. M. M'Intyre, *The Hidden Life of Prayer* [Minneapolis: Bethany Fellowship, 1969], p. 39).

[12]Of course, physical weakness will inevitably come with old age, and sometimes comes earlier due to infirmity, but this can be

Finally, sanctification affects our *physical bodies*. Paul says, "May the God of peace himself sanctify you wholly; and may your spirit and soul *and body* be kept sound and blameless at the coming of our Lord Jesus Christ" (1 Thess. 5:23). Moreover, Paul encourages the Corinthians, "Let us cleanse ourselves from every defilement of *body* and spirit, and make holiness perfect in the fear of God" (2 Cor. 7:1; cf. 1 Cor. 7:34). As we become more sanctified in our bodies, our bodies become more and more useful servants of God, more and more responsive to the will of God and the desires of the Holy Spirit (cf. 1 Cor. 9:27).[12] We will not let sin reign in our bodies (Rom. 6:12) nor allow our bodies to participate in any way in immorality (1 Cor. 6:13), but will treat our bodies with care and will recognize that they are the means by which the Holy Spirit works through us in this life. Therefore they are not to be recklessly abused or mistreated, but are to be made useful and able to respond to God's will: "Do you not know that your body is a temple of the Holy Spirit within you, which you have from God? You are not your own; you were bought with a price. So glorify God in your body" (1 Cor. 6:19–20).

E. Motives for Obedience to God in the Christian Life

Christians sometimes fail to recognize the wide range of motives for obedience to God that are found in the New Testament. (1) It is true that a desire to please God and express our love to him is a very important motive for obeying him—Jesus says, "If you love me, you will keep my commandments" (John 14:15), and, "He who has my commandments and keeps them, he it is who loves me" (John 14:21; cf. 1 John 5:3). But many other motives are also given to us: (2) the need to keep a clear conscience before God (Rom. 13:5; 1 Tim. 1:5, 19; 2 Tim. 1:3; 1 Peter 3:16); (3) the desire to be a "vessel for noble use" and have increased effectiveness in the work of the kingdom (2 Tim. 2:20–21); (4) the desire to see unbelievers come to Christ through observing our lives (1 Peter 3:1–2, 15–16); (5) the desire to receive present blessings from God on our lives and ministries (1 Peter 3:9–12); (6) the desire to avoid God's displeasure and discipline on our lives (sometimes called "the fear of God") (Acts 5:11; 9:31; 2 Cor. 5:11; 7:1; Eph. 4:30; Phil. 2:12; 1 Tim. 5:20; Heb. 12:3–11; 1 Peter 1:17; 2:17; cf. the state of unbelievers in Rom. 3:18); (7) the desire to seek greater heavenly reward (Matt. 6:19–21; Luke 19:17–19; 1 Cor. 3:12–15; 2 Cor. 5:9–10); (8) the desire for a deeper walk with God (Matt. 5:8; John 14:21; 1 John 1:6; 3:21–22; and, in the Old Testament, Ps. 66:18; Isa. 59:2); (9) the desire that angels would glorify God for our obedience (1 Tim. 5:21; 1 Peter 1:12); (10) the desire for peace (Phil. 4:9) and joy (Heb. 12:1–2) in our lives; and (11) the desire to do what God commands, simply because his commands are right, and we delight in doing what is right (Phil. 4:8; cf. Ps. 40:8).

F. The Beauty and Joy of Sanctification

It would not be right to end our discussion without noting that sanctification brings great joy to us. The more we grow in likeness to Christ, the more we will personally experience the "joy" and "peace" that are part of the fruit of the Holy Spirit (Gal. 5:22), and the more we will draw near to the kind of life that we will have in heaven. Paul says that as we become more and more obedient to God, "the return you get is sanctification and its end, eternal life" (Rom. 6:22). He realizes that this is the source of our true joy. "For the kingdom of God is not food and drink but righteousness and peace and joy in the Holy Spirit" (Rom. 14:17). As we grow in holiness we grow in conformity to the image of Christ, and more and more of the beauty of his character is seen in our own lives. This is the goal of perfect sanctification which we hope and long for, and which will be ours when Christ returns. "And every one who thus hopes in him purifies himself as he is pure" (1 John 3:3).

QUESTIONS FOR PERSONAL APPLICATION

1. Can you remember in your own experience the definite beginning to sanctification that occurred when you became a Christian? Did you sense a clear break from the ruling power and love of sin in your life? Do you really believe that you are even now dead to the ruling power and love of sin in your life? How can this truth of the Christian life be of help to you in specific areas of your life where you still need to grow in sanctification?

2. As you look back over the last few years of your Christian life, can you see a pattern of definite growth in sanctification? What are some things that you used to delight in which no longer interest you? What are some things that you used to have no interest in that now hold great interest for you?

3. As you have grown to greater maturity and holiness in the Christian life, have you become more conscious of the weight of sin that remains in your heart? If not, why has this not been so? Do you think that it would be helpful if you had a greater consciousness of the sin that remains in your own life? If you had this, what difference would it make in your own life?

4. How would it affect your life if you thought more about the fact that the Holy Spirit is continually at work in you to increase your sanctification? In living the Christian life, have you maintained a balance between your passive role and your active role in sanctification, or have you tended to emphasize one aspect over the other, and why? What might you do to correct this imbalance, if there is one in your life?

5. Have you thought previously that sanctification affects your intellect and the way you think? What areas of your intellect still need quite a bit of growth in sanctification? With regard to your emotions, in what areas do you know that God still needs to work to bring about greater sanctification? Are there areas or aspects of sanctification that need to be improved with respect to your physical body and its obedience to God's purposes?

6. Are there areas where you have struggled for years to grow in sanctification, but with no progress at all in your life? Has this chapter helped you regain hope for progress in

---

consistent with increased sanctification as God's power is "made perfect in weakness" (2 Cor. 12:9). Paul clearly teaches this when he says, "We have this treasure in earthen vessels, to show that the transcendent power belongs to God and not to us" (2 Cor. 4:7), and, "We do not lose heart. Though our outer nature is wasting away, our inner nature is being renewed every day" (2 Cor. 4:16).

those areas? (For Christians who have serious discouragement over lack of progress in sanctification, it is very important to talk personally to a pastor or other mature Christian about this situation, rather than letting it go on for a long period of time.)

7. Overall, has this chapter been an encouragement or discouragement to you in your Christian life?

SPECIAL TERMS

perfectionism
sanctification
sinless perfection

BIBLIOGRAPHY

Alexander, Donald L., ed. *Christian Spirituality: Five Views of Sanctification*. Downers Grove, Ill.: InterVarsity Press, 1988.

Berkouwer, G. C. *Faith and Sanctification*. Trans. by John Vriend. Grand Rapids: Eerdmans, 1952.

Bockmuehl, Klaus. "Sanctification." In *NDT*, pp. 613–16.

Chafer, Lewis Sperry. *He That Is Spiritual*. Rev. ed. Grand Rapids: Zondervan, 1967.

Coppedge, Allan. *The Biblical Principles of Discipleship*. Grand Rapids: Francis Asbury Press, 1989.

Downs, Perry G. *Teaching for Spiritual Growth: An Introduction to Christian Education*. Grand Rapids: Zondervan, 1994.

Hoekema, Anthony A. "Sanctification." In *Saved by Grace*. Grand Rapids: Eerdmans and Exeter: Paternoster, 1989, pp. 192–233.

Murray, John. "Sanctification." In *Redemption Accomplished and Applied*. Grand Rapids: Eerdmans, 1955, pp. 141–50.

Packer, J. I. *Keep in Step With the Spirit*. Old Tappan, N.J.: Revell, 1984.

Prior, K. *The Way of Holiness*. Downers Grove, Ill.: InterVarsity Press, 1967.

Ryle, J. C. *Holiness: Its Nature, Hindrances, Difficulties and Roots*. Westwood, N.J.: Revell, n.d.

White, R. E. O. "Sanctification." In *EDT*, pp. 969–71.

Willard, Dallas. *The Spirit of the Disciplines: Understanding How God Changes Lives*. San Francisco: Harper and Row, 1988.

Ziesler, J. A. *The Meaning of Righteousness in Paul*. Cambridge: Cambridge University Press, 1972.

SCRIPTURE MEMORY PASSAGE

Romans 6:11 – 14: *So you also must consider yourselves dead to sin and alive to God in Christ Jesus. Let not sin therefore reign in your mortal bodies, to make you obey their passions. Do not yield your members to sin as instruments of wickedness, but yield yourselves to God as men who have been brought from death to life, and your members to God as instruments of righteousness. For sin will have no dominion over you, since you are not under law but under grace.*

HYMN

"Take Time to Be Holy"

Take time to be holy, speak oft with thy Lord;
    Abide in him always, and feed on his Word.
Make friends of God's children; help those who are weak;
    Forgetting in nothing his blessing to seek.

Take time to be holy, the world rushes on;
    Spend much time in secret with Jesus alone.
By looking to Jesus, like him thou shalt be;
    Thy friends in thy conduct his likeness shall see.

Take time to be holy, let him be thy guide,
    And run not before him, whatever betide;
In joy or in sorrow, still follow thy Lord,
    And, looking to Jesus, still trust in his Word.

Take time to be holy, be calm in thy soul;
    Each thought and each motive beneath his control;
Thus led by his Spirit to fountains of love,
    Thou soon shalt be fitted for service above.

AUTHOR: WILLIAM D. LONGSTAFF, 1887

Chapter

BAPTISM IN AND FILLING WITH THE HOLY SPIRIT

Should we seek a "baptism in the Holy Spirit" after conversion? What does it mean to be filled with the Holy Spirit?

Systematic theology books have not traditionally included a chapter on baptism in the Holy Spirit or filling with the Holy Spirit as part of the study of the "order of salvation," the study of the various steps in which the benefits of salvation are applied to our lives.[1] But with the spread of Pentecostalism that began in 1901, the widespread influence of the charismatic movement in the 1960's and 1970's, and the remarkable growth of Pentecostal and charismatic[2] churches worldwide from 1970 to the present, the question of a "baptism in the Holy Spirit" distinct from regeneration has come into increasing prominence. I have put this chapter at this point in our study of the application of redemption for two reasons: (1) A proper understanding of this question must assume an understanding of regeneration, adoption, and sanctification, all of which have been discussed in previous chapters. (2) All the previous chapters on the application of redemption have discussed events that occur (or in the case of sanctification, that begin) at the point at which a person becomes a Christian. But this question concerns an event that occurs either at the point of conversion (according to one view) or sometime after conversion (according to another view). Moreover, people on both sides of the question agree that some kind of second experience has happened to many people after their conversion, and therefore one very important question is how to understand this experience in the light of Scripture and what scriptural categories properly apply to it.

EXPLANATION AND SCRIPTURAL BASIS

A. The Traditional Pentecostal Understanding

The topic of this chapter has become important today because many Christians say that they have experienced a "baptism in the Holy Spirit" that came after they became Christians and that brought great blessing in their lives. They claim that prayer and Bible study have become much more meaningful and effective, that they have discovered new joy in worship, and they often say that they have received new spiritual gifts (especially, and most frequently, the gift of speaking in tongues).

This traditional Pentecostal or charismatic position is supported from Scripture in the following way:

(1) Jesus' disciples were born-again believers long before the day of Pentecost, perhaps during Jesus' life and ministry, but certainly by the time that Jesus, after his resurrection, "breathed on them, and said to them, 'Receive the Holy Spirit'" (John 20:22).

(2) Jesus nevertheless commanded his disciples "not to depart from Jerusalem, but to wait for the promise of the Father" (Acts 1:4), telling them, "Before many days you shall be *baptized with the Holy Spirit*" (Acts 1:5). He told them, "You shall receive power when the Holy Spirit has come upon you" (Acts 1:8). The disciples then obeyed Jesus' command and waited in Jerusalem for the Holy Spirit to come upon them so that they would receive new empowering for witness and ministry.

(3) When the disciples had waited for ten days, the day of Pentecost came, tongues of fire rested above their heads, "And they were all filled with the Holy Spirit and began to speak in other tongues, as the Spirit gave them utterance" (Acts 2:4). This clearly shows that they received a baptism in (or with)[3] the Holy Spirit. Although the disciples were born again long before Pentecost, at Pentecost they received a

"baptism with the Holy Spirit" (Acts 1:5 and 11:16 refer to it this way) that was subsequent to conversion and resulted in great empowering for ministry as well as speaking in tongues.[4]

(4) Christians today, like the apostles, should ask Jesus for a "baptism in the Holy Spirit" and thus follow the pattern of the disciples' lives.[5] If we receive this baptism in the Holy

---

[1]See chapter 3, for a list of the elements in the order of salvation.

[2]I am using the terms *Pentecostal* and *charismatic* in the following way: *Pentecostal* refers to any denomination or group that traces its historical origin back to the Pentecostal revival that began in the United States in 1901 and that holds to the doctrinal positions (a) that baptism in the Holy Spirit is ordinarily an event subsequent to conversion, and (b) that baptism in the Holy Spirit is made evident by the sign of speaking in tongues, and (c) that all the spiritual gifts mentioned in the New Testament are to be sought and used today. Pentecostal groups usually have their own distinct denominational structures, the most prominent of which is the Assemblies of God.

Charismatic refers to any groups (or people) that trace their historical origin to the charismatic renewal movement of the 1960s and 1970s, seek to practice all the spiritual gifts mentioned in the New Testament (including prophecy, healing, miracles, tongues, interpretation, and distinguishing between spirits), and allow differing viewpoints on whether baptism in the Holy Spirit is subsequent to conversion and whether

tongues is a sign of baptism in the Holy Spirit. Charismatics will very often refrain from forming their own denomination, but will view themselves as a force for renewal within existing Protestant and Roman Catholic churches. There is no representative charismatic denomination in the United States today, but the most prominent charismatic spokesman is probably Pat Robertson with his Christian Broadcasting Network, the television program "The 700 Club," and Regent University (formerly CBN University).

In the 1980s yet a third renewal movement arose, called the *"third wave"* by missions professor C. Peter Wagner at Fuller Seminary (he referred to the Pentecostal renewal as the first wave of the Holy Spirit's renewing work in the modern church, and the charismatic movement as the second wave). "Third wave" people encourage the equipping of all believers to use New Testament spiritual gifts today, and say that the proclamation of the gospel should ordinarily be accompanied by "signs, wonders, and miracles," according to the New Testament pattern. They teach, however, that baptism in the Holy Spirit happens to all Christians at conversion, and that

Spirit, it will result in much more power for ministry for our own lives, just as it did in the lives of the disciples, and will often (or always, according to some teachers) result in speaking in tongues as well.

(5) Support for this pattern—in which people are first born again and then later are baptized in the Holy Spirit—is seen in several other instances in the book of Acts. It is seen, for example, in Acts 8, where the people of Samaria first became Christians when they "believed Philip as he preached good news about the kingdom of God and the name of Jesus Christ" (Acts 8:12), but only later received the Holy Spirit when the apostles Peter and John came from Jerusalem and prayed for them (Acts 8:14–17).[6]

Another example is found in Acts 19, where Paul came and found "some disciples" at Ephesus (Acts 19:1). But, "when Paul had laid his hands upon them, the Holy Spirit came on them; and they spoke with tongues and prophesied" (Acts 19:6).

All of these examples (Acts 2, 8, sometimes 10, and 19)[7] are cited by Pentecostals in order to show that a "baptism in the Holy Spirit" subsequent to conversion was a very common occurrence for New Testament Christians. Therefore, they reason, if it was common for Christians in Acts to have this second experience sometime after conversion, should it not be common for us today as well?

We can analyze this issue of the baptism in the Holy Spirit by asking three questions: (1) What does the phrase "baptism in the Holy Spirit" mean in the New Testament? (2) How should we understand the "second experiences" that came to born-again believers in the book of Acts? (3) Are there other biblical expressions, such as "filling with the Holy Spirit," that are better suited to describe an empowering with the Holy Spirit that comes after conversion?

B. What Does "Baptism in the Holy Spirit" Mean in the New Testament?

There are only seven passages in the New Testament where we read of someone being baptized in the Holy Spirit. (The English translations quoted here use the word *with* rather than *in*.)[8] The seven passages follow:

In the first four verses, John the Baptist is speaking of Jesus and predicting that he will baptize people in (or with) the Holy Spirit:

> Matthew 3:11: "I baptize you with water for repentance, but he who is coming after me is mightier than I, whose sandals I am not worthy to carry; he will *baptize you with the Holy Spirit* and with fire."

---

subsequent experiences are better called "filling" with the Holy Spirit. The most prominent representative of the "third wave" is John Wimber, senior pastor of the Vineyard Christian Fellowship in Anaheim, California, and leader of the Association of Vineyard Churches. Wimber's two most influential books, *Power Evangelism* (San Francisco: Harper and Row, 1986; rev. ed., 1992) and *Power Healing* (San Francisco: Harper and Row, 1987), both co-authored by Kevin Springer, are widely recognized as representative of distinctive "third wave" emphases.

The definitive reference work for these movements is now Stanley M. Burgess and Eduard M. van der Maas, eds., *New International Dictionary of Pentecostal and Charismatic Movements* (Grand Rapids: Zondervan, 2003).

Mark 1:8: "I have baptized you with water; but he will *baptize you with the Holy Spirit.*"

Luke 3:16: "I baptize you with water; but he who is mightier than I is coming, the thong of whose sandals I am not worthy to untie; he will *baptize you with the Holy Spirit* and with fire."

John 1:33: "He who sent me to baptize with water said to me, 'He on whom you see the Spirit descend and remain, this is he who *baptizes with the Holy Spirit.'*"

It is hard to draw any conclusions from these four passages with respect to what baptism with the Holy Spirit really is. We discover that Jesus is the one who will carry out this baptism and he will baptize his followers. But no further specification of this baptism is given.

The next two passages refer directly to Pentecost:

Acts 1:5: [Here Jesus says,] "John baptized with water, but before many days you shall be *baptized with the Holy Spirit.*"

Acts 11:16: [Here Peter refers back to the same words of Jesus that were quoted in the previous verse. He says,] "I remembered the word of the Lord, how he said, 'John baptized with water, but you shall be *baptized with the Holy Spirit.'*"

These two passages show us that whatever we may understand baptism in the Holy Spirit to be, it certainly happened at the day of Pentecost as recorded in Acts 2, when the Holy Spirit fell in great power on the disciples and those with them, and they spoke in other tongues, and about three thousand people were converted (Acts 2:14).

It is important to realize that all six of these verses use almost exactly the same expression in Greek, with the only differences being some variation in word order or verb tense

---

[3]It does not matter much whether we translate the Greek phrase *en pneumati* as "in the Spirit" or "with the Spirit" because both are acceptable translations, and people on all sides of this topic seem to use those two expressions rather interchangeably. I have used "in the Holy Spirit" ordinarily throughout this chapter, but the RSV translation which I quote here generally prefers to use "with the Holy Spirit." I do not make any distinction between these two phrases in the discussion of this chapter. (But see below, pp. 135–36, for a discussion of the frequent claim by Pentecostals that baptism *by* the Holy Spirit [as in 1 Cor. 12:13] is a different event than baptism *in* [or with] the Holy Spirit.)

[4]Most Pentecostal discussions of baptism in the Holy Spirit include the view that speaking in tongues is a "sign" that one has been baptized in the Holy Spirit, and that this sign will be given to all who have been baptized in the Holy Spirit, even though not all will later have the gift of speaking in tongues as a continuing gift in their lives.

[5]I personally heard such teaching on baptism in the Holy Spirit as a first-year university student in 1967, and later privately prayed, as instructed, first repenting of all known sin and once again yielding every area of my life to God, then ask-

ing Jesus to baptize me in the Holy Spirit. Though my understanding of that experience has since changed, so that I would explain it in different terms (see below), the result in my life was undoubtedly a positive and lasting one, including a much deeper love for Christ and much greater effectiveness in personal ministry.

[6]Another example sometimes cited is that of Cornelius in Acts 10. He was a devout man who prayed constantly to God (Acts 10:2), but when Peter came and preached to him and his household, Peter and those with him were amazed "because the gift of the Holy Spirit had been poured out even on the Gentiles. For they heard them speaking in tongues and extolling God" (Acts 10:45–46).

[7]The case of Paul in Acts 9:17 is sometimes mentioned as well, but it is not as clear-cut, since his violent persecution of the church prior to that time indicates that he was not born again before the Damascus Road experience. But some have seen a similar pattern in the distinction between his conversion on the Damascus Road and his receiving the Holy Spirit at the hands of Ananias three days later.

[8]See above, footnote 3.

to fit the sentence, and with one example having the preposition understood rather than expressed explicitly.[9]

The only remaining reference in the New Testament is in the Pauline epistles:

> 1 Corinthians 12:13 (NIV mg): "For we were all *baptized in one Spirit* into one body—whether Jews or Greeks, slave or free—and we were all given the one Spirit to drink."

Now the question is whether 1 Corinthians 12:13 refers to the same activity as these other six verses. In many English translations it appears to be different, for many translations are similar to the RSV, which says, "For *by one Spirit* we were all baptized into one body." Those who support the Pentecostal view of baptism in the Holy Spirit after conversion are quite eager to see this verse as referring to something other than baptism in the Holy Spirit, and they frequently emphasize the difference that comes out in the English translations. In all the other six verses, Jesus is the one who baptizes people and the Holy Spirit is the "element" (parallel to water in physical baptism) in which or with which Jesus baptizes people. But here in 1 Corinthians 12:13 (so the Pentecostal explanation goes) we have something quite different—here the person doing the baptizing is not Jesus but the Holy Spirit. Therefore, they say, 1 Corinthians 12:13 should not be taken into account when we ask what the New Testament means by "baptism in the Holy Spirit."

This point is very important to the Pentecostal position, because, if we admit that 1 Corinthians 12:13 refers to baptism *in* the Holy Spirit, then it is very hard to maintain that it is an experience that comes after conversion. In this verse Paul says that this baptism in/with/by the Holy Spirit made us members of the body of Christ—"We were all baptized *in* one Spirit into one body" (1 Cor. 12:13 NIV mg). But if this really is a "baptism in the Holy Spirit," the same as the event that was referred to in the previous six verses, then Paul is saying that it happened to all the Corinthians *when they became members of the body of Christ; that is, when they became Christians.* For it was that baptism that resulted in their being members of the body of Christ, the church. Such a conclusion would be very difficult for the Pentecostal position that holds that baptism in the Holy Spirit is something that occurs after conversion, not at the same time.

Is it possible to sustain the Pentecostal view that the other six verses refer to a baptism *by Jesus* in which he baptizes us in (or with) the Holy Spirit, but that 1 Corinthians 12:13 refers to something different, to a baptism *by the Holy Spirit*? Although the distinction seems to make sense from some English translations, it really cannot be supported by an examination of the Greek text, for there the expression is almost identical to the expressions we have seen in the other six verses. Paul says *en heni pneumati . . . ebaptisthemen* ("in one Spirit . . . we were baptized"). Apart from one small difference (he refers to "one Spirit" rather than "the Holy Spirit"),[10] all the other elements are the same: the verb is *baptizō,* and the prepositional phrase contains the same words (*en* plus the dative noun *pneumati*). If we translate this same Greek expression "baptize *in* the Holy Spirit" (or "baptize *with* the Holy Spirit") in the other six New Testament occurrences where we find it, then it seems only proper that

---

[9]The expression used in all six passages is the verb *baptizō*

we translate it in the same way in this seventh occurrence. And no matter how we translate, it seems hard to deny that the original readers would have seen this phrase as referring to the same thing as the other six verses, because for them the words were the same.

But why have modern English translations translated this verse to say, "By one Spirit we were all baptized into one body," thus giving apparent support to the Pentecostal interpretation? We should first note that the NASB gives "in" as a marginal translation, and the NIV margin gives both "with" and "in" as alternatives. The reason these translations have chosen the word "by" has apparently been a desire to avoid an appearance of two locations for the baptism in the same sentence. The sentence already says that this baptism was "into one body," and perhaps the translators thought it seemed awkward to say, "*in* one Spirit we were all baptized *into* one body." But this should not be seen as a great difficulty, for Paul says, referring to the Israelites, "all were baptized *into* Moses *in* the cloud and *in* the sea" (1 Cor. 10:2)—a very closely parallel expression where the cloud and the sea are the "elements" that surrounded or overwhelmed the people of Israel and *Moses* means the new life of participation in the Mosaic covenant and the fellowship of God's people (led by Moses) that the Israelites found themselves in after they had passed through the cloud and the sea. It is not that there were two locations for the same baptism, but one was the element in which they were baptized and the other was the location in which they found themselves after the baptism. This is very similar to 1 Corinthians 12:13: the Holy Spirit was the *element* in which they were baptized, and the body of Christ, the church, was the *location* in which they found themselves after that baptism.[11] It thus seems appropriate to conclude that 1 Corinthians 12:13 also refers to baptism "in" or "with" the Holy Spirit, and is referring to the same thing as the other six verses mentioned.

But this has a significant implication for us: it means that, as far as the apostle Paul was concerned, *baptism in the Holy Spirit occurred at conversion.* He says that all the Corinthians were baptized in the Holy Spirit and the result was that they became members of the body of Christ: "For we were all baptized in one Spirit into one body" (1 Cor. 12:13 NIV mg). "Baptism in the Holy Spirit," therefore, must refer to the activity of the Holy Spirit at the beginning of the Christian life when he gives us new spiritual life (in regeneration) and cleanses us and gives a clear break with the power and love of sin (the initial stage of sanctification). In this way "baptism in the Holy Spirit" refers to all that the Holy Spirit does at the beginning of our Christian lives. But this means that it cannot refer to an experience after conversion, as the Pentecostal interpretation would have it.[12]

But how, then, do we understand the references to baptism in the Holy Spirit in Acts 1:5 and 11:16, both of which refer to the day of Pentecost? Were these not instances where the disciples, having previously been regenerated by the Holy Spirit, now experienced a new empowering from the Holy Spirit that enabled them to minister effectively?

It is true that the disciples were "born again" long before Pentecost, and in fact probably long before Jesus breathed on them and told them to receive the Holy Spirit in John 20:22.[13]

("baptize") plus the prepositional phrase *en pneumati hagiō* ("in [or with] the Holy Spirit"), except that Mark omits the preposition *en*. Even so, there is no difference in meaning, because the dative noun alone can take the same sense as the preposition *en* plus the dative noun. Matthew and Luke also add "and with fire."

Jesus had said, "No one can come to me unless the Father who sent me draws him" (John 6:44), but the disciples certainly had come to Jesus and had followed him (even though their understanding of who he was increased gradually over time). Certainly when Peter said to Jesus, "You are the Christ, the Son of the living God" (Matt. 16:16), it was evidence of some kind of regenerating work of the Holy Spirit in his heart. Jesus told him, "Flesh and blood has not revealed this to you, but my Father who is in heaven" (Matt. 16:17). And Jesus had said to the Father regarding his disciples, "I have given them the words which you gave me, and *they have received them* and know in truth that I came from you; and they have believed that you sent me. . . . *I have guarded them,* and *none of them is lost* but the son of perdition, that the scripture might be fulfilled" (John 17:8, 12). The disciples had "little faith" (Matt. 8:26) at times, but they did have faith! Certainly they were regenerated long before the day of Pentecost.[14]

But we must realize that the day of Pentecost is much more than an individual event in the lives of Jesus' disciples and those with them. The day of Pentecost was the point of transition between the old covenant work and ministry of the Holy Spirit and the new covenant work and ministry of the Holy Spirit. Of course the Holy Spirit was at work throughout the Old Testament, hovering over the waters of the first day of creation (Gen. 1:2), empowering people for service to God and leadership and prophecy (Ex. 31:3; 35:31; Deut. 34:9; Judg. 14:6; 1 Sam. 16:13; Ps. 51:11, et al.). But during that time the work of the Holy Spirit in individual lives was, in general, a work of lesser power.

There are several indications of a less powerful and less extensive work of the Holy Spirit in the old covenant: the Holy Spirit only came to a few people with significant power for ministry (Num. 11:16–17, for example), but Moses longed for the day when the Holy Spirit would be poured out on all of God's people: "Would that all the LORD's people were prophets, that the LORD would put his spirit upon them!" (Num. 11:29). The equipping of the Holy Spirit for special ministries could be lost, as it was in the life of Saul (1 Sam. 16:14), and as David feared that it might be in his own life (Ps. 51:11). In terms of spiritual power in the lives of the people of God, there was little power over the dominion of Satan, resulting in very little effective evangelism of the nations around Israel, and no examples of ability to cast out demons.[15] The old covenant work of the Holy Spirit was almost completely confined to the nation of Israel, but in the new covenant there is created a new "dwelling place of God" (Eph. 2:22), the church, which unites both Gentiles and Jews in the body of Christ.

---

[10]In this context, in which he is talking repeatedly about the Holy Spirit and spiritual gifts, there can be little doubt that he is referring to the Holy Spirit.

[11]In addition to the fact that this Greek phrase found in 1 Cor. 12:13 is translated to refer to baptism in the Holy Spirit in all the other six occurrences, there is a grammatical argument that supports the translation "*in* one Spirit we were all baptized into one body" in 1 Cor. 12:13: if Paul had wanted to say that we were baptized *by* the Holy Spirit, he would have used a different expression. To be baptized "by" someone in the New Testament is always expressed by the preposition *hypo* followed by a genitive noun. This is the way New Testament writers say that people were baptized in the Jordan River "by" John the Baptist (Matt. 3:6; Mark 1:5; Luke 3:7) or that Jesus was baptized "by" John (Matt. 3:13; Mark 1:9), or that the Pharisees had not been baptized "by" John (Luke 7:30), or that John the Baptist told Jesus, "I need to be baptized by you" (Matt. 3:14). Therefore, if Paul had wanted to say that the Corinthians had all been baptized *by* the Holy Spirit he would have used *hypo* plus the genitive, not *en* plus the dative. (It is common in the New Testament for the agent who performs the action expressed by a passive verb to be named using *hypo* plus the genitive.) Further support for the view that 1 Cor. 12:13 means "in (or with) one Spirit" is found in M. J. Harris, "Prepositions and Theology in the Greek New Testament," in *NIDNTT*, vol. 3, p. 1210.

Moreover, the Old Testament people of God looked forward to a "new covenant" age when the work of the Holy Spirit would be much more powerful and much more widespread (Num. 11:29; Jer. 31:31–33; Ezek. 36:26–27; Joel 2:28–29).[16]

When the New Testament opens, we see John the Baptist as the last of the Old Testament prophets. Jesus said, "Among those born of women there has risen no one greater than John the Baptist; yet he who is least in the kingdom of heaven is greater than he . . . all the prophets and the law prophesied until John; and if you are willing to accept it, he is Elijah who is to come" (Matt. 11:11–14). John knew that he baptized with water, but Jesus would baptize with the Holy Spirit (Luke 3:16). John the Baptist, then, still was living in an "old covenant" experience of the working of the Holy Spirit.

In the life of Jesus, we first see the new covenant power of the Holy Spirit at work. The Holy Spirit descends on him at his baptism (Luke 3:21–22), and after his temptation Jesus "returned *in the power of the Spirit* into Galilee" (Luke 4:14). Then we begin to see what this new covenant power of the Holy Spirit will look like, because Jesus casts out demons with a word, heals all who are brought to him, and teaches with authority that people had not heard before (see Luke 4:16–44, et al.).

The disciples, however, do not receive this full new covenant empowering for ministry until the Day of Pentecost, for Jesus tells them to wait in Jerusalem, and promises, "*You shall receive power* when the Holy Spirit has come upon you" (Acts 1:8). This was a transition in the lives of the disciples as well (see John 7:39; 14:17; 16:7; Acts 2:16). The promise of Joel

---

[12]Howard M. Ervin, *Conversion-Initiation and the Baptism in the Holy Spirit* (Peabody, Mass.: Hendrickson, 1984), pp. 98–102, admits that 1 Cor. 12:13, however it is translated, does refer to the beginning of the Christian life (he says it is "initiatory," p. 101), but then he says that the next phrase, "we were made to drink of one Spirit" (his translation) refers to a subsequent empowering for service. He also says that Paul's use of the phrase "baptism in the Holy Spirit" is different from the sense the phrase takes in the other six occurrences in the New Testament. Thus, he apparently grants the non-Pentecostal interpretation of 1 Cor. 12:13, but still says that Paul uses the same phrase with different meaning. Yet this argument does not seem persuasive. It would be very unlikely if Luke, who was Paul's traveling companion throughout much of his missionary activity, and who was probably with Paul in Rome when he wrote the book of Acts (Acts 28:30–31), would use a phrase in a different sense than Paul, or that Paul would use this phrase in a different sense than the sense in which it was so prominently used by Matthew, Mark, Luke, and John.

Another attempt to avoid our conclusion on 1 Cor. 12:13 is found in John P. Baker, *Baptized in One Spirit* (Plainfield, N.J.: Logos Books, 1970), pp. 18–25, where he argues that 1 Cor. 12:13 does not mean that we were baptized *into* one body, but that we were baptized "*for* the one body of Christ" (p. 24). But Baker's argument is not convincing, because the word "for" at the beginning of v. 13 shows that it must be an argument that supports v. 12, where Paul says that we are many members, but one body. Yet in order for v. 13 to show that all Christians are a part of one body, it is necessary for v. 13 to communicate why

we are *all* members of one body, and Paul does this by showing that we are all baptized into one body. Baker's view, that this happens only to some "who are already members *of* the body of Christ to enable them to function effectively" (p. 24), is not convincing in view of Paul's statement that "all" Christians were baptized into one body. Moreover, baptism *for the benefit of* one body (which is essentially what Baker takes it to mean) gives a very unusual sense to the preposition *eis*—if Paul had meant this, we would have expected something like *heneka*, "for the sake of," or *hyper* plus the genitive, meaning "in behalf, for the sake of."

[13]When Jesus breathed on his disciples and said to them, "Receive the Holy Spirit" (John 20:22), it probably was an acted-out prophecy of what would happen to them at Pentecost. In this same context—in fact, in the verse immediately preceding—Jesus had told them something that would not happen until Pentecost: "As the Father has sent me, *even so I send you*" (John 20:21). But even though he said this before he had ascended into heaven, he did not really send them out to preach the gospel until the Day of Pentecost had come. Therefore his words were looking forward to what would happen at Pentecost. It is best to understand the words in the next sentence, "Receive the Holy Spirit," in the same way—he was speaking in advance of something that would happen on the Day of Pentecost. On that day they would receive the new covenant fullness and power of the Holy Spirit, a much greater empowering of the Holy Spirit than what they had experienced before.

that the Holy Spirit would come in new covenant fullness was fulfilled (Acts 2:16) as Jesus returned to heaven and then was given authority to pour out the Holy Spirit in new fullness and power (Acts 2:33).

What was the result in the lives of the disciples? These believers, who had had an old-covenant less-powerful experience of the Holy Spirit in their lives, received on the Day of Pentecost a more-powerful new-covenant experience of the Holy Spirit working in their lives.[17] They received much greater "power" (Acts 1:8), power for living the Christian life and for carrying out Christian ministry.

This transition from an old covenant experience of the Holy Spirit to a new covenant experience of the Holy Spirit can be seen in figure 10.1.[18]

In this diagram, the thinner line at the bottom represents the less-powerful work of the Holy Spirit in individuals' lives during the old covenant. The thicker line that begins at Pentecost shows the more-powerful work of the Holy Spirit in people's lives after that time. The lines for "this age" and "the age to come" overlap now because the powers of the age to come have broken into this present evil age, so that Christians live during an "overlap of the ages." The dotted lines prior to Pentecost indicate that in the life of Jesus the more-powerful work of the Holy Spirit had already begun in a way that anticipated (and even surpassed) what would come at Pentecost.[19]

This new covenant power gave the disciples more effectiveness in their witness and their ministry (Acts 1:8; Eph. 4:8, 11–13), much greater power for victory over the influence of sin in the lives of all believers (note the emphasis on the power of Christ's resurrection at work within us in Rom. 6:11–14; 8:13–14; Gal. 2:20; Phil. 3:10), and power for victory over Satan and demonic forces that would attack believers (2 Cor. 10:3–4; Eph. 1:19–21; 6:10–18; 1 John 4:4). This new covenant power of the Holy Spirit also resulted in a wide and hitherto unknown distribution of gifts for ministry to all believers (Acts 2:16–18; 1 Cor. 12:7, 11; 1 Peter 4:10; cf. Num. 11:17, 24–29). These gifts also had corporate implications because they were intended not to be used individualistically but for the corporate building up of the body of Christ (1 Cor. 12:7; 14:12). It also meant that the gospel was no longer effectively limited to the Jews only, but that all races and all nations would hear the gospel in power and would be united into the church, to the glory of God (Eph. 2:11–3:10).[20] The Day of Pentecost was certainly a remarkable time of transition in the whole history of redemption as recorded in Scripture. It was a remarkable day in the history

---

[14]I do not mean to say that believers' experience of regeneration in the old covenant was exactly the same as that of new covenant believers. While considerations listed in the following discussion indicate a less-powerful work of the Holy Spirit in the old covenant, defining the nature of the differences is difficult, since Scripture gives us little explicit information about it. But the fact that there was any saving faith at all in old covenant believers requires us to think that there was some kind of regenerating work of the Holy Spirit in them, enabling them to believe. (See the discussion of regeneration in chapter 5.)

[15]The closest thing to casting out demons in the Old Testament is the situation where the evil spirit troubling Saul departed from him whenever David played his lyre (1

Sam. 16:23), but this is hardly equivalent to the effective and lasting casting out of demons of which we see in the New Testament age.

[16]Of course, there were examples in the Old Testament where certain leaders were remarkably gifted by God and empowered by the Holy Spirit—Moses, David, Daniel, many of the writing prophets, and even Samson received unusual empowering from the Holy Spirit for specific ministries. But their experiences were not typical of the vast numbers of God's people who were saved by faith as they looked forward to the promised Messiah's coming, but who did not have the outpouring of the Holy Spirit in the new covenant power that we experience today.

of the world, because on that day the Holy Spirit began to function among God's people with new covenant power.

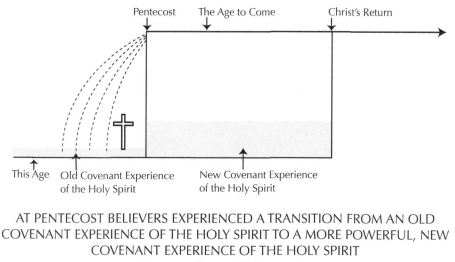

Pentecost   The Age to Come   Christ's Return

This Age   Old Covenant Experience   New Covenant Experience
of the Holy Spirit   of the Holy Spirit

AT PENTECOST BELIEVERS EXPERIENCED A TRANSITION FROM AN OLD COVENANT EXPERIENCE OF THE HOLY SPIRIT TO A MORE POWERFUL, NEW COVENANT EXPERIENCE OF THE HOLY SPIRIT
Figure 10.1

But this fact helps us understand what happened to the disciples at Pentecost. They received this remarkable new empowering from the Holy Spirit *because they were living at the time of the transition between the old covenant work of the Holy Spirit and the new covenant work of the Holy Spirit.* Though it was a "second experience" of the Holy Spirit, coming as it did long after their conversion, it is not to be taken as a pattern for us, for we are not living at a time of transition in the work of the Holy Spirit. In their case, believers with an old covenant empowering from the Holy Spirit became believers with a new covenant empowering from the Holy Spirit. But we today do not first become believers with a weaker, old covenant work of the Holy Spirit in our hearts and wait until some later time to receive a new covenant work of the Holy Spirit. Rather, we are in the same position as those who became Christians in the church at Corinth: when we become Christians we are all "*baptized in one Spirit* into one body" (1 Cor. 12:13)—just as the Corinthians were, and

---

[17]Ervin, *Conversion-Initiation*, pp. 14, 15–19, objects that the new covenant did not begin at Pentecost but earlier at the time of Jesus' death. This is certainly true, but it misses the point. We are not arguing that the new covenant itself began at the day of Pentecost, but the new covenant experience of the Holy Spirit began at Pentecost, because it was there that Jesus poured out the Holy Spirit in new covenant fullness and power (Acts 2:33; cf. 1:4–5).

Ervin also objects that the disciples at Pentecost received "power-in-mission" from the Holy Spirit, not entrance into the new covenant (pp. 17–18). But here Ervin has put forth a false dichotomy: it is not either/or, but both/and: at Pentecost the disciples both entered into a new covenant experience of the Holy Spirit and (of course) received a new empowering for ministry with that experience of the Holy Spirit.

[18]I have adapted this diagram from George Ladd, *A Theology of the New Testament* (Grand Rapids: Eerdmans, 1974), pp. 68–69.

[19]Because of their association with Jesus, the disciples also received some foretaste of the post-Pentecostal power of the Holy Spirit when they healed the sick and cast out demons (cf. Luke 9:1; 10:1, 8, 17–20, and many other verses).

just as were the new believers in many churches who were converted when Paul traveled on his missionary journeys.

In conclusion, the disciples certainly did experience "a baptism in the Holy Spirit" after conversion on the Day of Pentecost, but this happened because they were living at a unique point in history, and this event in their lives is therefore not a pattern that we are to seek to imitate.

What shall we say about the phrase "baptism in the Holy Spirit"? It is a phrase that the New Testament authors use to speak of coming into the new covenant power of the Holy Spirit. It happened at Pentecost for the disciples, but it happened at conversion for the Corinthians and for us.[21]

It is not a phrase the New Testament authors would use to speak of any post-conversion experience of empowering by the Holy Spirit.

C. How Should We Understand the "Second Experiences" in Acts?

But even if we have correctly understood the experience of the disciples at Pentecost as recorded in Acts 2, are there not other examples of people who had a "second experience" of empowering of the Holy Spirit after conversion, such as those in Acts 8 (at Samaria), Acts 10 (Cornelius' household), and Acts 19 (the Ephesian disciples)?

These are not really convincing examples to prove the Pentecostal doctrine of baptism in the Holy Spirit either. First, the expression "baptism in the Holy Spirit" is not ordinarily used to refer to any of these events,[22] and this should give us some hesitation in applying this phrase to them. But more importantly, a closer look at each case shows more clearly what was happening in these events.

In Acts 8:4–25 the Samaritan people "believed Philip as he preached good news about the kingdom of God and the name of Jesus Christ" and "they were baptized, both men and women" (Acts 8:12). Some have argued that this was not genuine saving faith on the part of the Samaritans.[23] However, there is no indication in the text that Philip had a deficient understanding of the gospel (he had been prominent in the Jerusalem church) or that Philip himself thought that their faith in Christ was inadequate, for he allowed them to be baptized (Acts 8:12).

A better understanding of this event would be that God, in his providence, sovereignly waited to give the new covenant empowering of the Holy Spirit to the Samaritans directly through the hands of the apostles (Acts 8:14–17)[24] so that it might be evident to the highest leadership in the Jerusalem church that the Samaritans were not second-class citizens but full members of the church. This was important because of the historical animosity between Jews and Samaritans ("Jews have no dealings with Samaritans," John 4:9), and because Jesus had specified that the spread of the gospel to Samaria would be the next major step after it had been preached in Jerusalem and the region of Judea that surrounded Jerusalem: "You shall be my witnesses in Jerusalem and in all Judea *and Samaria* and to the end of the earth" (Acts 1:8). Thus, the event in Acts 8 was a kind of "Samaritan Pentecost,"

[20]When the Holy Spirit came in power he ordinarily came to groups of people rather than to isolated individuals (so Acts 2:4; 8:17; 10:44; 19:6; but the conversion of Saul is different: see Acts 9:17–18). A new community, filled with love for one another, was the evident result of the outpouring of the Holy Spirit in this way (see Acts 2:41–47).

a special outpouring of the Holy Spirit on the people of Samaria, who were a mixed race of Jewish and Gentile ancestry, so that it might be evident to all that the full new covenant blessings and power of the Holy Spirit had come to this group of people as well, and were not confined to Jews only. Because this is a special event in the history of redemption, as the pattern of Acts 1:8 is worked out in the book of Acts, it is not a pattern for us to repeat today. It is simply part of the transition between the old covenant experience of the Holy Spirit and the new covenant experience of the Holy Spirit.

The situation in Acts 10 is less complicated, because it is not even clear that Cornelius was a genuine believer before Peter came and preached the gospel to him. Certainly he had not trusted in Christ for salvation. He is rather a Gentile who was one of the first examples of the way in which the gospel would go "to the end of the earth" (Acts 1:8).[25] Certainly Cornelius had not first believed in Christ's death and resurrection to save him and then later come into a second experience after his conversion.

In Acts 19, once again we encounter a situation of some people who had not really heard the gospel of salvation through Christ. They had been baptized into the baptism of John the Baptist (Acts 19:3), so they were probably people who had heard John the Baptist preach, or had talked to others who had heard John the Baptist preach, and had been baptized "into John's baptism" (Acts 19:3) as a sign that they were repenting of their sins and preparing for the Messiah who was to come. They certainly had not heard of Christ's death and resurrection, for they had not even heard that there was a Holy Spirit (Acts 19:2)!—a fact that no one who was present at Pentecost or who had heard the gospel after Pentecost could have failed to know. It is likely that they had not even heard that Jesus had come and lived and died, because Paul had to explain to them, "John baptized with the baptism of repentance, telling the people to believe in the one who was to come after him, *that is, Jesus*" (Acts 19:4). Therefore these "disciples" in Ephesus did not have new covenant understanding or new covenant faith, and they certainly did not have a new covenant empowering of the Holy Spirit—they were "disciples" only in the sense of followers of John the Baptist who were still waiting for the Messiah. When they heard of him they believed in him, and then received the power of the Holy Spirit that was appropriate to the gospel of the risen Lord Jesus Christ.

Because of this, these disciples at Ephesus are certainly not a pattern for us today either, for we do not first have faith in a Messiah that we are waiting for, and then later learn that

---

[21]My student James Renihan has argued (in a lengthy paper) that baptism in the Holy Spirit, while occurring at the same time as conversion, should nevertheless be considered a distinct element in the "order of salvation" (the list of things that happen to us in experiencing salvation; see chapter 3). He notes that baptism in the Holy Spirit is not exactly the same as any of the other elements in the order of salvation (such as regeneration or conversion), and may also be called "receiving the Holy Spirit" (see Acts 8:15–16; 19:2, 6; Rom. 8:9, 11; Gal. 3:2). Renihan's idea is clearly not the charismatic doctrine of a baptism in the Holy Spirit subsequent to conversion (for he would say it always accompanies genuine conversion and always occurs at the same time as conversion). The suggestion is an interesting one and,

while I have not presently adopted it in this chapter, I think it deserves further consideration. It would not be inconsistent with my overall argument in this chapter.

[22]The only exception is Acts 11:15–17. While this passage does not explicitly call the falling of the Holy Spirit on Cornelius' household a "baptism in the Holy Spirit," when Peter says, "the Holy Spirit fell on them *just as on us at the beginning*," and then recalls Jesus' words about baptism in the Holy Spirit, he clearly implies that the members of Cornelius's household were baptized in the Holy Spirit when he preached to them (see Acts 10:44–48).

[23]This is the argument of James Dunn, *Baptism in the Holy Spirit* (London: SCM, 1970), pp. 55–72.

Jesus has come and lived and died and risen again. We come into an understanding of the gospel of Christ immediately, and we, like the Corinthians, enter immediately into the new covenant experience of the power of the Holy Spirit.[26]

It seems therefore that there are no New Testament texts that encourage us to seek for a second experience of "baptism in the Holy Spirit" that comes after conversion.

D. What Terms Shall We Use to Refer to an Empowering by the Holy Spirit That Comes After Conversion?

The previous sections have argued that "baptism in the Holy Spirit" is not the term the New Testament authors would use to speak of a post-conversion work of the Spirit, and that the examples of "second experiences" of receiving the Holy Spirit in the book of Acts are not patterns for us to imitate in our Christian lives. But the question remains, "What is actually happening to the millions of people who claim that they have received this 'baptism in the Holy Spirit' and that it has brought much blessing to their lives? Could it be that this has been a genuine work of the Holy Spirit but that the biblical categories and biblical examples used to illustrate it have been incorrect? Might it be that there are other biblical expressions and biblical teachings that point to this kind of work of the Holy Spirit after conversion and help us understand it more accurately?" I think there are, but before we look at these, it is appropriate to comment on the importance of having a correct understanding at this point.

1. Harm Comes to the Church From Teaching Two-Class Christianity. At various times in the history of the church Christians have attempted to divide the church into two categories of believers. This is in effect what happens with the Pentecostal doctrine of baptism in the Holy Spirit. It might be pictured as in figure 10.2, which shows the world divided into Christians and non-Christians, and then shows Christians divided into two categories, ordinary believers and Spirit-baptized believers.

But such a division of Christians into two categories is not a unique understanding that is found only in Pentecostal teaching in the twentieth century. In fact, much Pentecostal teaching came out of earlier holiness groups that had taught that Christians could either be ordinary believers or "sanctified" believers. Other groups have divided Christians using different categories, such as ordinary believers and those who are "Spirit filled," or ordinary believers and those who are "disciples," or "carnal" and "spiritual" Christians. In fact, the Roman Catholic Church has long had not two but three categories: ordinary believers, priests, and saints. All of these divisions into different categories of Christians can be seen in figure 10.3.[27]

Although those who teach the classical Pentecostal view of baptism in the Holy Spirit may deny that they are attempting to divide Christians into two categories, such a division is implicit every time they ask whether someone has been baptized in the Holy Spirit or not.

---

[24]In this section I am largely following the careful discussion of John Stott, *Baptism and Fulness,* 2d ed. (Leicester and Downers Grove, Ill.: InterVarsity Press, 1976), pp. 31–34.

[25]Even if we did regard him as someone who first had a kind of old covenant faith in the Jewish Messiah who was to come, this would only show that he is one more example of someone who first had an old covenant experience of the Holy Spirit and then came into a new covenant experience of the Holy Spirit.

Such a question strongly suggests that there are two groups of Christians, those who have had this experience of "baptism in the Holy Spirit" and those who have not.

What is the problem with viewing Christians as existing in two categories like this? The problem is that it contributes to a "we-they" mentality in churches, and leads to jealousy, pride, and divisiveness. No matter how much these people who have received this special empowering of the Holy Spirit try to be thoughtful and considerate of those who have not, if they genuinely love their fellow brothers and sisters in Christ, and if this has been a very helpful experience in their own Christian lives, they cannot help but give the impression that they would like others to share this experience as well. Even if they are not proud in their hearts (and it seems to me that most are not) with respect to this experience, such a conviction that there is a second category of Christians will inevitably give an impression of pride or spiritual superiority. Yet there will very likely be a sense of jealousy on the part of those who have not had such an experience. In this way, a view of two groups within the church is fostered, and the repeated charge of divisiveness that is made against the charismatic movement is given some credibility. In fact, divisions often do occur in churches.

The major objection to this position is that the New Testament itself teaches no such two-level or two-class Christianity. Nowhere in the Epistles do we read of Paul or Peter telling a church that is having problems, "You all need to be baptized in the Holy Spirit." Nowhere do we hear of the risen Lord Jesus speaking to the troubled and weak churches in Revelation 2–3, "Ask me to baptize you in the Holy Spirit." It is hard to avoid the conclusion that the two-level or two-class view taught by all of these groups throughout history does not have a solid foundation in the New Testament itself.

2. There Are Many Degrees of Empowering, Fellowship With God, and Personal Christian Maturity. Is there a better model for understanding the varying degrees of maturity and power and fellowship with God that Christians experience? If we are willing to eliminate the categories that make us think of Christians in one group or another, a better model is possible, as represented in figure 10.4.

This chart shows the world as divided into non-Christians and Christians, but among Christians there are not categories into which we can place believers and divide them into set groups. Rather, there are Christians at all points along a scale of increasing Christian maturity (sanctification), increasing closeness of fellowship in their walk with God (an aspect of adoption), and greater experiences of the power of the Holy Spirit at work in their lives and ministries.

---

[26]Regarding Acts 19:1–7, Ervin, *Conversion-Initiation*, pp. 55–59, objects that these disciples were first baptized and then, when Paul laid his hands on them, they were empowered with the Holy Spirit. We may admit that this is true, but the two events were so closely connected in time that it is hard to make a clear separation between them, and they certainly do not fit the common Pentecostal pattern of instruction and prayer, sometimes weeks or months or years after conversion, seeking a subsequent baptism in the Holy Spirit. If we had asked them later if their baptism in the Holy Spirit was "subsequent" to their conversion, they would probably have said that it was at the same time, so closely connected were these events in the actual historical sequence.

The Christian life should be one of *growth in all of these areas* as we progress throughout life. For many people that growth will be gradual and progressive, and will extend over all the years of their lives. We could represent it by the arrow in figure 10.5.[28]

a. How Should We Understand Contemporary Experience? What then has happened to people who say they have experienced a "baptism in the Holy Spirit" that has brought great

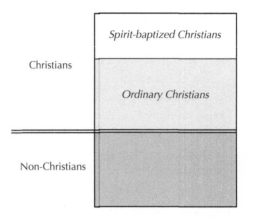

CHRISTIANS DIVIDED INTO TWO CATEGORIES:
ORDINARY AND SPIRIT-BAPTIZED
Figure 10.2

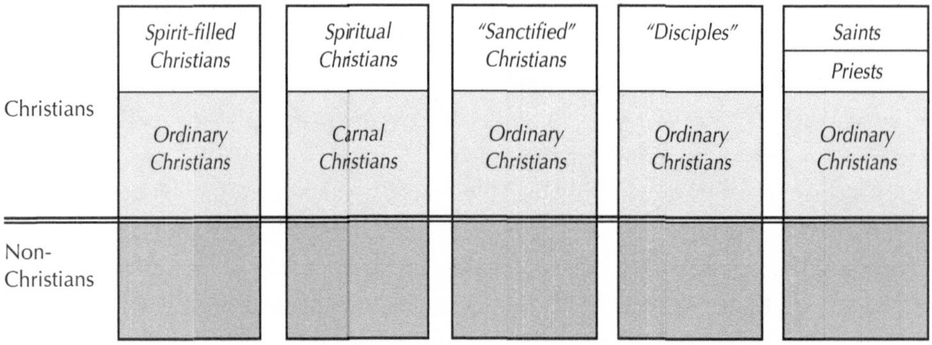

	Spirit-filled Christians	Spiritual Christians	"Sanctified" Christians	"Disciples"	Saints
					Priests
Christians	Ordinary Christians	Carnal Christians	Ordinary Christians	Ordinary Christians	Ordinary Christians
Non-Christians					

OTHER WAYS PEOPLE HAVE CLASSIFIED CHRISTIANS SO AS
TO DIVIDE THEM INTO TWO (OR THREE) CATEGORIES
Figure 10.3

---

[27]I have not included in this diagram another division that is sometimes reflected, not in any official teaching, but in attitude and practice, in Reformed circles: the division between ordinary Christians and those who are "truly Reformed."

blessing to their lives? We must understand first what is commonly taught about the need to prepare for baptism in the Holy Spirit. Very often people will be taught that they should confess all known sins, repent of any remaining sin in their lives, trust Christ to forgive those sins, commit every area of their lives to the Lord's service, yield themselves fully to him, and believe that Christ is going to empower them in a new way and equip them with new gifts for ministry. Then after that preparation, they are encouraged to ask Jesus in prayer to baptize them in the Holy Spirit. But what does this preparation do? It is a guaranteed prescription for significant growth in the Christian life! Such confession, repentance, renewed commitment, and heightened faith and expectation, if they are genuine, can only bring positive results in a person's life. If any Christian is sincere in these steps of preparation to receive baptism in the Holy Spirit, there will certainly be growth in sanctification and deeper fellowship with God. In addition to that, we may expect that at many of these times the Holy Spirit will graciously bring a measure of the additional fullness and empowering that sincere Christians are seeking, even though their theological understanding and vocabulary may be imperfect in the asking. If this happens, they may well realize increased power for ministry and growth in spiritual gifts as well. We could say that a person has moved from point A to point B in figure 10.6 and has made one very large step forward in the Christian life.

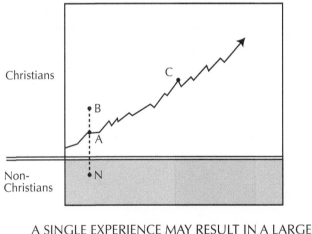

A SINGLE EXPERIENCE MAY RESULT IN A LARGE
STEP OF GROWTH IN THE CHRISTIAN LIFE
Figure 10.6

Of course prayer and Bible study and worship will seem more meaningful. Of course there will be more fruitfulness in evangelism and other kinds of ministry. But it is important to recognize that someone who moves from point A to point B on the chart is not now in a separate category of Christians, such as a group of those who have been "baptized

---

[28]To be more precise we need to recognize that we can grow in some aspects of the Christian life without growing in others, and a single chart is therefore inadequate to show all of this. For example, Christians can grow in power but not in holiness (as the Corinthian church had done), or people can grow in knowledge but not in power, or knowledge but not in holiness of life

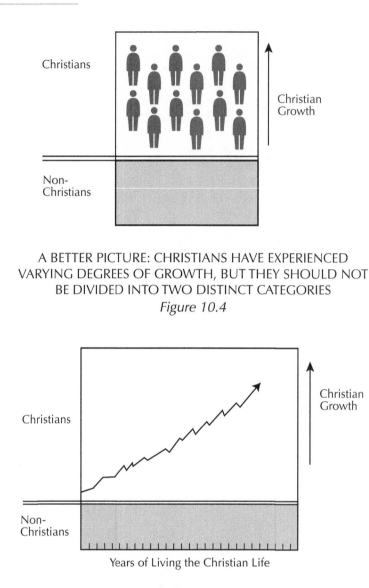

A BETTER PICTURE: CHRISTIANS HAVE EXPERIENCED
VARYING DEGREES OF GROWTH, BUT THEY SHOULD NOT
BE DIVIDED INTO TWO DISTINCT CATEGORIES
Figure 10.4

FOR MOST CHRISTIANS GROWTH WILL BE GRADUAL AND
PROGRESSIVE AND WILL EXTEND OVER THEIR WHOLE LIVES
Figure 10.5

(something that tragically happens to some—but certainly not all—students in theological seminaries, and to some pastors who place excessive emphasis on academic pursuits). Or a person can grow in personal fellowship with God but not in knowledge of Scripture (something that happens with an extensive "pietistic" emphasis). Or someone can grow in holiness of life but not in power or use of spiritual gifts. All sorts of combinations like this are possible, but we would need several charts to show them in a schematic way. For the sake of simplicity I have simply represented "Christian growth" in general on this chart.

in the Holy Spirit" and who are therefore different from those who have not had such an experience. There might be another Christian in the same church who has never had such a large step of growth but who has nonetheless been making steady progress for the last forty years of his or her Christian life and has come to point C on the chart above. Though that person has never had a single experience that Pentecostals would call a "baptism in the Holy Spirit," he or she is still much farther along the path of Christian growth than the younger Christian who has recently been "baptized in the Holy Spirit" (according to Pentecostal terminology) and moved from point A to point B. Although the Christian who moved from point A to point B is not farther along in the Christian life than another person who is at point C, the person who moved to point B is certainly farther along *than he or she was before,* and this is certainly a positive result in his or her life. Thus, with this understanding of the Christian life, we have no divisions of Christians into two categories.

Before we leave this chart, one more observation should be made: in many cases the charismatic movement has brought teaching on the baptism of the Holy Spirit into more liberal churches where, for many years, there has not been a clear proclamation of the gospel of salvation by faith in Christ alone, and where people have not been taught that they can believe the Bible completely as God's Word to us. In such cases, many of the people in those churches have never experienced saving faith—they are at point N on the chart above, actually non-Christians and not born again.[29] Now when a representative of a charismatic renewal comes to these churches and tells them that they can experience new vitality in their Christian lives, and then tells them that the preparation is to repent of all known sins, ask Christ for forgiveness of those sins and trust him to forgive them, and commit their lives totally to Christ as their Lord, they eagerly respond to those directions. Then they pray and ask Jesus to baptize them in the Holy Spirit. The actual result is that they move from point N on the chart to point A or perhaps even point B, because of their sincerity and deep eagerness to draw closer to God. While they think that they have been baptized by the Holy Spirit as a second experience in their Christian lives, what has in fact happened is that they have become Christians for the first time. (They have been "baptized in the Holy Spirit" in the true New Testament sense!) The next day it is almost impossible to keep them silent, they are so excited. Suddenly, reading the Bible has become meaningful. Suddenly prayer has become real. Suddenly they know the presence of God in their lives. Suddenly worship has become an experience of deep joy, and often they have begun to experience spiritual gifts that they had not known before. It is no wonder that the charismatic renewal has brought such excitement (and often much controversy) to many Roman Catholic parishes and to many mainline, more liberal Protestant denominations. Though we may differ with the way this teaching is actually presented, no one should fault the good results that have come about as a result of it in these churches.

b. What Terms Should We Use Today? Now we can understand why our use of terms to describe this experience and the category of understanding we put it in are so important. If we use the traditional Pentecostal terminology of "baptism of the Holy Spirit," then we almost inevitably end up with two-category Christianity, for this is seen as a common experience that *can* and indeed *should* happen to Christians at one point in time, and, once it has happened, does not need to be repeated. It is seen as a single experience of empowering for ministry that is distinct from the experience of becoming a Christian, and people either have received that experience or they have not. Especially when the experience is described in terms of what happened to the disciples at Pentecost in Acts 2 (which was clearly a one-time experience for them), the Samaritans in Acts 8, and the Ephesian disciples in Acts 19, it is clearly implied that this is a one-time event that empowers people for ministry but that also puts them in a separate category or group than the one they were in before this experience. The use of the term "*the* baptism in the Holy Spirit" inevitably implies two groups of Christians.

But if we are correct in understanding the experience that has come to millions of people in the charismatic renewal as a large step of growth in their Christian lives, then some other term than "baptism in the Holy Spirit" would seem to be more appropriate. There might be several terms that we could use, so long as they allow for repetition, varying degrees of intensity, and further development beyond that one experience, and so long as they do not suggest that all truly obedient Christians should have the same experience.[30] We have already used one expression, "*a large step of growth* in several aspects of the Christian life." Because this phrase speaks of "*a large step of growth*" it cannot be misunderstood to refer to a single experience that puts Christians in a new category. And because it is referred to as a large step of growth, it clearly implies that others may experience such growth in smaller steps over a longer period of time but reach the same point in the Christian life.[31]

Another term that may be helpful is "a new *empowering for ministry.*" It is certainly true that many who have received such a charismatic experience do find new power for ministry in their Christian lives, including the ability to use spiritual gifts that had not been theirs before. However, the problem with this phrase is that it does not say anything about the deepened fellowship with God, the greater effectiveness in prayer and Bible study, and the new joy in worship that often also result from this experience.

c. What Is "Being Filled With the Spirit"? Yet an even more commonly used term in the New Testament is "*being filled with the Holy Spirit.*" Because of its frequent use in contexts that speak of Christian growth and ministry, *this seems to me to be the best term to use* to describe genuine "second experiences" today (or third or fourth experiences, etc.). Paul tells the Ephesians, "Do not get drunk with wine, for that is debauchery; but *be filled with the Spirit*" (Eph. 5:18). He uses a present tense imperative verb that could more explicitly be translated, "Be continually being filled with the Holy Spirit," thus implying that this is something that should repeatedly be happening to Christians. Such fullness of the Holy Spirit will result in *renewed worship and thanksgiving* (Eph. 5:19–20), and in renewed relationships to others, especially those in authority over us or those under our authority (Eph. 5:21–6:9). In addition, since the Holy Spirit is the Spirit who sanctifies us, such a filling will often result in *increased sanctification.* Furthermore, since the Holy Spirit is the one who empowers us for Christian service and gives us spiritual gifts, such filling will often result in *increased power for ministry* and increased effectiveness and perhaps diversity in the use of *spiritual gifts.*

---

[29]However, in many cases, both in some Protestant churches and in Roman Catholic churches, people have been told that they received Christ and became Christians at their baptism when they were infants.

We see examples of repeated filling with the Holy Spirit in the book of Acts. In Acts 2:4, the disciples and those with them were "all *filled with the Holy Spirit*." Later, when Peter was standing before the Sanhedrin, we read, "Then Peter, *filled with the Holy Spirit*, said to them . . ." (Acts 4:8). But a little later, when Peter and the other apostles had returned to the church to tell what had happened (Acts 4:23) they joined together in prayer. After they had prayed they were again filled with the Holy Spirit, a sequence of events that Luke makes clear: "*After they prayed, the place where they were meeting was shaken. And they were all filled with the Holy Spirit and spoke the word of God boldly*" (Acts 4:31 NIV). Even though Peter had been filled with the Holy Spirit at Pentecost (Acts 2:4) and had later been filled with the Holy Spirit before speaking to the Sanhedrin (Acts 4:8), he was once again filled with the Holy Spirit after the group of Christians he was meeting with had prayed.

Therefore, it is appropriate to understand filling with the Holy Spirit *not as a one-time event* but as *an event that can occur over and over again* in a Christian's life. It may involve a momentary empowering for a specific ministry (such as apparently happened in Acts 4:8; 7:55), but it may also refer to a long-term characteristic of a person's life (see Acts 6:3; 11:24). In either case such filling can occur many times in a person's life: even though Stephen, as an early deacon (or apostolic assistant), was a man "full of the Spirit and of wisdom" (Acts 6:3, 5), when he was being stoned he apparently received a fresh new filling of the Holy Spirit in great power (Acts 7:55).

Someone might object that a person who is already "full" of the Holy Spirit cannot become more full—if a glass is full of water no more water can be put into it. But a water glass is a poor analogy for us as real people, for God is able to cause us to grow and to be able to contain much more of the Holy Spirit's fullness and power. A better analogy might be a balloon, which can be "full" of air even though it has very little air in it. When more air is blown in, the balloon expands and in a sense it is "more full." So it is with us: we can be filled with the Holy Spirit and at the same time be able to receive much more of the Holy Spirit as well. It was only Jesus himself to whom the Father gave the Spirit without measure (John 3:34).

The divisiveness that comes with the term *"baptism in the Holy Spirit"* could easily be avoided by using any of the alternative terms mentioned in this section. People could be thankful for "a new fullness of the Holy Spirit" or "a new empowering for ministry" or "a significant step in growth" in some aspect of another Christian's life. There would be no separating into "we" and "they," for we would recognize that we are all part of one body with no separate categories.[32] In fact, many charismatics and even some traditional Pentecostals today are using the term "baptism in the Holy Spirit" far less frequently, preferring to use other terms such as "being filled with the Holy Spirit" instead.[33]

Moreover, many people who have had no single dramatic experience (such as what Pentecostals have called a baptism in the Holy Spirit) have nonetheless begun to experience new freedom and joy in worship (often with the advent of modern worship or praise songs in their churches), and to use a wider variety of spiritual gifts with effectiveness and edification for themselves and their churches (including gifts such as healing, prophecy, working

---

[30]The same criteria could be used to find replacement terms for some of the other "two-category" views mentioned above, or else to explain the terms that are used so as to avoid misunderstanding.

[31]Paul does say that we "are to grow up *in every way* into him who is the head, into Christ" (Eph. 4:15).

of miracles, discernment of spirits, and the ability to exercise authority over demonic forces with prayer and a word of rebuke spoken directly to the evil spirits). Sometimes the gift of speaking in tongues and the gift of interpretation have been used as well, but in other cases they have not. All of this is to say that the differences between Pentecostals and charismatics on the one hand, and more traditional and mainstream evangelical Christians on the other hand, seem to me to be breaking down more and more, and there are fewer and fewer differences between them.

Someone may object that it is specifically this experience of praying for a baptism in the Holy Spirit that catapults people into a new level of power in ministry and effectiveness in use of spiritual gifts. Since this experience has been so helpful in the lives of millions of people, should we so quickly dismiss it? In response, it must be said that, if the terminology "baptism in the Holy Spirit" is changed for something more representative of New Testament teaching, there should be no objection at all to people coming into churches, and to encouraging people to prepare their hearts for spiritual renewal by sincere repentance and renewed commitment to Christ and by believing that the Holy Spirit can work much more powerfully in their lives.[34] There is nothing wrong with teaching people to pray and to seek this greater infilling of the Holy Spirit, or to expect and ask the Lord for an outpouring of more spiritual gifts in their lives, for the benefit of the body of Christ (see 1 Cor. 12:31; 14:1, 12). In fact, most evangelical Christians in every denomination genuinely long for greater power in ministry, greater joy in worship, and deeper fellowship with God. Many would also welcome increased understanding of spiritual gifts, and encouragement to grow in the use of them. If Pentecostal and charismatic Christians would be willing to teach on these things without the additional baggage of two-level Christianity that is implied by the term "baptism in the Holy Spirit," they might find a new era of greatly increased effectiveness in bringing teaching on these other areas of the Christian life to evangelicals generally.

3. Being Filled With the Holy Spirit Does Not Always Result in Speaking in Tongues. One remaining point needs to be made with respect to the experience of being filled with the Holy Spirit. Because there were several cases in Acts where people received the new covenant power of the Holy Spirit and began to speak with tongues at the same time (Acts 2:4; 10:46; 19:6; probably also implied in 8:17–19 because of the parallel with the experience of the disciples in Acts 2), Pentecostal teaching has commonly maintained that the outward sign of baptism in the Holy Spirit is speaking in tongues (that is, speaking in languages that are not understood by and have not been learned by the person speaking, whether known human languages or other kinds of angelic or heavenly or miraculously given languages).

But it is important to realize that there are many cases where being filled with the Holy Spirit *did not* result in speaking in tongues. When Jesus was filled with the Spirit in Luke 4:1, the result was strength to overcome the temptations of Satan in the wilderness. When the temptations were ended, and Jesus "returned in the power of the Spirit into Galilee"

---

[32]It is my personal opinion that most of the divisiveness that has come with the influence of charismatic renewal in many churches has not come because of spiritual gifts but because of a misunderstanding of what is happening and the implications of two groups of Christians that come with the term "baptism in the Holy Spirit."

[33]John Wimber, who does not like to identify himself as a Pentecostal or a charismatic, says with much wisdom, "I have

(Luke 4:14), the results were miracles of healing, casting out of demons, and teaching with authority. When Elizabeth was filled with the Holy Spirit, she spoke a word of blessing to Mary (Luke 1:41–45). When Zechariah was filled with the Holy Spirit, he prophesied (Luke 1:67–79). Other results of being filled with the Holy Spirit were powerful preaching of the gospel (Acts 4:31), (perhaps) wisdom and Christian maturity and sound judgment (Acts 6:3), powerful preaching and testimony when on trial (Acts 4:8), a vision of heaven (Acts 7:55), and (apparently) faith and maturity of life (Acts 11:24). Several of these cases may also imply the fullness of the Holy Spirit to empower some kind of ministry, especially in the context of the book of Acts, where the empowering of the Holy Spirit is frequently seen to result in miracles, preaching, and works of great power.[35]

Therefore, while an experience of being filled with the Holy Spirit may result in the gift of speaking in tongues, or in the use of some other gifts that had not previously been experienced, it also may come without the gift of speaking in tongues. In fact, many Christians throughout history have experienced powerful infillings of the Holy Spirit that have not been accompanied by speaking in tongues. With regard to this gift as well as all other gifts, we must simply say that the Holy Spirit "apportions each one individually as he wills" (1 Cor. 12:11).

QUESTIONS FOR PERSONAL APPLICATION

1. Before reading this chapter, what was your understanding of "baptism in the Holy Spirit"? How has your understanding changed, if at all?

2. Has your own Christian life included one or more events that you could call "a large step of growth" in some area or another in the Christian life? Or has it rather been one of small but continuing steps in sanctification, in fellowship with God, and in use of spiritual gifts and power in ministry?

3. Have you known people who have claimed they received a "baptism in the Holy Spirit" after conversion? In your evaluation, has the result in their lives been mostly positive, or mostly negative, or has it been rather mixed? If you have had such an experience yourself, do you think that understanding it as a one-time "baptism in the Holy Spirit" was essential to the experience, or could the same results have come in your Christian life if it had been called "being filled with the Holy Spirit"? Do you

---

discovered that the argument concerning the baptism of the Spirit usually comes down to a question of labels. Good medicine may be incorrectly labeled, which is probably true in this case. The Pentecostals' experience of God is better than their explanation of it" (John Wimber with Kevin Springer, *Power Evangelism*, p. 145). In recent years I have noticed in personal conversation with professors at institutions affiliated with the charismatic movement that there is an increasing tendency to talk about filling with the Holy Spirit rather than baptism in the Holy Spirit to represent what has happened to those within the charismatic movement.

[34]My student Jack Mattern, though not himself a charismatic, has told me that in over a decade of working with students on university campuses, he has found a great hunger among Christians to know how they may be filled with the Holy Spirit. He rightly points out that effective teaching on this area must include the need (1) to yield our lives fully to God (Rom. 12:1; Gal. 2:20), (2) to depend fully on God for power to live the Christian life (Rom. 8:13; Gal. 2:20; 3:2–3), and (3) to obey the Lord's commands in our lives (1 John 2:6). These elements are similar to the steps of preparation mentioned above in the discussion of common charismatic teaching. In any case, to these steps could certainly be added a prayer that the Holy Spirit would fill us, in accordance with the will of God as expressed in Eph. 5:18. There should be no objection to teaching Christians to pray daily in accordance with these principles.

think it would be right to seek for an experience of filling with the Holy Spirit in your own life now? How might someone go about doing this?

4. We all realize that it is possible to overemphasize something good in the Christian life to such an extent that our lives become unbalanced and not as effective in ministry as they might be. If we think of the various ways in which we can grow in the Christian life (knowledge of the Word and sound doctrine, prayer, love for God, love for other Christians and for non-Christians, trust in God each day, worship, holiness of life, use of spiritual gifts, effective power of the Holy Spirit in our witness and ministry, daily fellowship with God, etc.), in what areas do you think you need to ask God for more growth in your own life? Would it be appropriate to ask him for a new fullness of the Holy Spirit to accompany growth in those areas?

5. With regard to this topic of baptism in or being filled with the Holy Spirit, do you think that evangelical churches generally have been moving toward more divisiveness or more unity on this issue?

SPECIAL TERMS

baptism by the Holy Spirit
baptism in the Holy Spirit
baptism with the Holy Spirit
being filled with the Holy Spirit
Pentecost

new covenant experience of the
  Holy Spirit
old covenant experience of the
  Holy Spirit
two-class Christianity

BIBLIOGRAPHY

Bennett, Dennis and Rita. *The Holy Spirit and You.* Plainfield, N.J.: Logos, 1971.

Bruner, Frederick Dale. *A Theology of the Holy Spirit: The Pentecostal Experience and the New Testament Witness.* Grand Rapids: Eerdmans, 1970.

Dunn, James D. G. *Baptism in the Holy Spirit.* London: SCM, 1970.

Ervin, Howard M. *Conversion-Initiation and the Baptism in the Holy Spirit: A Critique of James D. G. Dunn, "Baptism in the Holy Spirit."* Peabody, Mass.: Hendrickson, 1984.

_____. *Spirit Baptism.* Peabody, Mass.: Hendriksen, 1987.

Gaffin, Richard. *Perspectives on Pentecost.* Phillipsburg, N.J.: Presbyterian and Reformed, 1979.

Green, Michael. *Baptism: Its Purpose, Practice and Power.* Downers Grove, Ill.: InterVarsity Press, 1987, pp. 127–41.

_____. "The Spirit's Baptism." In *I Believe in the Holy Spirit.* London: Hodder and Stoughton, and Grand Rapids: Eerdmans, 1975, pp. 123–47.

Hoekema, Anthony A. *Holy Spirit Baptism.* Grand Rapids: Eerdmans, (1972).

---

[35]Scripture does not specify what result there was in the life of John the Baptist, who was "filled with the Holy Spirit, even from his mother's womb" (Luke 1:15), but "the hand of the Lord was with him" (Luke 1:66), and "the child grew and became strong in spirit" (Luke 1:80).

Lloyd-Jones, Martyn. *Joy Unspeakable: Power and Renewal in the Holy Spirit*. Ed. by Christopher Catherwood. Wheaton, Ill.: Shaw, 1984.

McGee, Gary B., ed. *Initial Evidence*. Peabody, Mass.: Hendrickson, 1991.

Packer, J. I. "Baptism in the Spirit." In *NDT*, pp. 73–74.

_____. *Keep in Step With the Spirit*. Old Tappan, N.J.: Revell, and Leicester: Inter-Varsity Press, 1984.

Stott, John. *Baptism and Fulness*. Leicester and Downers Grove, Ill.: InterVarsity Press, 1976.

Unger, Merrill F. *The Baptizing Work of the Holy Spirit*. Wheaton, Ill.: Van Kampen Press, 1953.

White, R. E. O. "Baptism of the Spirit." In *EDT*, pp. 121–22.

SCRIPTURE MEMORY PASSAGE

1 Corinthians 12:12–13: *For just as the body is one and has many members, and all the members of the body, though many, are one body, so it is with Christ. For by [or "in"] one Spirit we were all baptized into one body—Jews or Greeks, slaves or free—and all were made to drink of one Spirit.*

HYMN

"Spirit of God, Descend Upon My Heart"

Spirit of God, descend upon my heart;
    Wean it from earth, through all its pulses move;
Stoop to my weakness, mighty as thou art,
    And make me love thee as I ought to love.

Hast thou not bid us love thee, God and King?
    All, all thine own, soul, heart, and strength and mind.
I see thy cross—there teach my heart to cling:
    O let me seek thee, and O let me find.

Teach me to feel that thou art always nigh;
    Teach me the struggles of the soul to bear,
To check the rising doubt, the rebel sigh;
    Teach me the patience of unanswered prayer.

Teach me to love thee as thine angels love,
    One holy passion filling all my frame;
The baptism of the heav'n descended dove
    My heart an altar, and thy love the flame.

AUTHOR: GEORGE CROLY, 1854

Alternative hymn: "Spirit of the Living God"

Chapter

THE PERSEVERANCE OF THE SAINTS (REMAINING A CHRISTIAN)

Can true Christians lose their salvation?
How can we know if we are truly born again?

EXPLANATION AND SCRIPTURAL BASIS

Our previous discussion has dealt with many aspects of the full salvation that Christ has earned for us and that the Holy Spirit now applies to us. But how do we know that we shall continue to be Christians throughout our lives? Is there anything that will keep us from falling away from Christ, anything to guarantee that we will remain Christians until we die and that we will in fact live with God in heaven forever? Or might it be that we will turn away from Christ and lose the blessings of our salvation? The topic of the perseverance of the saints speaks to these questions. *The perseverance of the saints means that all those who are truly born again will be kept by God's power and will persevere as Christians until the end of their lives, and that only those who persevere until the end have been truly born again.*

This definition has two parts to it. It indicates first that there is assurance to be given to those who are truly born again, for it reminds them that God's power will keep them as Christians until they die, and they will surely live with Christ in heaven forever. On the other hand, the second half of the definition makes it clear that continuing in the Christian life is one of the evidences that a person is truly born again. It is important to keep this aspect of the doctrine in mind as well, lest false assurance be given to people who were never really believers in the first place.

It should be noted that this question is one on which evangelical Christians have long had significant disagreement. Many within the Wesleyan/Arminian tradition have held that it is possible for someone who is truly born again to lose his or her salvation, while Reformed Christians have held that that is not possible for someone who is *truly* born again.[1] Most Baptists have followed the Reformed tradition at this point; however, they have frequently used the term "*eternal security*" or the "*eternal security of the believer*" rather than the term "*perseverance of the saints.*"

A. All Who Are Truly Born Again Will Persevere to the End

There are many passages that teach that those who are truly born again, who are genuinely Christians, will continue in the Christian life until death and will then go to be with Christ in heaven. Jesus says,

> I have come down from heaven, not to do my own will, but the will of him who sent me; and this is the will of him who sent me, that I should lose nothing of all that he has given me, but raise it up at the last day. For this is the will of my Father, that *every one who* sees the Son and *believes in* him should have eternal life; and *I will raise him up at the last day.* (John 6:38 – 40)

Here Jesus says that everyone who believes in him will have eternal life. He says that he will raise that person up at the last day—which, in this context of believing in the Son and having eternal life, clearly means that Jesus will raise that person up to eternal life with him (not just raise him up to be judged and condemned). It seems hard to avoid the conclusion that everyone who truly believes in Christ will remain a Christian up to the day of final resurrection into the blessings of life in the presence of God.[2] Moreover,

this text emphasizes that Jesus does the will of the Father, which is that he should "*lose nothing* of all that he has given me" (John 6:39). Once again, those given to the Son by the Father will not be lost.

Another passage emphasizing this truth is John 10:27 – 29, in which Jesus says:

> My sheep hear my voice, and I know them, and they follow me; and I give them eternal life, and *they shall never perish,* and no one shall snatch them out of my hand. My Father, who has given them to me, is greater than all, and no one is able to snatch them out of the Father's hand.

Here Jesus says that those who follow him, those who are his sheep, are given eternal life. He further says that "no one shall snatch them out of my hand" (v. 28). Now some have objected to this that even though no one else can take Christians out of Christ's hand, we might remove ourselves from Christ's hand. But that seems to be pedantic quibbling over words—does not "no one" also include the person who is in Christ's hand? Moreover, we know that our own hearts are far from trustworthy. Therefore if the possibility remained that we could remove ourself from Christ's hand, the passage would hardly give the assurance that Jesus intends by it.

But more importantly, the most forceful phrase in the passage is "*they shall never perish*" (v. 28). The Greek construction (*ou mē* plus aorist subjunctive) is especially emphatic and might be translated more explicitly, "and they shall certainly not perish forever." This emphasizes that those who are Jesus' "sheep" and who follow him, and to whom he has given eternal life, shall never lose their salvation or be separated from Christ—they shall "never perish."[3]

There are several other passages that say those who believe have "eternal life." One example is John 3:36: "He who believes in the Son *has eternal life*" (cf. also John 5:24; 6:47; 10:28; 1 John 5:13). Now if this is truly eternal life that believers have, then it is life that lasts forever with God. It is a gift of God that comes with salvation (it is put in contrast to condemnation and eternal judgment in John 3:16–17, 36; 10:28). Arminians have objected that "eternal life" is simply a quality of life, a type of life in relationship with God, which one can have for a time and then lose. But this objection does not seem to be convincing in view of the clear nuance of unending time involved in the adjective *eternal* (Gk. *aiōnios,* "eternal, without end").[4] Certainly there is a special quality about this life, but the emphasis in the adjective *eternal* is on the fact that it is the opposite of death; it is the opposite of judgment and separation from God; it is life that goes on forever in the presence of God. And he who believes in the Son has this "*eternal* life" (John 3:36).

Evidence in Paul's writings and the other New Testament epistles also indicates that those who are truly born again will persevere to the end. There remains "no condemnation for those who are in Christ Jesus" (Rom. 8:1); therefore, it would be unjust for God to give any kind of eternal punishment to those who are Christians—no condemnation remains for them, for the entire penalty for their sins has been paid.

Then in Romans 8:30, Paul emphasizes the clear connection between God's eternal purposes in predestination and his working out of those purposes in life, together with his final realization of those purposes in "glorifying" or giving final resurrection bodies to those whom he has brought into union with Christ: "And those whom he predestined he also called; and those whom he called he also justified; and those whom he justified he also glorified." Here Paul sees the future event of glorification as such a certainty in God's settled purpose that he can speak of it as if it were already accomplished ("he also glorified"). This is true of all those who are called and justified—that is, all those who truly become Christians.

Further evidence that God keeps those who are born again safe for eternity is the "seal" that God places upon us. This "seal" is the Holy Spirit within us, who also acts as God's "guarantee" that we will receive the inheritance promised to us: "In him you also, who have heard the word of truth, the gospel of your salvation, and have believed in him, were *sealed with the promised Holy Spirit,* which is the *guarantee* of our inheritance until we acquire

---

[1]The doctrine of the perseverance of the saints is represented by "P" in the acronym TULIP, which is often used to summarize the "five points of Calvinism." (See full list in chapter 3, n. 10.)

[2]Grant R. Osborne, "Exegetical Notes on Calvinist Texts," in *Grace Unlimited,* ed. Clark H. Pinnock (Minneapolis: Bethany Fellowship, 1975), pp. 170–71, does not give an alternative explanation for Jesus' statement, "I will raise him up at the last day," when he deals with this passage. But he does say that in this context v. 35 emphasizes the fact that eternal life is dependent on the individual person "coming and believing" in Christ (p. 171) and that the present tense verbs used for "believe" in these passages imply not merely an initial decision of faith, but rather continuing in that state.

I regret having to differ with my friend and colleague on this question, but there is something to be said in response:

while no one would deny that it is necessary for people themselves to believe in Christ for eternal life, and while it is also true that Jesus here speaks not just of initial saving faith but of a faith that continues over time, the verse does not go so far as to specify that "everyone who believes continuously *until his or her death* will have eternal life," but rather simply says that "he who is *presently in a state of believing* in Christ" will have eternal life and Jesus will raise him up at the last day. The verse speaks about all who presently are in a state of believing in Christ, and it says that all of them will be raised up by Christ at the last day. No further objections to this specific verse are given in Osborne's second essay, "Soteriology in the Gospel of John," in *The Grace of God, the Will of Man: A Case for Arminianism* (Grand Rapids: Zondervan, 1989), p. 248.

possession of it, to the praise of his glory" (Eph. 1:13–14). The Greek word translated "guarantee" in this passage (*arrabōn*) is a legal and commercial term that means "first installment, deposit, down payment, pledge" and represents "a payment which obligates the contracting party to make further payments."[5] When God gave us the Holy Spirit within, he committed himself to give all the further blessings of eternal life and a great reward in heaven with him. This is why Paul can say that the Holy Spirit is the "*guarantee of our inheritance until we acquire possession of it*" (Eph. 1:14). All who have the Holy Spirit within them, all who are truly born again, have God's unchanging promise and guarantee that the inheritance of eternal life in heaven will certainly be theirs. God's own faithfulness is pledged to bring it about.[6]

Another example of assurance that believers will persevere to the end is found in Paul's statement to the Philippians: "I am sure that he who began a good work in you will bring it to completion at the day of Jesus Christ" (Phil. 1:6). It is true that the word "you" here is plural (Gk. *hymas*), and thus he is referring to Christians in the Philippian church generally, but he is still talking about the specific believers to whom he is writing, and saying that God's good work that began in them will continue and will be completed at the day Christ returns.[7] Peter tells his readers that they are those "who *by God's power are guarded* through faith for a salvation ready to be revealed in the last time" (1 Peter 1:5). The word *guarded* (Gk. *phroureō*) can mean both "kept from escaping" and "protected from attack," and perhaps both kinds of guarding are intended here: God is preserving believers from escaping out of his kingdom, and he is protecting them from external attacks.

The present participle that Peter uses gives the sense "You are continually being guarded."[8] He stresses that this is by God's power. Yet God's power does not work apart from the personal faith of those being guarded, but through their faith. ("Faith," *pistis*, is regularly a personal activity of individual believers in Peter's epistles; see 1 Peter 1:7, 9, 21; 5:9; 2 Peter 1:1, 5; and commonly in the New Testament.) The parallel examples of God working "through" someone or something in Peter's writings (1 Peter 1:3, 23; 2 Peter 1:4; and probably also 1 Peter 1:12; 2:14; 3:1) suggest that the believer's personal faith or trust in God is the means God uses to guard his people. Thus we might give the sense of the verse by saying that "God is continually using his power to guard his people by means of their

---

[3]The Greek word used here for "perish" is *apollymi*, the same term John uses in John 3:16 to say that "whoever believes in him should not perish but have eternal life."

Grant Osborne, in "Exegetical Notes on Calvinist Texts," p. 172, says that this verse must not be interpreted apart from the teaching about the vine and the branches in John 15:1–7, but he gives no alternative explanation for the phrase "they shall never perish," and gives no reason why we should fail to understand it to mean that these people will certainly have life with God forever in heaven. In his subsequent article, "Soteriology in the Gospel of John," Osborne again mentions John 10:28, but gives no alternative explanation for it other than to say that this passage emphasizes God's sovereignty, but other passages in John emphasize the faith-response that works together with God's sovereignty. These articles do not seem to provide a reason why

we should not understand these words in an ordinary sense, indicating that one who believes in Christ will certainly never fall away.

Of course, those who believe in the doctrine of the perseverance of the saints (such as myself) would affirm that the *way* God keeps us safe is by causing us to continue to believe in Christ (see discussion below), so to say that Scripture also emphasizes the necessity of continuing in faith is not to object to the doctrine of perseverance of the saints as it has been expressed by Reformed theologians frequently in the history of the church. In other words, there is a way to believe in both sets of texts without concluding that people who are truly born again can lose their salvation.

[4]*BAGD*, p. 28.

faith," a statement that seems to imply that God's power in fact energizes and continually sustains individual, personal faith.[9]

This guarding is not for a temporary goal but for a salvation ready to be revealed in the last time. "Salvation" is used here not of past justification or of present sanctification (speaking in theological categories) but of the future full possession of all the blessings of our redemption—of the final, complete fulfillment of our salvation (cf. Rom. 13:11; 1 Peter 2:2). Though already prepared or "ready," it will not be "revealed" by God to mankind generally until the "last time," the time of final judgment.

This last phrase makes it difficult if not impossible to see any end to God's guarding activity. If God's guarding has as its purpose the preservation of believers until they receive their full, heavenly salvation, then it is safe to conclude that God will accomplish that purpose and they will in fact attain that final salvation. Ultimately their attainment of final salvation depends on God's power. Nevertheless, God's power continually works "through" their faith. Do they wish to know whether God is guarding them? If they continue to trust God through Christ, God is working and guarding them, and he should be thanked.

This emphasis on God's guarding in combination with our faith provides a natural transition to the second half of the doctrine of perseverance.

B. Only Those Who Persevere to the End Have Been Truly Born Again

While Scripture repeatedly emphasizes that those who are truly born again will persevere to the end and will certainly have eternal life in heaven with God, there are other passages that speak of the necessity of continuing in faith throughout life. They make us realize that what Peter said in 1 Peter 1:5 is true, namely, that God does not guard us *apart from* our faith, but only by working *through* our faith so that he enables us to continue to believe in him. In this way, those who continue to trust in Christ gain assurance that God is working in them and guarding them.

One example of this kind of passage is John 8:31–32: "Jesus then said to the Jews who had believed in him, '*If you continue in my word,* you are truly my disciples, and you will

---

[5]Ibid., p. 109.

[6]Osborne, "Exegetical Notes on Calvinist Texts," p. 181, answers this verse by saying that Paul also teaches personal responsibility, since "the Christian is warned not to 'grieve' the Spirit (cf. 1 Thess. 4:8)" and "the danger of apostasy is real, and he dare not 'grieve' the Spirit." But once again this objection provides no alternative interpretation to the verse at hand, but simply refers to other verses that teach personal responsibility, a fact that a Reformed theologian would also be eager to affirm.

Arminian theologians frequently assume that if they affirm human responsibility and the need for continuing in faith they have thereby negated the idea that God's sovereign keeping and protection is absolutely certain and eternal life is guaranteed. But they often do this without providing any other convincing interpretations for the texts cited to demonstrate the doctrine of perseverance of the saints, or any

explanation that would show why we should not take these words as absolute guarantees that those who are born again will certainly persevere to the end. Rather than assuming that passages on human responsibility negate the idea of God's sovereign protection, it seems better to adopt the Reformed position that says that God's sovereign protection is consistent with human responsibility, because it works through human responsibility and guarantees that we will respond by maintaining the faith that is necessary to persevere.

[7]Osborne rightly rejects the idea that this refers only to the fact that the church will continue. He says, "Paul does intend that the promise extend to the individual. He will be kept by God with a view to the final salvation, but this does not obviate the need for perseverance" ("Exegetical Notes on Calvinist Texts," p. 182).

know the truth, and the truth will make you free.'" Jesus is here giving a warning that one evidence of genuine faith is continuing in his word, that is, continuing to believe what he says and living a life of obedience to his commands. Similarly, Jesus says, "*He who endures to the end* will be saved" (Matt. 10:22), as a means of warning people not to fall away in times of persecution.

Paul says to the Colossian Christians that Christ has reconciled them to God, "in order to present you holy and blameless and irreproachable before him, *provided that you continue in the faith,* stable and steadfast, not shifting from the hope of the gospel which you heard" (Col. 1:22–23). It is only natural that Paul and the other New Testament writers would speak this way, for they are addressing groups of people who profess to be Christians, without being able to know the actual state of every person's heart. There may have been people at Colossae who had joined in the fellowship of the church, and perhaps even professed that they had faith in Christ and had been baptized into membership of the church, but who never had true saving faith. How is Paul to distinguish such people from true believers? How can he avoid giving them false assurance, assurance that they will be saved eternally when in fact they will not, unless they come to true repentance and faith? Paul knows that those whose faith is not real will eventually fall away from participation in the fellowship of the church. Therefore he tells his readers that they will ultimately be saved, "*provided that you continue in the faith*" (Col. 1:23). Those who continue show thereby that they are genuine believers. But those who do not continue in the faith show that there was no genuine faith in their hearts in the first place.

A similar emphasis is seen in Hebrews 3:14 (NASB): "For we have become partakers of Christ, *if we hold fast the beginning of our assurance firm to the end.*" This verse provides an excellent perspective on the doctrine of perseverance. How do we know if "we have become partakers of Christ"? How do we know if this being joined to Christ has happened to us at some time in the past?[10] One way in which we know that we have come to genuine faith in Christ is if we continue in faith until the end of our lives.

Attention to the context of Hebrews 3:14 will keep us from using this and other similar passages in a pastorally inappropriate way. We must remember that there are other evidences elsewhere in Scripture that give Christians assurance of salvation,[11] so *we should not think that assurance that we belong to Christ is impossible until we die.* However, continuing in faith is the one means of assurance that is named here by the author of Hebrews. He mentions this to warn his readers that they should not fall away from Christ, because he is writing to a situation where such a warning is needed. The beginning of that section, just two verses earlier, said, "Take care, brethren, lest there be in any of you an evil, unbelieving heart, leading you to fall away from the living God" (Heb. 3:12). In fact, in all of the passages where continuing to believe in Christ to the end of our lives is mentioned as one indication of genuine faith, the purpose is never to make

---

[8]The following three paragraphs are taken from Wayne Grudem, *The First Epistle of Peter* (Leicester: Inter-Varsity Press, and Grand Rapids: Eerdmans, 1988), pp. 58–59.

[9]The translation by J. N. D. Kelly, "as a result of . . . faith," is an extremely unlikely rendering of the very common construction *dia* with the genitive (the few examples of this construction meaning "as a result of" which are suggested in, *BAGD*, p. 180, IV, are all ambiguous, and Kelly himself gives no examples: see J. N. D. Kelly, *A Commentary on the Epistles of Peter and Jude,* Black's New Testament Commentaries [London: Black, 1969], p. 52).

those who are presently trusting in Christ worry that some time in the future they might fall away (and we should never use these passages that way either, for that would be to give wrongful cause for worry in a way that Scripture does not intend). Rather, the purpose is always *to warn those who are thinking of falling away or have fallen away* that if they do this it is a strong indication that they were never saved in the first place. Thus, the necessity for continuing in faith should just be used as a warning against falling away, a warning that those who fall away give evidence that their faith was never real.

John clearly states that when people fall away from fellowship with the church and from belief in Christ they thereby show that their faith was not real in the first place and that they were never part of the true body of Christ. Speaking of people who have left the fellowship of believers, John says, "They went out from us, but they were not of us; for *if they had been of us, they would have continued with us;* but they went out, that it might be plain that they all are not of us" (1 John 2:19). John says that those who have departed showed by their actions that they "were not of us"—that they were not truly born again.

C. Those Who Finally Fall Away May Give Many External Signs of Conversion

Is it always clear which people in the church have genuine saving faith and which have only an intellectual persuasion of the truth of the gospel but no genuine faith in their hearts? It is not always easy to tell, and Scripture mentions in several places that *unbelievers* in fellowship with the visible church can give some external signs or indications that make them look or sound like genuine believers. For example, Judas, who betrayed Christ, must have acted almost exactly like the other disciples during the three years he was with Jesus. So convincing was his conformity to the behavior pattern of the other disciples, that at the end of three years of Jesus' ministry, when he said that one of his disciples would betray him, they did not all turn and suspect Judas, but they rather "began to say to him one after another, 'Is it I?'" (Matt. 26:22; cf. Mark 14:19; Luke 22:23; John 13:22). However, Jesus himself knew that there was no genuine faith in Judas' heart, because he said at one point, "Did I not choose you, the twelve, and one of you is a devil?" (John 6:70). John later wrote in his gospel that "Jesus knew from the first who those were that did not believe, and who it was that would betray him" (John 6:64). But the disciples themselves did not know.

Paul also speaks of "*false brethren* secretly brought in" (Gal. 2:4), and says that in his journeys he has been "in danger from *false brethren*" (2 Cor. 11:26). He also says that the servants of Satan "*disguise themselves* as servants of righteousness" (2 Cor. 11:15). This does not mean that all unbelievers in the church who nevertheless give some signs of true conversion are servants of Satan secretly undermining the work of the church, for some may be in process of considering the claims of the gospel and moving toward real faith, others may have heard only an inadequate explanation of the gospel message, and others may not have come under genuine conviction of the Holy Spirit yet. But Paul's statements do mean

---

[10]The author uses the perfect tense verb *gegonamen*, "we have become" (at some time in the past, with results that continue into the present).

[11]See the list of evidences of salvation given in section D below.

that some unbelievers in the church will be false brothers and sisters sent to disrupt the fellowship, while others will simply be unbelievers who will eventually come to genuine saving faith. In both cases, however, they give several external signs that make them look like genuine believers.

We can see this also in Jesus' statement about what will happen at the last judgment:

> Not every one who says to me, "Lord, Lord," shall enter the kingdom of heaven, but he who does the will of my Father who is in heaven. On that day many will say to me, "Lord, Lord, did we not prophesy in your name, and cast out demons in your name, and do many mighty works in your name?" And then will I declare to them, "*I never knew you;* depart from me, you evildoers." (Matt. 7:21–23)

Although these people prophesied and cast out demons and did "many mighty works" in Jesus' name, the ability to do such works did not guarantee that they were Christians. Jesus says, "I never knew you." He does not say, "I knew you at one time but I no longer know you," nor "I knew you at one time but you strayed away from me," but rather, "I *never* knew you." They never were genuine believers.

A similar teaching is found in the parable of the sower in Mark 4. Jesus says, "Other seed fell on rocky ground, where it had not much soil, and immediately it sprang up, since it had no depth of soil; and when the sun rose it was scorched, and since it had no root it withered away" (Mark 4:5–6). Jesus explains that the seed sown upon rocky ground represents people who "when they hear the word, immediately receive it with joy; and *they have no root in themselves,* but endure for a while; then, when tribulation or persecution arises on account of the word, immediately they fall away" (Mark 4:16–17). The fact that they "have no root in themselves" indicates that there is no source of life within these plants; similarly, the people represented by them have no genuine life of their own within. They have an appearance of conversion and they apparently have become Christians because they receive the word "with joy," but when difficulty comes, they are nowhere to be found—their apparent conversion was not genuine and there was no real saving faith in their hearts.

The importance of continuing in faith is also affirmed in the parable of Jesus as the vine, in which Christians are portrayed as branches (John 15:1–7). Jesus says:

> I am the true vine, and my Father is the vinedresser. Every branch of mine that bears no fruit, he takes away, and every branch that does bear fruit he prunes, that it may bear more fruit. . . . If a man does not abide in me, he is cast forth as a branch and withers; and the branches are gathered, thrown into the fire and burned. (John 15:1–2, 6)

Arminians have argued that the branches that do not bear fruit are still true branches on the vine—Jesus refers to "Every branch *of mine* that bears no fruit" (v. 2). Therefore the branches that are gathered and thrown into the fire and burned must refer to true believers that were once part of the vine but fell away and became subject to eternal judgment. But that is not a necessary implication of Jesus' teaching at this point. The imagery of the vine used in this parable is limited in how much detail it can teach. In fact, if Jesus had wanted to teach that there were true and false believers associated with him, and if he wanted to use the analogy of a vine and branches, then the only way he could refer to people who do not have genuine life in themselves would be to speak of branches that bear no fruit (somewhat after the analogy of the seeds that fell on rocky ground and had "no root in themselves" in Mark 4:17). Here in John 15 the branches that do not bear fruit, though they are in some way connected to Jesus and give an outward appearance of being genuine branches, nonetheless give indication of their true state by the fact that they bear no fruit. This is similarly indicated by the fact that the person "does not abide" in Christ (John 15:6) and is cast off as a branch and withers. If we try to press the analogy any further, by saying, for example, that all branches on a vine really are alive or they would not be there in the first place, then we are simply trying to press the imagery beyond what it is able to teach—and in that case there would be nothing in the analogy that could represent false believers in any case. The point of the imagery is simply that those who bear fruit thereby give evidence that they are abiding in Christ; those who do not, are not abiding in him.

Finally, there are two passages in Hebrews that also affirm that those who finally fall away may give many external signs of conversion and may look in many ways like Christians. The first of these, Hebrews 6:4–6, has frequently been used by Arminians as proof that believers can lose their salvation. But on closer inspection such an interpretation is not convincing. The author writes,

> For it is impossible to restore again to repentance those who have once been enlightened, who have tasted the heavenly gift, and have become partakers of the Holy Spirit, and have tasted the goodness of the word of God and the powers of the age to come, if they then commit apostasy, since they crucify the Son of God on their own account and hold him up to contempt. (Heb. 6:4–6)

The author continues with an example from agriculture:

> For land which has drunk the rain that often falls upon it, and brings forth vegetation useful to those for whose sake it is cultivated, receives a blessing from God. But if it bears thorns and thistles, it is worthless and near to being cursed; its end is to be burned. (Heb. 6:7–8)

In this agricultural metaphor, those who receive final judgment are compared to land that bears no vegetation or useful fruit, but rather bears thorns and thistles. When we recall the other metaphors in Scripture where good fruit is a sign of true spiritual life and fruitlessness is a sign of false believers (for example, Matt. 3:8–10; 7:15–20; 12:33–35), we already have an indication that the author is speaking of people whose most trustworthy evidence of their spiritual condition (the fruit they bear) is negative, suggesting that the author is talking about people who are not genuinely Christians.

Some have objected that the long description of things that have happened to these people who fall away means that they must have been genuinely born again. But that is not a convincing objection when we look at the individual terms used. The author says they have "once been *enlightened*" (Heb. 6:4). But this enlightening simply means that they came to understand the truths of the gospel, not that they responded to those truths with genuine saving faith.[12]

Similarly, the word *once* that is used to speak of those who "have once been enlightened" is the Greek term *hapax,* which is used, for example, in Philippians 4:16 of the Philippians' sending Paul a gift "*once* and again," and in Hebrews 9:7 of entrance in the Holy of Holies "*once* a year." Therefore, this word does not mean that something happened "once" and can never be repeated, but simply that it happened once, without specifying whether it will be repeated or not.[13]

The text further says that these people "have *tasted* the heavenly gift" and that they "have *tasted* the goodness of the word of God and the powers of the age to come" (Heb. 6:4–5). Inherent in the idea of tasting is the fact that the tasting is temporary and one might or might not decide to accept the thing that is tasted. For example, the same Greek word (*geuomai*) is used in Matthew 27:34 to say that those crucifying Jesus "offered him wine to drink, mingled with gall; but when he *tasted* it, he would not drink it." The word is also used in a figurative sense meaning "come to know something."[14] If we understand it in this figurative sense, as it must be understood here since the passage is not talking about tasting literal food, then it means that these people have come to understand the heavenly gift (which probably means here that they had experienced some of the power of the Holy Spirit at work) and to know something of the Word of God and the powers of the age to come. It does not necessarily mean that they had (or did not have) genuine saving faith, but may simply mean that they came to understand it and have some experience of spiritual power.[15]

The text also further says that these people "have become *partakers* of the Holy Spirit" (Heb. 6:4). The question here is the exact meaning of the word *metochos,* which is here translated "partaker." It is not always clear to English-speaking readers that this term has a range of meaning and may imply very close participation and attachment, or may only imply a loose association with the other person or persons named. For example, the context shows that in Hebrews 3:14 to become a "partaker" of Christ means to have a very close participation with him in a saving relationship.[16] On the other hand, *metochos* can also be used in a much looser sense, simply to refer to associates or companions. We read that when the disciples took in a great catch of fish so that their nets were breaking, "they beckoned to their *partners* in the other boat to come and help them" (Luke 5:7). Here it simply refers to those who were companions or partners with Peter and the other disciples in their fishing work.[17] Ephesians 5:7 uses a closely related word (*symmetochos,* a compound of *metochos* and the preposition *syn* ["with"]) when Paul warns Christians about the sinful acts of unbelievers and says, "do not associate with them" (Eph. 5:7). He is not concerned that their total nature will be transformed by the unbelievers, but simply that they will associate with them and have their own witness compromised and their own lives influenced to some degree by them.

By analogy, Hebrews 6:4–6 speaks of people who have been "*associated with*" the Holy Spirit, and thereby had their lives influenced by him, but it need not imply that they had a redeeming work of the Holy Spirit in their lives, or that they were regenerated. By similar analogy with the example of the fishing companions in Luke 5:7, Peter and the disciples could be *associated with* them and even to some degree influenced by them without having a thoroughgoing change of life caused by that association. The very word *metochos* allows for a range of influence from fairly weak to fairly strong, for it only means "one who participates with or shares with or accompanies in some activity." This was apparently what had happened to these people spoken of in Hebrews 6, who had been associated with the church and as such associated with the work of the Holy Spirit, and no doubt had been influenced by him in some ways in their lives.[18]

Finally, the text says that it is impossible "to restore again to *repentance*" people who have experienced these things and have then committed apostasy. Some have argued that if this is a repentance to which they need to be restored again, then it must be genuine repentance. But this is not necessarily the case. First, we must realize that "repentance" (Gk. *metanoia*) does not need to refer to inward heart repentance unto salvation. For example, Hebrews 12:17 uses this word to speak of a change of mind that Esau sought concerning the sale of his birthright, and refers to it as "repentance" (*metanoia*). This would not have been a repentance for salvation, but simply a change of mind and an undoing of the transaction regarding his birthright. (Note also the example of Judas' repentance in Matt. 27:3 — howbeit with a different Greek word.)

The cognate verb "to repent" (Gk. *metanoeō*) is sometimes used to refer not to saving repentance, but just to sorrow for individual offenses in Luke 17:3–4: "If your brother sins, rebuke him, and *if he repents* forgive him; and if he sins against you seven times in the day, and turns to you seven times, and says, 'I repent,' you must forgive him." We conclude that "repentance" simply means a sorrow for actions that have been done or for sins that have been committed. Whether or not it is a genuine saving repentance, a "repentance unto salvation," may not be always evident right away. The author of Hebrews is not concerned to specify whether it is a genuine repentance or not. He is simply saying that if someone has a sorrow for sin and comes to understand the gospel and experiences these various blessings of the Holy Spirit's work (no doubt in fellowship with the church), and then turns away, it

---

[12]The word *enlightened* translates the Greek term *phōtizō*, which refers to learning in general, not necessarily a learning that results in salvation—it is used in John 1:9 of "enlightening" every man that comes into the world, in 1 Cor. 4:5 of the enlightening that comes at the final judgment, and in Eph. 1:18 of the enlightening that accompanies growth in the Christian life. The word is not a "technical term" that means that the people in question were saved.

After completing the following discussion of Hebrews 6:4–6, I wrote a much more extensive study, with additional analysis, supporting data, and interaction with other literature: see Wayne Grudem, "Perseverance of the Saints: A Case Study From Heb. 6:4–6 and the Other Warning Passages of Hebrews," in *Still Sovereign*, ed. Tom Schreiner and Bruce Ware (Grand Rapids: Baker, 2000).

[13]This is not the same word as *ephapax*, which is more regularly used in the New Testament of nonrepeatable events (Rom. 6:10; Heb. 7:27; 9:12; 10:10).

[14]*BAGD*, p. 157. They mention other examples of *geuomai* ("taste"), such as Herodotus 6.5, where the people of Miletus had "tasted of freedom," but it was certainly not their own possession. They also cite Dio Chrysostom, 32.72, where he speaks of the people of Alexandria in a time when they "had a taste of

warfare" in an encounter with Roman troops who were simply harassing them and not actually engaging in genuine war. Josephus, *The Jewish War*, 2.158, speaks about the theological views of the Essenes "whereby they irresistibly attract all who have once *tasted* their philosophy." Here again Josephus makes it clear that those who have "once tasted" have not yet made the Essene philosophy their own, but are simply very strongly attracted to it. By analogy, in Heb. 6 those who have "tasted" the heavenly gift and the word of God and the powers of the age to come may be strongly attracted to these things, or they may not be, but mere tasting does not mean that they have made it their own—quite the contrary, if all the author can say of them is that they have "tasted" these things, it suggests that they have not made what they tasted to be their own.

[15]The word *tasted* is also used in Heb. 2:9 to say that Jesus "tasted death," indicating that he came to know it by experience (but "tasted" is an apt word because he did not remain dead). The same could be true of those who had some experience of heavenly gifts, as can be true even of unbelievers (cf. Matt. 7:22; 1 Cor. 7:14; 2 Peter 2:20–22). In Heb. 6:4–5 these people's experience of the Holy Spirit's power and of the Word of God was of course a *genuine*

will not be possible to restore such a person again to a place of sorrow for sin. But this does not necessarily imply that the repentance was genuine saving repentance in the first place.

At this point we may ask what kind of person is described by all of these terms. These are no doubt people who have been affiliated closely with the fellowship of the church. They have had some sorrow for sin (repentance). They have clearly understood the gospel (they have been enlightened). They have come to appreciate the attractiveness of the Christian life and the change that comes about in people's lives because of becoming a Christian, and they have probably had answers to prayer in their own lives and felt the power of the Holy Spirit at work, perhaps even using some spiritual gifts in the manner of the unbelievers in Matthew 7:22 (they have become "associated with" the work of the Holy Spirit or have become "partakers" of the Holy Spirit and have tasted the heavenly gift and the powers of the age of come). They have been exposed to the true preaching of the Word and have appreciated much of its teachings (they have tasted the goodness of the Word of God).

But then in spite of all this, if they "commit apostasy" and "crucify the Son of God on their own account and hold him up to contempt" (Heb. 6:6), then they are willfully rejecting all of these blessings and turning decidedly against them. Perhaps all of us have known in our own churches people who (sometimes by their own profession) have long been affiliated with the fellowship of the church but are not themselves born-again Christians. They have thought about the gospel for years and have continued to resist the wooing of the Holy Spirit in their lives, perhaps through an unwillingness to give up lordship of their lives to Jesus and preferring to cling to it themselves.

Now the author tells us that *if these people willfully turn away from all of these temporary blessings,* then it will be impossible to restore them again to any kind of repentance or sorrow for sin. Their hearts will be hardened and their consciences calloused. What more could be done to bring them to salvation? If we tell them Scripture is true they will say that they know it but they have decided to reject it. If we tell them God answers prayer and changes lives they will respond that they know that as well, but they want nothing of it. If we tell them that the Holy Spirit is powerful to work in people's lives and the gift of eternal life

---

experience (just as Jesus *genuinely* died), but that by itself does not show that the people had an experience of regeneration.

[16]The same Greek word *metochos* is used in Heb. 3:14, even though the English text of the RSV says "We share in Christ."

[17]Heb. 1:9 also uses the same word to speak of "comrades" (RSV) or "companions" (NIV, NASB).

[18]The other uses of *metochos* in Hebrews (3:1 and 12:8) do suggest closer association or participation, but even 12:8, which talks about people becoming partakers in discipline, certainly allows for the fact that some may receive that discipline but not be transformed by it. In any case, the evidence is not strong enough to make us think that the author of Hebrews used this word as a "technical term" that always referred to a saving kind of participation (it did not in Heb. 1:9 and 12:8), and our understanding of the sense of the word must be governed by an examination of the range of meaning it can take in the Greek literature of the New Testament and in other literature

that shares a similar vocabulary with the writers of the New Testament.

The usage of the Septuagint is also instructive with respect to this word, since in several instances it only refers to companionship, not any kind of regenerating or life-changing experience with God or with the Holy Spirit. For instance, in 1 Sam. 20:30, Saul accuses Jonathan of being a "partner" with David. In Ps. 119:63, the psalmist says he is a "companion" of all those who fear God. Eccl. 4:10 says that two are better than one, for if they fall, the one will lift up his "partner." Prov. 28:24, in the translations of Aquila, Symmachus, and Theodotian, uses this word to say that a man who rejects his father or mother is a "companion" of ungodly men. Examples of somewhat stronger association are seen in Esth. 8:13; Prov. 29:10; Hos. 4:17; 3 Macc. 3:21. The conclusion of this examination of the term *metochos* is that, while it can be used of very close association with saving results in a person's life, it can also be used simply of is good beyond description, they will say that they understand that, but they want nothing of it. Their repeated familiarity with the things of God and their experience of many influences of the Holy Spirit has simply served to harden them against conversion.

Now the author of Hebrews knows that there are some in the community to which he writes who are in danger of falling away in just this way (see Heb. 2:3; 3:8, 12, 14–15; 4:1, 7, 11; 10:26, 29, 35–36, 38–39; 12:3, 15–17). He wants to warn them that, though they have participated in the fellowship of the church and experienced a number of God's blessings in their lives, yet if they fall away after all that, there is no salvation for them. This does not imply that he thinks that true Christians could fall away—Hebrews 3:14 implies quite the opposite. But he wants them to gain assurance of salvation through their continuing in faith, and thereby implies that if they fall away it would show that they never were Christ's people in the first place (see Heb. 3:6: "We are his house *if* we hold fast our confidence and pride in our hope").

Therefore the author wants to give a severe warning to those in danger of slipping away from their Christian profession. He wants to use the strongest language possible to say, "Here is how far a person can come in experiencing *temporary blessings* and still not really be saved." He is warning them to watch out, because depending on temporary blessings and experiences is not enough. To do this he talks not of any true change of heart or any good fruit produced, but simply about the temporary blessings and experiences that have come to these persons and have given them some understanding of Christianity.

For this reason he immediately passes from this description of those who commit apostasy to a further analogy that shows that these people who fell away never had any genuine fruit in their lives. As we explained above, verses 7–8 speak of these people in terms of *"thorns and thistles,"* the kind of crop that is brought forth on land that has no worthwhile life in itself even though it receives repeated blessings from God (in terms of the analogy, even though rain frequently falls upon it). We should notice here that people who commit apostasy are not compared to a field that once bore good fruit and now does not, but that they are like *land that never bore good fruit,* but only thorns and thistles. The land may look good before the crops start to come up, but the fruit gives the genuine evidence, and it is bad.

Strong support for this interpretation of Hebrews 6:4–8 is found in the verse immediately following. Though the author has been speaking very harshly about the possibility of falling away, he then returns to speak to the situation of the great majority of the hearers, whom he thinks to be genuine Christians. He says, "Though we speak thus, *yet in your case,* beloved, *we feel sure of better things that belong to salvation*" (Heb. 6:9). But the question is "better things" than what? The plural "better things" forms an appropriate contrast to the "good things" that have been mentioned in verses 4–6: the author is

associating or participating with someone else. Therefore the term itself does not require that the people in Heb. 6:4–6 had saving participation with the Holy Spirit or had been regenerated. It simply means they had in some ways been associated with and influenced by the Holy Spirit.

The people who prophesied and cast out demons and did many mighty works in Jesus' name in Matt. 7:22 are good examples of people who certainly did have some sharing in the work of the Holy Spirit or who had become "partakers" of the Holy Spirit in this sense, but had not been saved: Jesus says, "I never knew you" (Matt. 7:23).

convinced that most of his readers have experienced better things than simply the partial and temporary influences of the Holy Spirit and the church talked about in verses 4–6.

In fact, the author talks about these things by saying (literally) that they are "better things, *also belonging to salvation*" (Gk. *kai echomena sōtērias*).[19] These are not only the temporary blessings talked about in verses 4–6, but these are better things, things having not only temporary influence, but "also belonging to salvation." In this way the Greek word *kai* ("also") shows that salvation is something that was not part of the things mentioned in verses 4–6 above. Therefore this word *kai,* which is not explicitly translated in the RSV or NIV (but the NASB comes close),[20] provides a crucial key for understanding the passage. If the author had meant to say that the people mentioned in verses 4–6 were truly saved, then it is very difficult to understand why he would say in verse 9 that he is convinced of *better things* for them, things that belong to salvation, or that have salvation in addition to those things mentioned above. He thus shows that he can use a brief phrase to say that people "have salvation" if he wishes to do so (he does not need to pile up many phrases), and he shows, moreover, that the people whom he speaks of in verses 4–6 are not saved.[21]

What exactly are these "better things"? In addition to salvation mentioned in verse 9, they are things that give real evidence of salvation—genuine fruit in their lives (v. 10), full assurance of hope (v. 11), and saving faith, of the type exhibited by those who inherit the promises (v. 12). In this way he reassures those who are genuine believers—those who show fruit in their lives and show love for other Christians, who show hope and genuine faith that is continuing at the present time, and who are not about to fall away. He wants to reassure these readers (who are certainly the great majority of the ones to whom he writes) while still issuing a strong warning to those among them who may be in danger of falling away.

A similar teaching is found in Hebrews 10:26–31. There the author says, "If we deliberately keep on sinning after we have received the knowledge of the truth, no sacrifice for sins is left" (v. 26 NIV). A person who rejects Christ's salvation and "has treated as an unholy thing the blood of the covenant that sanctified him" (v. 29 NIV) deserves eternal punishment. This again is a strong warning against falling away, but it should not be taken as proof that someone who has truly been born again can lose his or her salvation. When the author talks about the blood of the covenant "that sanctified him," the word *sanctified* is used simply to refer to "external sanctification, like that of the ancient Israelites, by outward connection with God's people."[22] The passage does not talk about someone who is genuinely saved, but someone who has received some beneficial moral influence through contact with the church.[23]

One other passage in John's writings has been claimed to teach the possibility of loss of salvation. In Revelation 3:5, Jesus says, "He who conquers shall be clad thus in white garments, and *I will not blot his name out of the book of life.*" Some have claimed that when Jesus says this he implies that it is possible that he would blot out the names of some people from the book of life, people who had already had their names written in it and were thus already saved. But the fact that Jesus emphatically states that he will *not* do something should not be taken as teaching that he will do that same thing in other cases! The same kind of Greek construction[24] is used to give an emphatic negation in John 10:28, where Jesus says, "I give them eternal life, and *they shall never perish.*" This does not mean that there are some of Jesus' sheep who do not hear his voice and follow him and who will perish; it is simply affirming that his sheep certainly will not perish. Similarly, when God says, "I will never fail you nor forsake you" (Heb. 13:5), it does not imply that he will leave or forsake others; it just emphatically states that he will not leave nor forsake his people. Or, in even a closer parallel, in Matthew 12:32, Jesus says, "Whoever speaks against the Holy Spirit *will not be forgiven,* either in this age *or in the age to come."* This does not imply that some sins will be forgiven in the age to come (as Roman Catholics claim in support for the doctrine of purgatory)[25] — that is simply an error in reasoning: to say that something will not happen in the age to come does not imply that it might happen in the age to come! In the same way, Revelation 3:5 is just a strong assurance that those who are clad in the white garments and who have remained faithful to Christ will not have their names blotted out of the book of life.[26]

Finally, one passage from the Old Testament is sometimes used to argue that people can lose their salvation: the story of the Holy Spirit departing from King Saul. But Saul should not be taken as an example of someone who lost his salvation, for when "the Spirit of the LORD departed from Saul" (1 Sam. 16:14), it was immediately after Samuel had anointed David king and "the Spirit of the LORD came mightily upon David from that day forward" (1 Sam. 16:13). In fact, the Spirit of the Lord coming upon David is reported in the immediately previous sentence to the one in which we read that the Spirit departed from Saul. This close connection means that Scripture is not here talking about a total loss of all work of the Holy Spirit in Saul's life, but simply about the withdrawing of the Holy Spirit's function of empowering Saul as king.[27] But that does not mean that Saul was eternally condemned. It is simply very hard to tell from the pages of the Old Testament whether Saul, throughout his life, was (a) an unregenerate man who had leadership capabilities and was used by God as a demonstration of the fact that someone worthy to be king in the eyes of the world was not thereby suited to be king over the Lord's people, or (b) a regenerate man with poor understanding and a life that increasingly strayed from the Lord.

D. What Can Give a Believer Genuine Assurance?

If it is true, as explained in the previous section, that those who are unbelievers and who finally fall away may give many external signs of conversion, then what will serve as evidence of genuine conversion? What can give real assurance to a real believer? We can list three categories of questions that a person could ask of himself or herself.

---

[19]*BAGD,* p. 334, III, translates the middle participle of *echō* as "hold oneself fast, cling to," and lists Heb. 6:9 as the only New Testament example of this form used "of inner belonging and close association" (cf. *LSJ,* p. 750, C: "hold oneself fast, cling closely"). However, even if we translated the middle voice in the same way as the active, the phrase would mean, "things also having salvation," and my argument in this section would not be affected.

[20]The NASB translates, "*and* things that accompany salvation."

[21]Someone might object that the phrase "better things" does not contrast with the temporary blessings in vv. 4–6, but with the judgment mentioned that is coming to the thorns and thistles who are about to be "burned" in v. 8. But it is unlikely that the author would refer to not being cursed simply as "better things." The comparative "better" (*kreisson*) is used thirteen times in Hebrews, and it regularly contrasts something *better* with something *good* (better covenant, better sacrifice, etc.); similarly, here it suggests a comparison with things that are already good (such as the blessings in vv. 4–6), much more than it suggests a contrast with the horrible fate of eternal judgment in v. 8.

1. Do I Have a Present Trust in Christ for Salvation? Paul tells the Colossians that they will be saved on the last day, "provided that you *continue in the faith,* stable and steadfast, not shifting from the hope of the gospel which you heard" (Col. 1:23). The author of Hebrews says, "We share in Christ, if only we hold our first confidence firm to the end" (Heb. 3:14) and encourages his readers to be imitators of those "who *through faith* and patience inherit the promises" (Heb. 6:12). In fact, the most famous verse in the entire Bible uses a present tense verb that may be translated, "whoever continues believing in him" may have eternal life (see John 3:16).

Therefore a person should ask himself or herself, "Do I today have trust in Christ to forgive my sins and take me without blame into heaven forever? Do I have confidence in my heart that he has saved me? If I were to die tonight and stand before God's judgment seat, and if he were to ask me why he should let me into heaven, would I begin to think of my good deeds and depend on them, or would I without hesitation say that I am depending on the merits of Christ and am confident that he is a sufficient Savior?"

This emphasis on *present* faith in Christ stands in contrast to the practice of some church "testimonies" where people repeatedly recite details of a conversion experience that may have happened 20 or 30 years ago. If a testimony of saving faith is genuine, it should be a testimony of faith that is active this very day.

2. Is There Evidence of a Regenerating Work of the Holy Spirit in My Heart? The evidence of the work of the Holy Spirit in our hearts comes in many different forms. Although we should not put confidence in the demonstration of miraculous works (Matt. 7:22), or long hours and years of work at some local church (which may simply be building with "wood, hay, straw" [in terms of 1 Cor. 3:12] to further one's own ego or power over others, or to attempt to earn merit with God), there are many other evidences of a real work of the Holy Spirit in one's heart.

First, there is a subjective testimony of the Holy Spirit within our hearts bearing witness that we are God's children (Rom. 8:15–16; 1 John 4:13). This testimony will usually be accompanied by a sense of being led by the Holy Spirit in paths of obedience to God's will (Rom. 8:14).

---

[22] A. H. Strong, *Systematic Theology* (Valley Forge, Pa.: Judson Press, 1907), p. 884. Strong mentions an appropriate parallel use of the verb "sanctify" in 1 Cor. 7:14, which speaks about the unbelieving husband being "sanctified" by the believing wife (1 Cor. 7:14, where the same Greek word, *hagiazō,* is used). Outward ceremonial sanctification is also referred in Heb. 9:13; cf. Matt. 23:17, 19.

[23] Ex. 24:7–8 speaks of the blood of the covenant that set apart the people as God's people even though not all were truly born again. In the context of Heb. 10, such imagery, taken from the Old Testament process of sanctifying a people so that they could come before God to worship, is an appropriate background.

[24] The construction uses *ou mē* plus the aorist subjunctive to express emphatic negation.

[25] See discussion of the doctrine of purgatory in chapter 12, section C.1.a.

[26] A different kind of book is probably in view in Ex. 32:33, where God says to Moses, "Whoever has sinned against me, him will I blot out of my book." Here the New Testament idea of the "book of life" is not mentioned. Rather, the image is one of God keeping a record of those currently dwelling among his people, much as an earthly king would do. To "blot out" someone's name from such a book would imply that the person had died. Using this imagery, Ex. 32:33 is best understood to mean that God will take the life of anyone who sins against him (see v. 35). Eternal destiny is not in view in this passage.

In addition, if the Holy Spirit is genuinely at work in our lives, he will be producing the kind of character traits that Paul calls "the fruit of the Spirit" (Gal. 5:22). He lists several attitudes and character traits that are produced by the Holy Spirit: "love, joy, peace, patience, kindness, goodness, faithfulness, gentleness, self-control" (Gal. 5:22–23). Of course, the question is not, "Do I perfectly exemplify all of these characteristics in my life?" but rather, "Are these things a general characteristic of my life? Do I sense these attitudes in my heart? Do others (especially those closest to me) see these traits exhibited in my life? Have I been growing in them over a period of years?" There is no suggestion in the New Testament that any non-Christian, any unregenerate person, can convincingly fake these character traits, especially for those who know the person most closely.

Related to this kind of fruit is another kind of fruit—the results of one's life and ministry as they have influence on others and on the church. There are some people who profess to be Christians but whose influence on others is to discourage them, to drag them down, to injure their faith, and to provoke controversy and divisiveness. The result of their life and ministry is not to build up others and to build up the church, but to tear it down. On the other hand, there are those who seem to edify others in every conversation, every prayer, and every work of ministry they put their hand to. Jesus said, regarding false prophets, "You will know them by their fruits.... Every sound tree bears good fruit, but the bad tree bears evil fruit.... Thus you will know them by their fruits" (Matt. 7:16–20).

Another evidence of work of the Holy Spirit is continuing to believe and accept the sound teaching of the church. Those who begin to deny major doctrines of the faith give serious negative indications concerning their salvation: "No one who denies the Son has the Father.... If what you heard from the beginning abides in you, then you will abide in the Son and in the Father" (1 John 2:23–24). John also says, "Whoever knows God listens to us, and he who is not of God does not listen to us" (1 John 4:6). Since the New Testament writings are the current replacement for the apostles like John, we might also say that whoever knows God will continue to read and to delight in God's Word, and will continue to believe it fully. Those who do not believe and delight in God's Word give evidence that they are not "of God."

Another evidence of genuine salvation is a continuing present relationship with Jesus Christ. Jesus says, "Abide in me, and I in you" and, "If you abide in me, and my words abide in you, ask whatever you will, and it shall be done for you" (John 15:4, 7). This abiding in Christ will include not only day-by-day trust in him in various situations, but also certainly regular fellowship with him in prayer and worship.

Finally, a major area of evidence that we are genuine believers is found in a life of obedience to God's commands. John says, "He who says 'I know him' but disobeys his commandments is a liar, and the truth is not in him; but whoever keeps his word, in him truly love for God is perfected. By this we may be sure that we are in him: he who says he abides in him ought to walk in the same way in which he walked" (1 John 2:4–6). A perfect life is not necessary, of course. John is rather saying that in general our lives ought to be ones

---

[27]We should give a similar interpretation to David's prayer in Ps. 51:11: "Take not your holy Spirit from me." David is praying that the Holy Spirit's anointing for kingship would not be removed from him, and that the presence and power of God on his life would not depart; he is not praying against a loss of eternal salvation.

of imitation of Christ and likeness to him in what we do and say. If we have genuine saving faith, there will be clear results in obedience in our lives (see also 1 John 3:9–10, 24; 5:18). Thus James can say, "Faith by itself, if it has no works, is dead" and "I by my works will show you my faith" (James 2:17–18). One large area of obedience to God includes love for fellow Christians. "He who loves his brother abides in the light" (1 John 2:10). "We know that we have passed out of death into life, because we love the brethren. He who does not love abides in death" (1 John 3:14; cf. 3:17; 4:7). One evidence of this love is continuing in Christian fellowship (1 John 2:19), and another is giving to a brother in need (1 John 3:17; cf. Matt. 25:31–46).

3. Do I See a Long-Term Pattern of Growth in My Christian Life? The first two areas of assurance dealt with present faith and present evidence of the Holy Spirit at work in our lives. But Peter gives one more kind of test that we can use to ask whether we are genuinely believers. He tells us that there are some character traits which, if we keep on increasing in them, will guarantee that we will "never fall" (2 Peter 1:10). He tells his readers to add to their faith "virtue . . . knowledge . . . self-control . . . steadfastness . . . godliness . . . brotherly affection . . . love" (2 Peter 1:5–7). Then he says that these things are to belong to his readers and to continually "abound" in their lives (2 Peter 1:8). He adds that they are to "be the more zealous to confirm your call and election" and says then that "*if you do this* (literally, "these things," referring to the character traits mentioned in vv. 5–7) *you will never fall*" (2 Peter 1:10).

The way that we confirm our call and election, then, is to continue to grow in "these things." This implies that our assurance of salvation can be something that increases over time in our lives. Every year that we add to these character traits in our lives, we gain greater and greater assurance of our salvation. Thus, though young believers can have a quite strong confidence in their salvation, that assurance can increase to even deeper certainty over the years in which they grow toward Christian maturity.[28] If they continue to add these things they will confirm their call and election and will "never fall."

The result of these three questions that we can ask ourselves should be to give strong assurance to those who are genuinely believers. In this way the doctrine of the perseverance of the saints will be a tremendously comforting doctrine. No one who has such assurance should wonder, "Will I be able to persevere to the end of my life and therefore be saved?" Everyone who gains assurance through such a self-examination should rather think, "I am truly born again; therefore, I will certainly persevere to the end, because I am being guarded 'by God's power' working through my faith (1 Peter 1:5) and therefore I will never be lost. Jesus will raise me up at the last day and I will enter into his kingdom forever" (John 6:40).

On the other hand, this doctrine of the perseverance of the saints, if rightly understood, should cause genuine worry, and even fear, in the hearts of any who are "backsliding" or straying away from Christ. Such persons must clearly be warned that only those who persevere to the end have been truly born again. If they fall away from their profession of faith in Christ and life of obedience to him, they may not really be saved—in fact, the *evidence* that they are giving *is that they are not saved,* and they never really were saved. Once they stop trusting in Christ and obeying him (I am speaking in terms of outward evidence) they have no genuine assurance of salvation, and they should consider themselves unsaved, and turn to Christ in repentance and ask him for forgiveness of their sins.

At this point, in terms of pastoral care with those who have strayed away from their Christian profession, we should realize that *Calvinists and Arminians* (those who believe in the perseverance of the saints and those who think that Christians can lose their salvation) *will both counsel a "backslider" in the same way.* According to the Arminian this person was a Christian at one time but is no longer a Christian. According to the Calvinist, such a person never really was a Christian in the first place and is not one now. But in both cases the biblical counsel given would be the same: "You do not appear to be a Christian now—you must repent of your sins and trust in Christ for your salvation!" Though the Calvinist and Arminian would differ on their interpretation of the previous history, they would agree on what should be done in the present.[29]

But here we see why the phrase *eternal security* can be quite misleading. In some evangelical churches, instead of teaching the full and balanced presentation of the doctrine of the perseverance of the saints, pastors have sometimes taught a watered-down version, which in effect tells people that all who have once made a profession of faith and been baptized are "eternally secure." The result is that some people who are not genuinely converted at all may "come forward" at the end of an evangelistic sermon to profess faith in Christ, and may be baptized shortly after that, but then they leave the fellowship of the church and live a life no different from the one they lived before they gained this "eternal security." In this way people are given false assurance and are being cruelly deceived into thinking they are going to heaven when in fact they are not.[30]

QUESTIONS FOR PERSONAL APPLICATION

1. Do you have assurance that you are truly born again? What evidence do you see in your own life to give you that assurance? Do you think that God wants true believers to go on throughout life worrying about whether they are really born again, or to have firm assurance that they are his people? (See 1 John 5:13.) Have you seen a pattern of growth in your Christian life over time? Are you trusting in your own power to keep on believing in Christ, or in God's power to keep your faith active and alive?

2. If you have doubts about whether you are truly born again, what is it in your life that is giving reason for those doubts? What would Scripture encourage you to do to resolve those doubts (see 2 Peter 1:5–11; also Matt. 11:28–30; John 6:37)? Do you think that Jesus now knows about your doubts and understands them? What do you think he would like you to do now to gain greater assurance of salvation?

3. Have you known people, perhaps in your church, whose "fruit" is always destructive or divisive or harmful to the ministry of the church and the faith of others? Do they have very much influence, perhaps even positions of leadership in the church? Do you

---

[28]Cf. 1 Tim. 3:13, which says, that those who have "served well" as deacons gain "great assurance in their faith in Christ Jesus" (NIV).

think that an evaluation of the fruit of one's life and influence on others should be a qualification for church leadership? Is it possible that people would profess agreement with every true Christian doctrine and still not be born again? What are some more reliable evidences of genuine conversion other than intellectual adherence to sound doctrine?

SPECIAL TERMS

assurance of salvation
eternal security
perseverance of the saints

BIBLIOGRAPHY

Berkouwer, G. C. *Faith and Perseverance.* Trans. by Robert D. Knudsen. Grand Rapids: Eerdmans, 1958.

Carson, D. A. "Reflections on Christian Assurance." In *WTJ* 54 (1992), pp. 1–29.

Demarest, B. A. "Assurance." In *EDT,* pp. 91–92.

Grudem, Wayne. "The Perseverance of the Saints: A Case Study From Heb. 6:4–6 and the Other Warning Passages of Hebrews." In *Still Sovereign.* Ed. Tom Schreiner and Bruce Ware. Grand Rapids: Baker, 2000.

Guthrie, William. *The Christian's Great Interest.* London: Banner of Truth, 1969. See esp. Part I, *The Trial of a Saving Interest in Christ,* which was first published as a separate book in 1658.

Hoekema, Anthony A. "The Perseverance of True Believers." In *Saved by Grace.* Grand Rapids: Eerdmans, and Exeter: Paternoster, 1989, pp. 234–56.

Kearsley, R. "Perseverance." In *NDT,* pp. 506–7.

Marshall, I. H. *Kept by the Power of God.* Minneapolis: Bethany, 1969.

McKnight, Scot. "The Warning Passages of Hebrews," *TrinJ* 13, n.s. (1992), pp. 21–59.

Murray, John. "Perseverance." In *Redemption Accomplished and Applied.* Grand Rapids: Eerdmans, 1955, pp. 151–60.

Shank, Robert. *Life in the Son.* 2d ed. Minneapolis: Bethany, 1989.

White, R. E. O. "Perseverance." In *EDT,* pp. 844–45.

---

[29]Of course, both the Calvinist and the Arminian would allow for the possibility that the "backslidden" person is truly born again and had just fallen into sin and doubt. But both would agree that it is pastorally wise to assume that the person is not a Christian until some evidence of present faith is forthcoming.

[30]Of course, not all who use the phrase *eternal security* make mistakes of this sort, but the phrase is certainly open to such misunderstanding.

SCRIPTURE MEMORY PASSAGE

John 10:27–28: *My sheep hear my voice, and I know them, and they follow me; and I give them eternal life, and they shall never perish, and no one shall snatch them out of my hand.*

HYMN

"Call Jehovah Thy Salvation"

(Use tune of "Come, Thou Long Expected Jesus.")

Call Jehovah thy salvation, rest beneath th' Almighty's shade,
    In his secret habitation dwell, and never be dismayed:
There no tumult shall alarm thee, thou shalt dread no hidden snare:
    Guile nor violence can harm thee, in eternal safeguard there.

From the sword at noonday wasting, from the noisome pestilence,
    In the depth of midnight blasting, God shall be thy sure defence:
He shall charge his angel legions watch and ward o'er thee to keep;
    Though thou walk through hostile regions, though in desert
        wilds thou sleep.

Since, with pure and firm affection thou on God hast set thy love,
    With the wings of his protection he will shield thee from above:
Thou shalt call on him in trouble, he will hearken, he will save;
    Here for grief reward thee double, crown with life beyond
        the grave.

AUTHOR: JAMES MONTGOMERY, 1822

Chapter

DEATH AND THE INTERMEDIATE STATE

What is the purpose of death in the Christian life?
What happens to our bodies and souls
when we die?

EXPLANATION AND SCRIPTURAL BASIS

A. Why Do Christians Die?

Our treatment of the application of redemption must include a consideration of death and the question of how Christians should view their own death and the death of others. We also must ask what happens to us between the time that we die and the time that Christ returns to give us new resurrection bodies.

1. Death Is Not a Punishment for Christians. Paul tells us clearly that there is "no condemnation for those who are in Christ Jesus" (Rom. 8:1). All the penalty for our sins has been paid. Therefore, even though we know that Christians die, we should not view the death of Christians as a punishment from God or in any way a result of a penalty due to us for our sins.[1] It is true that the penalty for sin is death, but that penalty no longer applies to us—not in terms of physical death, and not in terms of spiritual death or separation from God. All of that has been paid for by Christ. Therefore there must be another reason than punishment for our sins if we are to understand why Christians die.

2. Death Is the Final Outcome of Living in a Fallen World. In his great wisdom, God decided that he would not apply to us the benefits of Christ's redemptive work all at once. Rather, he has chosen to apply the benefits of salvation to us gradually over time (as we have seen in chapters 4–11). Similarly, he has not chosen to remove all evil from the world immediately, but to wait until the final judgment and the establishment of the new heaven and new earth. In short, we still live in a fallen world and our experience of salvation is still incomplete.

The last aspect of the fallen world to be removed will be death. Paul says:

> Then comes the end, when he delivers the kingdom to God the Father after destroying every rule and every authority and power. For he must reign until he has put all his enemies under his feet. *The last enemy to be destroyed is death.* (1 Cor. 15:24–26)

When Christ returns,

> then shall come to pass the saying that is written:

> "Death is swallowed up in victory."
> "O death, where is your victory?
> O death, where is your sting?" (1 Cor. 15:54–55)

But until that time death remains a reality even in the lives of Christians. Although death does not come to us as a penalty for our individual sins (for that has been paid by Christ), it does come to us as a result of living in a fallen world, where the effects of sin have not all been removed. Related to the experience of death are other results of the fall that harm our physical bodies and signal the presence of death in

the world—Christians as well as non-Christians experience aging, illnesses, injuries, and natural disasters (such as floods, violent storms, and earthquakes). Although God often answers prayers to deliver Christians (and also non-Christians) from some of these effects of the fall for a time (and thereby indicates the nature of his coming kingdom), nevertheless, Christians eventually experience all of these things to some measure, and, until Christ returns, all of us will grow old and die. The "last enemy" has not yet been destroyed. And God has chosen to allow us to experience death before we gain all the benefits of salvation that have been earned for us.

3. God Uses the Experience of Death to Complete Our Sanctification. Throughout our Christian lives we know that we never have to pay any penalty for sin, for that has all been taken by Christ (Rom. 8:1). Therefore, when we do experience pain and suffering in this life, we should never think it is because God is *punishing* us (for our harm). Sometimes suffering is simply a result of living in a sinful, fallen world, and sometimes it is because God is *disciplining* us (for our good), but in all cases we are assured by Romans 8:28 that "God causes *all things* to work together for good to those who love God, to those who are called according to His purpose" (NASB).

---

[1]Even the death of some Corinthian Christians who had been abusing the Lord's Supper (1 Cor. 11:30) is viewed by Paul as a disciplining or chastening process, not as a result of condemnation: he says, "When we are judged by the Lord, we are being disciplined so that we will not be condemned with the world" (v. 32 NIV).

(In this discussion I am using the word *punishment* to mean retribution from God which is intended to do us harm, and *discipline* to mean hardship through which God intends to do us good.)

The positive purpose for God's discipline is clear in Hebrews 12, where we read:

> The Lord disciplines him whom he loves. . . . He disciplines us for our good, that we may share his holiness. For the moment all discipline seems painful rather than pleasant; later it yields the peaceful fruit of righteousness to those who have been trained by it. (Heb. 12:6, 10–11)

Not all discipline is in order to correct us from sins that we have committed; it can also be allowed by God to strengthen us in order that we may gain greater ability to trust God and resist sin in the challenging path of obedience. We see this clearly in the life of Jesus, who, though he was without sin, yet "learned obedience *through what he suffered*" (Heb. 5:8). He was made perfect *"through suffering"* (Heb. 2:10). Therefore we should see all the hardship and suffering that comes to us in life as something that God brings to us *to do us good,* strengthening our trust in him and our obedience, and ultimately increasing our ability to glorify him.

Consequently, we should view the aging and weakness and sometimes sickness leading up to death as another kind of discipline that God allows us to go through in order that through this process our sanctification might be furthered and ultimately completed when we go to be in the Lord's presence. The challenge that Jesus gives to the church in Smyrna could really be given to every believer: *"Be faithful unto death,* and I will give you the crown of life" (Rev. 2:10). Paul says his goal in life is that he may become like Christ: "that I may know him and the power of his resurrection, and may share his sufferings, *becoming like him in his death"* (Phil. 3:10). Paul thought about the way in which Jesus died, and made it his goal to exemplify the same characteristics in his life when it came time for him to die—that in whatever circumstances he found himself, he, like Christ, would continue obeying God, trusting God, forgiving others, and caring for the needs of those around him, thus in every way bringing glory to God even in his death. Therefore when in prison, without knowing whether he would die there or come out alive, he could still say, "it is my eager expectation and hope that I shall not be at all ashamed, but that with full courage now as always *Christ will be honored* in my body, whether by life *or by death"* (Phil. 1:20).

The understanding that death is not in any way a punishment for sin, but simply something God brings us through in order to make us more like Christ, should be a great encouragement to us. It should take away from us the fear of death that haunts the minds of unbelievers (cf. Heb. 2:15). Nevertheless, although God will bring good to us through the process of death, we must still remember that death is not natural; it is not right; and in a world created by God it is something that ought not to be. It is an enemy, something that Christ will finally destroy (1 Cor. 15:26).

4. Our Experience of Death Completes Our Union With Christ. Another reason why God allows us to experience death, rather than taking us immediately to heaven when we become Christians, is that through death we imitate Christ in what he did and thereby experience closer union with him. Paul can say that we are fellow heirs with Christ "provided we *suffer with him* in order that we may also be glorified with him" (Rom. 8:17). And Peter tells his readers not to be surprised at the fiery testing that comes on them, but encourages them, "rejoice in so far as *you share Christ's sufferings,* that you may also rejoice and be glad when his glory is revealed" (1 Peter 4:13). As we noted above, such union with Christ in suffering includes union with him in death as well (see Phil. 3:10). Jesus is the "pioneer and perfecter of our faith" (Heb. 12:2), and we follow after him as we run the race of life. Peter writes, "Christ also suffered for you, leaving you an example, that you should follow in his steps" (1 Peter 2:21).

5. Our Obedience to God Is More Important Than Preserving Our Own Lives. If God uses the experience of death to deepen our trust in him and to strengthen our obedience to him, then it is important that we remember that the world's goal of preserving one's own physical life at all costs is not the highest goal for a Christian: obedience to God and faithfulness to him in every circumstance is far more important. This is why Paul could say, "I am ready not only to be imprisoned but even to die at Jerusalem for the name of the Lord Jesus" (Acts 21:13; cf. 25:11). He told the Ephesian elders, "I do not account my life of any value nor as precious to myself, if only I may accomplish my course and the ministry which I received from the Lord Jesus, to testify to the gospel of the grace of God" (Acts 20:24).

It was this conviction—that obedience to God is far more important than the preservation of life—that gave Paul courage to go back into the city of Lystra after he had just been stoned and left for dead (Acts 14:20), and then return there again shortly thereafter (Acts 14:21–22). He endured many sufferings and dangers (2 Cor. 11:23–27), often risking his life, in order to obey Christ fully. Therefore he could say at the end of his life, with a note of great triumph, "The time of my departure has come. *I have fought the good fight,* I have finished the race, I have kept the faith" (2 Tim. 4:6–7). This same conviction empowered Old Testament saints to accept martyrdom rather than sin: "Some were tortured, refusing to accept release, that they might rise again to a better life" (literally, "that they might obtain a better resurrection," Heb. 11:35). This conviction also gave Peter and the other apostles courage, when facing the threat of death, to say, "We must obey God rather than men" (Acts 5:29). Certainly this was the point of Jesus' command to the church at Smyrna, "*Be faithful unto death,* and I will give you the crown of life" (Rev. 2:10). We also read that there will be rejoicing in heaven when the faithful saints have conquered the devil "by the blood of the Lamb and by the word of their testimony, for *they loved not their lives even unto death*" (Rev. 12:11).

The persuasion that we may honor the Lord even in our death, and that faithfulness to him is far more important than preserving our lives, has given courage and motivation to martyrs throughout the history of the church. When faced with a choice of preserving their own lives and sinning, or giving up their own lives and being faithful, they chose to give up their own lives—"they loved not their lives even unto death" (Rev. 12:11). Even in times where there is little persecution and little likelihood of martyrdom, it would be good for us to fix this truth in our minds once for all, for if we are willing to give up even our lives for faithfulness to God, we shall find it much easier to give up everything else for the sake of Christ as well.

B. How Should We Think of Our Own Death and the Death of Others?

1. Our Own Death. The New Testament encourages us to view our own death not with fear but with joy at the prospect of going to be with Christ. Paul says, "We would rather be away from the body and at home with the Lord" (2 Cor. 5:8). When he is in prison, not knowing whether he will be executed or released, he can say:

> For to me to live is Christ, and *to die is gain.* If it is to be life in the flesh, that means fruitful labor for me. Yet which I shall choose I cannot tell. I am hard pressed between the two. *My desire is to depart and be with Christ,* for that is far better. (Phil. 1:21–23)

We also read John's word in Revelation, "And I heard a voice from heaven saying, 'Write this: Blessed are the dead who die in the Lord henceforth.' 'Blessed indeed,' says the Spirit, 'that they may rest from their labors, for their deeds follow them!'" (Rev. 14:13).

Believers need have no fear of death, therefore, for Scripture reassures us that not even "death" will "separate us from the love of God in Christ Jesus our Lord" (Rom. 8:38–39; cf. Ps. 23:4). In fact, Jesus died in order that he might "deliver all those who through fear of death were subject to lifelong bondage" (Heb. 2:15).[2] This verse reminds us that a clear testimony to our lack of fear of death will provide a strong witness for Christians in an age that tries to avoid talking about death and has no answer for it.

2. The Death of Christian Friends and Relatives. While we can look forward to our own death with a joyful expectation of being in Christ's presence, our attitude will be somewhat different when we experience the death of Christian friends and relatives. In these cases we will experience genuine sorrow—but mixed with joy that they have gone to be with the Lord.

It is not wrong to express real sorrow at the loss of fellowship with loved ones who have died, and sorrow also for the suffering and hardship that they may have gone through prior to death. Sometimes Christians think it shows lack of faith if they mourn deeply for a brother or sister Christian who has died. But Scripture does not support that view, because when Stephen was stoned, we read that "Devout men buried Stephen, *and made great lamentation over him*" (Acts 8:2). If there ever was certainty that someone went to be with the Lord, it occurred in the case of Stephen. As he died, he said, "Behold, I see the heavens opened, and the Son of man standing at the right hand of God" (Acts 7:56). Then when he was dying, he prayed, "Lord Jesus, receive my spirit," and, "Lord, do not hold this sin against them" (Acts 7:59–60). And this occurred in Jerusalem, with all the apostles still present, those apostles who had seen Jesus himself after he had been raised from the dead. There was no lack of faith on anyone's part that Stephen was in heaven experiencing great joy in the presence of the Lord. Yet in spite of this, "Devout men buried Stephen, *and made great lamentation over him*" (Acts 8:2). Their sorrow showed the genuine grief that they felt at the loss of fellowship with someone whom they loved, and it was not wrong to express this sorrow—it was right. Even Jesus, at the tomb of Lazarus, "wept" (John 11:35), experiencing sorrow at the fact that Lazarus had died, that his sisters and others were experiencing such grief, and also, no doubt, at the fact that there was death in the world at all, for ultimately it is unnatural and ought not to be in a world created by God.

The Ephesian elders, whom Paul had taught personally for three years, later "*wept* and embraced Paul and kissed him, sorrowing most of all because of the word he had spoken, that they should see his face no more" (Acts 20:37–38). And Paul himself, in the same letter in which he expressed such a desire to depart from this life and be with Christ, said that if Epaphroditus had died, he himself would have had "*sorrow upon sorrow*" (Phil. 2:27). Moreover, King David, the man after God's own heart, the man who in his psalms frequently spoke of living forever with God, nonetheless had great sorrow when he learned that Saul and Jonathan had died (2 Sam. 1:11–27).

Nevertheless, the sorrow that we feel is clearly mingled with hope and joy. Paul does not tell the Thessalonians that they should not grieve *at all* concerning their loved ones who have died, but he writes, "that you may not grieve *as others do* who have no hope" (1 Thess. 4:13) — they should not grieve in the same way, with the same bitter despair, that unbelievers have. But certainly they should grieve. He assures them that Christ "died for us so that whether we wake or sleep we might live with him" (1 Thess. 5:10), and thereby encourages them that those who have died have gone to be with the Lord. That is why Scripture can say, "Blessed are the dead who die in the Lord henceforth . . . that they may rest from their labors" (Rev. 14:13). In fact, Scripture even tells us, "Precious in the sight of the LORD is the death of his saints" (Ps. 116:15).

Therefore, though we have genuine sorrow when Christian friends and relatives die, we also can say with Scripture, "O death, where is your victory? O death, where is your sting? . . . Thanks be to God, who gives us the victory through our Lord Jesus Christ" (1 Cor. 15:55–57). Though we mourn, our mourning should be mixed with worship of God and thanksgiving for the life of the loved one who has died. Worship is especially important at this time, as we see in the examples of David and of Job. When David's child died, he stopped praying for the child's health, and worshiped God: "Then David arose from the earth, and washed, and anointed himself, and changed his clothes; and he went into the house of the Lord, *and worshiped*" (2 Sam. 12:20).

Similarly, when Job heard of the death of his ten children,

> Then Job arose, and rent his robe, and shaved his head, and fell upon the ground, *and worshiped*. And he said, "Naked I came from my mother's womb, and naked shall I return; the LORD gave, and the LORD has taken away; blessed be the name of the LORD." (Job 1:20–21)

3. The Death of Unbelievers. When unbelievers die, the sorrow we feel is not mingled with the joy of assurance that they have gone to be with the Lord forever. This sorrow, especially regarding those we have been close to, is very deep and real. Paul himself, when thinking about some of his Jewish brothers who had rejected Christ, said, "I am speaking the truth

---

[2]Louis Berkhof is certainly correct to say that the burial of Jesus "did not merely serve to prove that Jesus was really dead, but also to remove the terrors of the grave for the redeemed and to sanctify the grave for them" (*Systematic Theology* [Grand Rapids: Eerdmans, 1939, 1941], p. 340).

in Christ, I am not lying; my conscience bears me witness in the Holy Spirit, that *I have great sorrow and unceasing anguish in my heart.* For I could wish that I myself were accursed and cut off from Christ for the sake of my brethren, my kinsmen by race" (Rom. 9:1–3).

Yet it also must be said that we often do not have absolute certainty that a person has persisted in refusal to trust in Christ all the way to the point of death. The knowledge of one's impending death often will bring about genuine heart searching on the part of the dying person, and sometimes words of Scripture or words of Christian testimony that have been heard long ago will be recalled and the person may come to genuine repentance and faith. Certainly, we do not have any assurance that this has happened unless there is explicit evidence for it, but it is also good to realize that in many cases we have only probable but not absolute knowledge that those whom we have known as unbelievers have persisted in their unbelief until the point of death. In some cases we simply do not know.

Nevertheless, after a non-Christian has died, it would be wrong to give any indication to others that we think that person has gone to heaven. This would simply be to give misleading information and false assurance, and to diminish the urgency of the need for those who are still alive to trust in Christ. It is much better, as we have opportunity, to focus on the fact that the sorrow that we feel at the loss of someone whom we love causes us to reflect on our own life and destiny as well. In fact, the times when we are able to talk as a friend to the loved ones of an unbeliever who has died are often times when the Lord will open up opportunities to talk about the gospel with those who are still living.

Moreover, it is often very helpful in such circumstances to speak with genuine thankfulness about the good qualities that we have noticed and been encouraged by in the life of the person who has died.[3] A good example of that is seen in David's reaction when King Saul died. Even though Saul had become an evil king and had pursued David and tried to kill him many times, once Saul had died, David spoke freely and publicly about the good things Saul had done:

> Your glory, O Israel, is slain upon your high places! How are the mighty fallen! . . . Saul and Jonathan . . . they were swifter than eagles, they were stronger than lions. You daughters of Israel, weep over Saul, who clothed you daintily in scarlet, who put ornaments of gold upon your apparel. How are the mighty fallen in the midst of battle! (2 Sam. 1:19–25)[4]

C. What Happens When People Die?

1. The Souls of Believers Go Immediately Into God's Presence. Death is a temporary cessation of bodily life and a separation of the soul from the body. Once a believer has died, though his or her physical body remains on the earth and is buried, at the moment of death the soul (or spirit) of that believer goes immediately into the presence of God with rejoicing. When Paul thinks about death he says, "We would rather be *away from the body and at home with the Lord*" (2 Cor. 5:8). To be away from the body is to be at home with the Lord. He also says that his desire is "to *depart and be with Christ,* for that is far better" (Phil. 1:23). And Jesus said to the thief who was dying on the cross next to him, "*Today* you will be with me in Paradise" (Luke 23:43).[5] The author of Hebrews says that when Christians come together to worship they come not only into the presence of God in heaven, but also into the presence of "the spirits of just men made perfect" (Heb. 12:23).[6] However, as we shall see in more detail in the next chapter, God will not leave our dead bodies in the earth forever, for when Christ returns the souls of believers will be reunited with their bodies, their bodies will be raised from the dead, and they will live with Christ eternally.

a. The Bible Does Not Teach the Doctrine of Purgatory: The fact that the souls of believers go immediately into God's presence means that *there is no such thing as purgatory.* In Roman Catholic teaching, purgatory is the place where the souls of believers go to be further purified from sin until they are ready to be admitted into heaven. According to this view, the sufferings of purgatory are given to God in substitute for the punishment for sins that believers should have received in time, but did not. Speaking of purgatory, Ott says:

> Suffrages operate in such a matter that the satisfactory value of the good works is offered to God in substitution for the temporal punishment for sins which the poor souls still have to render. It operates by way of remission of temporal punishments due to sins.[7]

But this doctrine is not taught in Scripture, and it is in fact contrary to the verses quoted immediately above. The Roman Catholic Church has found support for this doctrine, not in the pages of canonical Scripture, and as Protestants have accepted it since the Reformation, but in the writings of the Apocrypha, particularly in 2 Maccabees 12:42–45:

> [Judas Maccabeus, the leader of the Jewish forces] also took a collection, man by man, to the amount of 2,000 drachmas of silver, and sent it to Jerusalem to provide for a sin offering. In doing this he acted very well and honorably, taking into account the resurrection. For if he were not expecting that those who had fallen would rise again, it would have been superfluous and foolish *to pray for the dead.* But if he was looking to the splendid reward that is laid up for those who fall asleep in godliness, it was a holy and pious thought. Therefore *he made atonement for the dead, that they might be delivered from their sin.*

Here it is clear that prayer for the dead is approved, and also making an offering to God to deliver the dead from their sin. But in response it must be said that this literature is not equal to Scripture in authority, and should not be taken as an authoritative source of doctrine. Moreover, it contradicts the clear statements about departing and being with Christ quoted above, and thereby opposes the clear teaching of New Testament Scripture. Furthermore, when it talks about the offering of Judas making "atone-

---

[3]It is right to thank God for the benefits of common grace in the lives of unbelievers; see the discussion of common grace in chapter 2.

[4]Even this requires honesty and mature judgment, however, for if we are called upon to perform a funeral service for someone whose life has been widely known as evil and destructive, we do not want to give people the impression that what a person does in this life makes no difference, or that we are ignorant of the noticeably bad qualities of such a person, or we will lose credibility with those who hear us. As an example of the inevitable reaction of people to the death of someone clearly evil, such as Adolf Hitler, note Prov. 11:10, "When the wicked perish there are shouts of gladness."

ment [Gk. *exilasmos* ('propitiation')] for the dead" it contradicts the explicit teaching of the New Testament that Christ alone made atonement for us. Finally, this passage in 2 Maccabees is difficult to square even with Roman Catholic teaching, because it teaches that soldiers who had died in the mortal sin of idolatry (which cannot be forgiven, according to Catholic teaching) should have prayers and sacrifices offered for them with the possibility that they will be delivered from their suffering.

Roman Catholic theology finds support for the doctrine of purgatory primarily in the passage from 2 Maccabees quoted above, and in the teaching of the tradition of the church.[8] Other passages cited by Ott in support of the doctrine of purgatory are 2 Timothy 1:18; Matthew 5:26; 1 Corinthians 3:15; and Matthew 12:32. In 2 Timothy 1:18, Paul says, concerning Onesiphorus, "When he arrived in Rome he searched for me eagerly and found me—may the Lord grant him to find mercy from the Lord on that Day—and you well know all the service he rendered at Ephesus" (2 Tim. 1:17–18). The claim of those who find support for the doctrine of purgatory is that "Onesiphorus . . . apparently was no longer among the living at the time of the Second Epistle to Timothy."[9] This seems to be based on the fact that Paul refers not to Onesiphorus himself but "the household of Onesiphorus" (2 Tim. 1:16); however, that phrase does not prove that Onesiphorus had died, but only that Paul was wishing blessings not only on him but on his entire household. This would not be unusual since Onesiphorus had served in Ephesus where Paul had worked for three years (2 Tim. 1:18; cf. 4:19). To build support for purgatory on the idea that Onesiphorus had already died is simply to build it on an assumption that cannot be supported with clear evidence. (It is not unusual for Paul to express a wish that some Christians would be blessed in the Day of Judgment—see 1 Thess. 5:23.)

In Matthew 12:32, Jesus says, "Whoever speaks against the Holy Spirit will not be forgiven, either in this age or in the age to come." Ott says that this sentence "leaves open the possibility that sins are forgiven not only in this world but in the world to come."[10] However, this is simply an error in reasoning: to say that something will not happen in the age to come does not imply that it might happen in the age to come![11] What is needed to prove the doctrine of purgatory is not a negative statement such as this but a positive statement that says that people suffer for the purpose of continuing purification after they die. But Scripture nowhere says this.

In 1 Corinthians 3:15 Paul says that on the Day of Judgment, the work that everyone has done will be judged and tested by fire, and then says, "*If any man's work is burned up, he will suffer loss, though he himself will be saved, but only as through fire.*" But this

---

[5]Paradise is simply another name for heaven.

[6]It must be said, however, that the fact that we go to be with Christ immediately when we die should not be taken as an encouragement to anyone to think that suicide would be right. God says, "You shall not murder" (Ex. 20:13 NIV), and that means that we must not murder ourselves any more than we should murder others.

On the other hand, there are many faithful Christians who in wartime or shipwrecks or other trying circumstances have laid down their own lives for the sake of others, thus fulfilling Jesus' teaching, "Greater love has no man than this, that a man lay down his life for his friends" (John 15:13).

The larger principle is that as long as we remain in this life we are to be faithful to Christ in serving him and in prayer, for he calls us to be "faithful unto death" (Rev. 2:10). And though Paul, in thinking about his own personal desires, wanted to go to be with Christ, he realized that for the sake of the Philippians and for others that he ministered to, to stay alive would be "more necessary" on their behalf (Phil. 1:24).

[7]Ludwig Ott, *Fundamentals of Catholic Dogma*, trans. Patrick Lynch (Rockford, Ill.: TAN, 1960), p. 322.

does not speak of a *person* being burned or suffering punishment, but simply of *his work* as being tested by fire—that which is good will be like gold, silver, and precious stones that will last forever (v. 12). Moreover, Ott himself admits that this is something that occurs not during this age but during the day of "the general judgment,"[12] and this further indicates that it can hardly be used as a convincing argument for purgatory. Finally, in Matthew 5:26, after warning people to make friends quickly with their accusers while they are going to the court, lest the accuser hand them to the judge and the judge to the guard and they be put in prison, Jesus then says, "You will never get out till you have paid the last penny." Ott understands this as a parable teaching a "time-limited condition of punishment in the other world."[13] But surely there is no indication in context that this is a parable—Jesus is giving practical teaching about reconciliation of human conflicts and the avoidance of situations that naturally lead to anger and personal injury (see Matt. 5:21–26). Other passages of Scripture that have sometimes been referred to in support of the doctrine of purgatory[14] simply do not speak directly about this idea at all, and can all easily be understood in terms of punishment and deliverance from distress in this life, or of a life of eternal blessing with God in heaven in the life to come.

An even more serious problem with this doctrine is that it teaches that we must add something to the redemptive work of Christ, and that his redemptive work for us was not enough to pay the penalty for all our sins. But this is certainly contrary to the teaching of Scripture. Moreover, in a pastoral sense, the doctrine of purgatory robs believers of the great comfort that should be theirs in knowing that those who have died have immediately gone into the presence of the Lord, and knowing that they also, when they die, will "depart and be with Christ, for that is far better" (Phil. 1:23).

b. The Bible Does Not Teach the Doctrine of "Soul Sleep": The fact that souls of believers go immediately into God's presence also means that *the doctrine of soul sleep is incorrect.* This doctrine teaches that when believers die they go into a state of unconscious existence, and the next thing that they are conscious of will be when Christ returns and raises them to eternal life. This doctrine has been taught occasionally by one person or another in the history of the church, including some Anabaptists at the Reformation, and some of the Irvingites in England in the nineteenth century. In fact, one of John Calvin's first writings was a tract against this doctrine, a doctrine that has never found wide acceptance in the church.

Support for the doctrine of soul sleep has generally been found in the fact that Scripture several times speaks of the state of death as "sleep" or "falling asleep" (Matt. 9:24; 27:52; John 11:11; Acts 7:60; 13:36; 1 Cor. 15:6, 18, 20, 51; 1 Thess. 4:13; 5:10). Moreover, certain passages seem to teach that the dead do not have a conscious existence (see Pss. 6:5; 115:17 [but see v. 18!]; Eccl. 9:10; Isa. 38:19). But when Scripture represents death as "sleep" it is simply a metaphorical expression used to indicate that death is only temporary for Christians, just as sleep is temporary. This is clearly seen, for example, when Jesus tells his disciples about the death of Lazarus. He says, "Our friend Lazarus has fallen asleep, but

---

[8]Ibid., pp. 321–22, 482–85.

[9]Ibid., p. 321.

[10]Ibid., p. 483.

[11]This is a similar mistake to the one made by those who argue that, since Jesus says he will not blot someone's name out of the book of life (Rev. 3:5), it implies that he might blot the names of others out of the book of life (see chapter 11, p. 169).

[12]Ott, *Fundamentals of Catholic Dogma*, p. 483.

I go to awake him out of sleep" (John 11:11). We should notice that Jesus does not here say, "The soul of Lazarus is sleeping," nor, in fact, does any passage in Scripture say that the soul of a person is sleeping or unconscious (a statement that would be necessary to prove the doctrine of soul sleep). Rather Jesus simply says that *Lazarus* has fallen asleep. Then John explains, "Now Jesus had spoken of his death, but they thought that he meant taking rest in sleep. Then Jesus told them plainly, 'Lazarus is dead'" (John 11:12–13). The other passages that speak about people sleeping when they die are likewise to be interpreted as simply a metaphorical expression to teach that death is temporary.

As for the passages that indicate that the dead do not praise God, or that there is a ceasing of conscious activity when people die, these are all to be understood from the perspective of life in this world. From our perspective it appears that once people die, they do not engage in these activities any longer. But Psalm 115 presents the full biblical perspective on this viewpoint. It says, "The dead do not praise the LORD, nor do any that go down into silence." But then it continues in the very next verse with a contrast indicating that those who believe in God will bless the LORD forever: *"But we will bless the LORD from this time forth and for evermore.* Praise the LORD!" (Ps. 115:17–18).

Finally, the passages quoted above demonstrating that the souls of believers go immediately into God's presence and enjoy fellowship with him there (2 Cor. 5:8; Phil. 1:23; Luke 23:43; and Heb. 12:23) all indicate that there is conscious existence and fellowship with God immediately after death for the believer. Jesus did not say, "Today you will no longer have consciousness of anything that is going on," but, "Today *you will be with me in Paradise*" (Luke 23:43). Certainly the conception of paradise understood at that time was not one of unconscious existence but one of great blessing and joy in the presence of God.[15] Paul did not say, "My desire is to depart and be unconscious for a long period of time," but rather, "My desire is to depart *and be with Christ*" (Phil. 1:23)—and he certainly knew that Christ was not an unconscious, sleeping Savior, but one who was actively living and reigning in heaven. To be with Christ was to enjoy the blessing of fellowship in his presence, and that is why to depart and be with him was "far better" (Phil. 1:23). That is why he says, "We would rather be away from the body and at home with the Lord" (2 Cor. 5:8).

The fact that Hebrews 12:1 says, "We are surrounded by so great a cloud of witnesses," just after an entire chapter spent on the discussion of the faith of Old Testament saints who had died (Heb. 11), and the fact that the author encourages us to run the race of life with perseverance because we are surrounded by this great cloud of witnesses, both suggest that those who have died and gone before have some awareness of what is going on in the earth. Scripture says very little about this, probably because it does not want us to speak to those who have died or to pray to them or to contact them in any way (note Saul's great sin in this in 1 Sam. 28:7–25). Nonetheless, Hebrews 12:1–2 does give us this slight hint, probably as an encouragement to us to continue also to be faithful to God as were those who have died and gone to heaven before us. Similarly, at the end of Hebrews 12, the author tells us that when we worship we come into the presence of God in heaven, and we come not to "the

---

[13]Ibid. p. 484.

[14]Berkhof mentions that Roman Catholics have some-   1 Cor. 15:29.
times referred to Isa. 4:4; Mic. 7:8; Zech. 9:11; Mal. 3:2–3; and

spirits of just men who are sleeping in an unconscious state" but "to innumerable angels in festal gathering, and to the assembly of the first-born who are enrolled in heaven, and to a judge who is God of all, and to the spirits of just men made perfect, and to Jesus, the mediator of a new covenant" (Heb. 12:22–24).[16]

Revelation 6:9–11 and 7:9–10 also clearly show the souls or spirits of those who have died and who have gone to heaven praying and worshiping, for they cry out with a loud voice, "O Sovereign Lord, holy and true, how long before you will judge and avenge our blood on those who dwell upon the earth?" (Rev. 6:10), and they are seen "standing before the throne and before the Lamb, clothed in white robes, with palm branches in their hands, and crying out with a loud voice, 'Salvation belongs to our God who sits upon the throne, and to the Lamb!'" (Rev. 7:9–10). All of these passages deny the doctrine of soul sleep, for they make it clear that the souls of believers experience conscious fellowship with God in heaven immediately upon death.

c. Did Old Testament Believers Enter Immediately Into God's Presence? Some have said that, although the souls of believers *since Christ's resurrection* go immediately into God's presence in heaven, the souls of believers who died *before Christ's resurrection* did not enjoy the blessings of heaven but went into a place of waiting for Christ's work of redemption to be complete. Sometimes this is called the *limbus patrum,* or simply limbo.[17] This view has been especially common in Roman Catholic theology, but it has also been held by some Lutherans. Some of the support for this doctrine comes from a particular view of the idea of Christ's descent into hell.

Not many Scripture references talk about the state of Old Testament believers after they had died, but those that give us any indication of their state all point in the direction of immediate conscious enjoyment in the presence of God, not of a time of waiting away from God's presence. "Enoch walked with God; and he was not, for *God took him*" (Gen. 5:24; cf. Heb. 11:5). Elijah was not taken to a place on the border of hell, but he "went up by a whirlwind *into heaven*" (2 Kings 2:11; cf. Matt. 17:3, where Moses and Elijah appear, talking with Jesus). And David is confident that he will "*dwell in the house of the LORD for ever*" (Ps. 23:6; cf. 16:10–11; 17:15; 115:18). Moreover, when Jesus answers the Sadducees, he reminds them that God says, "I am the God of Abraham, and the God of Isaac, and the God of Jacob" and then says, "He is not God of the dead, but of the living" (Matt. 22:32), thus implying that Abraham, Isaac, and Jacob were living even at that very moment, and that God was their God. Moreover, in the story of the rich man and Lazarus, Jesus does not say that Lazarus is unconscious, but reports Abraham as saying about Lazarus, "Now he is comforted here" (Luke 16:25). Abraham himself is portrayed as dwelling consciously in a place that is very desirable—that the rich man longed to go to—certainly not a place on the fringe of hell. It is important to notice that since this is before Christ's resurrection, Lazarus was in the same situation as the Old Testament saints.

---

[15]See the other uses of the word *Paradise* in 2 Cor. 12:3 and Rev. 2:7, where the word clearly refers to heaven itself where God is and lives and reigns.

Therefore it seems likely that Old Testament believers also entered immediately into heaven and enjoyed a time of fellowship with God upon their death. However, it may well have been true that additional rich blessings and much greater rejoicing came to them when Christ returned to heaven at his ascension. But this does not mean that they were transported to heaven for the first time, or that that was the first time they enjoyed the blessing of God's presence.

d. Should We Pray for the Dead? Finally, the fact that the souls of believers go immediately into God's presence means that *we should not pray for the dead*. Although this idea is taught in 2 Maccabees 12:42–45 (see above), it is nowhere taught in the Bible itself. Moreover, there is no indication that this was the practice of any Christians at the time of the New Testament, nor should it have been. Once *believers* die they enter into God's presence and they are in a state of perfect happiness with him. What good would it do to pray for them anymore? Final heavenly reward will be based on deeds done in this life, as Scripture repeatedly testifies (1 Cor. 3:12–15; 2 Cor. 5:10, et al.). Further, the souls of *unbelievers* who die go to a place of punishment and eternal separation from the presence of God. It would do no good to pray for them either, since their final destiny has been settled by their sin and their rebellion against God in this life. To pray for the dead therefore is simply to pray for something that God has told us has already been decided.[18] Moreover, to teach that we should pray for the dead, or to encourage others to do so, would be to encourage false hope that the destinies of people might be changed after they die, something which Scripture nowhere encourages us to think. It may lead people to much useless anxiety and much time essentially wasted in prayers that will have absolutely no results, and will thereby divert attention from prayers that could be made for events for this life and could have great effect in advancing the work of the kingdom. We should spend time praying according to God's will.

2. The Souls of Unbelievers Go Immediately to Eternal Punishment. Scripture never encourages us to think that people will have a second chance to trust in Christ after death. In fact, the situation is quite the contrary. Jesus' story about the rich man and Lazarus gives no hope that people can cross from hell to heaven after they have died: though the rich man in hell called out, "Father Abraham, have mercy upon me, and send Lazarus to dip the end of his finger in water and cool my tongue; for I am in anguish in this flame," Abraham replied to him, "Between us and you a great chasm has been fixed, in order that those who would pass from here to you may not be able, and *none may cross from there to us*" (Luke 16:24–26).

---

[16]The phrase "the communion of saints" in the Apostles' Creed refers to the fact that we have in some sense a communion or fellowship with those who have died and gone before into heaven, an idea that is affirmed in Heb. 12:23. This does not imply that we can be aware of them, but simply that when we worship we join in worship that is already going on in heaven.

[17]Strictly speaking, Roman Catholic theologians have held that there are two limbos, a place where unbaptized infants go when they die called *limbus infantum,* and a place where Old Testament believers went when they died called *limbus patrum.* The Latin word *limbus* means "border"; these were thought to be places on the border of hell where people were excluded from the presence of God but also did not experience conscious suffering. There is no explicit support in Scripture for either doctrine.

The book of Hebrews connects death with the consequence of judgment in close sequence: "just as it is appointed for men to die once, and after that comes judgment . . ." (Heb. 9:27). Moreover, Scripture never represents the final judgment as depending on anything done after we die, but only on what has happened in this life (Matt. 25:31–46; Rom. 2:5–10; cf. 2 Cor. 5:10). Some have argued for a second chance to believe in the gospel on the basis of Christ's preaching to the spirits in prison in 1 Peter 3:18–20 and the preaching of the gospel "even to the dead" in 1 Peter 4:6, but those are inadequate interpretations of the verses in question, and, on closer inspection, do not support such a view.[19]

We should also realize that the idea that there will be a second chance to accept Christ after death is based on the assumption that everyone deserves a chance to accept Christ and that eternal punishment only comes to those who consciously decide to reject him. But certainly that idea is not supported by Scripture: we all are sinners by nature and choice, and no one actually deserves any of God's grace or deserves any opportunity to hear the gospel of Christ—those come only because of God's unmerited favor. Condemnation comes not only because of a willful rejection of Christ, but also because of the sins that we have committed and the rebellion against God that those sins represent (see John 3:18).

The idea that people have a second chance to accept Christ after death would also destroy most motivation for evangelism and missionary activity today, and is not consistent with the intense missionary zeal that was felt by the New Testament church as a whole, and that was especially exemplified in the missionary travels of the apostle Paul.

The fact that there is conscious punishment for unbelievers after they die and that this punishment goes on forever is certainly a difficult doctrine for us to contemplate. But the passages teaching it appear so clear that it seems that we must affirm it if we are to affirm what Scripture teaches. Jesus says that at the day of final judgment he will say to those at his left hand, "Depart from me, you cursed, into the *eternal fire* prepared for the devil and his angels," and he says that "they will go away into *eternal punishment,* but the righteous into eternal life" (Matt. 25:41, 46).

These passages show that we cannot accept as faithful to Scripture the doctrine of *annihilationism.* This is a doctrine that says that unbelievers, either immediately upon death, or else after suffering for a period of time, will simply cease to exist—God will "annihilate" them and they will no longer be. Although the idea initially sounds attractive to us, and it avoids the emotional difficulty connected with affirming eternal conscious punishment for the wicked, such an idea is not explicitly affirmed in any passages of Scripture, and seems so clearly to be contradicted by those passages that connect the eternal blessing of the righteous with the eternal punishment of the wicked (Matt. 25:46) and that talk about punishment extending to the wicked day and night forever (Rev. 14:11; 20:10).

Although unbelievers pass into a state of eternal punishment immediately upon death, their bodies will not be raised until the day of final judgment. On that day, their bodies will be raised and reunited with their souls, and they will stand before God's throne for final

---

[18]Further indication that it is not right to pray for the dead is seen in the fact that David prayed intensely for his little son before that son died, but after he had died, David rose from prayer and washed and changed his clothes and "went into the house of the Lord and worshiped . . . and he ate" (2 Sam. 12:20; cf. v. 23). David realized that once the child had died his task of praying for him was done. When I speak of "praying for the dead" in this section, I mean praying that God would change their status or destiny. Of course there is nothing wrong with *thanking God* for the lives of people after they have died.

judgment to be pronounced upon them in the body (see Matt. 25:31–46; John 5:28–29; Acts 24:15; and Rev. 20:12, 15).

QUESTIONS FOR PERSONAL APPLICATION

1. Have you thought very much about the possibility of your own death? Has there been an element of fear connected with those thoughts? What, if anything, do you fear about death? Do you think that these fears have come from the influence of the world around you or from Scripture? How would the teachings of Scripture encourage you to deal with these fears?

2. Has this chapter changed your feelings about your own death in any way? Can you honestly contemplate it now as something that will bring you nearer to Christ and increase your own trust in God and faithfulness to him? How would you express your hopes regarding your own death?

3. Do you think you would have the courage to refuse to sin even if it meant being thrown to the lions in a Roman coliseum, or burned at the stake during the Reformation, or thrown in prison for years in some foreign country today? Do you think the Christian martyrs throughout history had thought that they would have enough courage when put to the test? What happened to them to equip them for this suffering (read 1 Cor. 10:13)? If you can obtain a copy, you may wish to read the account of the martyrdom of Polycarp, a stirring testimony of faith in God and of God's faithfulness in the second century A.D.[20] Have you settled in your own mind that obedience to Christ is more important than preserving your own life? What would make you hesitant to believe this or act on this conviction?

4. If you have experienced the death of a believer who was close to you, do you think that your reaction to that death was one of sorrow mingled with joy? How has this chapter influenced the way you feel about that situation, if at all?

5. Have you previously believed in the doctrine of purgatory? If you no longer believe in it now, can you describe the way the doctrine made you feel, and the way you now feel emotionally about the fact that that doctrine is not true and there is no such place as purgatory?

6. If death itself is viewed as part of the process of sanctification, then how should we view the process of growing older and weaker in this world? Is that the way the world views aging? What about you?

[19]See Wayne Grudem, *1 Peter,* TNTC (Grand Rapids: Eerdmans, 1988), pp. 155–62, 170–72, 203–39.

SPECIAL TERMS

annihilationism
communion of saints
death
limbo

limbus patrum
purgatory
soul sleep

BIBLIOGRAPHY

Beckwith, Roger T. "Purgatory." In *NDT*, pp. 549–50.

Cooper, John W. *Body, Soul and Life Everlasting: Biblical Anthropology and the Monism-Dualism Debate.* Grand Rapids: Eerdmans, 1989, pp. 81–103, 121–253.

Davids, P. H. "Death." In *EDT*, pp. 299–300.

Feinberg, John S. "1 Peter 3:18–20, Ancient Mythology, and the Intermediate State." *WTJ.* Vol. 48, no. 2 (Fall 1986), pp. 303–36.

Grudem, Wayne. "Christ Preaching Through Noah: 1 Peter 3:19–20 in the Light of Dominant Themes in Jewish Literature." In *The First Epistle of Peter.* Tyndale New Testament Commentaries. Leicester: Inter-Varsity Press, and Grand Rapids: Eerdmans, 1988, pp. 203–39.

Harris, Murray J. "Death." In *NDT*, p. 188.

_____. "Intermediate State." In *NDT*, pp. 339–40.

Hoekema, Anthony A. *The Bible and the Future.* Grand Rapids: Eerdmans, 1979, pp. 79–108.

Smith, S. M. "Intermediate State." In *EDT*, pp. 562–64.

SCRIPTURE MEMORY PASSAGE

Philippians 1:20–24: *As it is my eager expectation and hope that I shall not be at all ashamed, but that with full courage now as always Christ will be honored in my body, whether by life or by death. For to me to live is Christ, and to die is gain. If it is to be life in the flesh, that means fruitful labor for me. Yet which I shall choose I cannot tell. I am hard pressed between the two. My desire is to depart and be with Christ, for that is far better. But to remain in the flesh is more necessary on your account.*

HYMN

"My Jesus I Love Thee"

My Jesus, I love thee, I know thou art mine;

---

[20]One version of *The Martyrdom of Polycarp* is available in *The Apostolic Fathers,* 2 vols., ed. Kirsopp Lake, Loeb Classical Library (Cambridge, Mass.: Harvard University Press, 1913), pp. 307–45. It is also available in *The Ante-Nicene Fathers,* ed. A. Roberts and J. Donaldson (10 vols.; Grand Rapids: Eerdmans, 1979 [reprint]).

For thee all the follies of sin I resign.

My gracious Redeemer, my Savior art thou;

If ever I loved thee, my Jesus 'tis now.

I love thee because thou hast first loved me,

And purchased my pardon on Calvary's tree.

I love thee for wearing the thorns on thy brow;

If ever I loved thee, my Jesus, 'tis now.

I'll love thee in life, I will love thee in death;

And praise thee as long as thou lendest me breath;

And say, when the death-dew lies cold on my brow:

If ever I loved thee, my Jesus, 'tis now.

In mansions of glory and endless delight,

I'll ever adore thee in heaven so bright;

I'll sing with the glittering crown on my brow:

If ever I loved thee, my Jesus, 'tis now.

AUTHOR: WILLIAM R. FEATHERSTONE, 1864

Chapter

GLORIFICATION (RECEIVING A RESURRECTION BODY)

When will we receive resurrection bodies?
What will they be like?

EXPLANATION AND SCRIPTURAL BASIS

When Christ redeemed us he did not just redeem our spirits (or souls) — he redeemed us as whole persons, and this includes the redemption of our bodies. Therefore the application of Christ's work of redemption to us will not be complete until our bodies are entirely set free from the effects of the fall and brought to that state of perfection for which God created them. In fact, the redemption of our bodies will only occur when Christ returns and raises our bodies from the dead. But at this present time, Paul says that we wait for *"the redemption of our bodies,"* and then adds, "for in this hope we were saved" (Rom. 8:23–24). The stage in the application of redemption when we receive resurrection bodies is called *glorification.* Referring to that future day Paul says that we will be *"glorified* with him" (Rom. 8:17). Moreover, when Paul traces the steps in the application of redemption, the last one he names is glorification: "And those whom he predestined he also called; and those whom he called he also justified; and those whom he justified he also *glorified"* (Rom. 8:30).

The day we are glorified will be a day of great victory because on that day the last enemy, death, will be destroyed, just as Scripture predicts: "For he must reign until he has put all his enemies under his feet. The last enemy to be destroyed is death" (1 Cor. 15:25–26). In the context of a discussion of the resurrection of our bodies when Christ returns, Paul says, "Then shall come to pass the saying that is written: 'Death is swallowed up in victory.' 'O death, where is your victory? O death, where is your sting?'" (1 Cor. 15:54–55). When our bodies are raised from the dead we will experience complete victory over the death that came as a result of the fall of Adam and Eve. Then our redemption will be complete.

We may therefore define *glorification* as follows: *Glorification is the final step in the application of redemption. It will happen when Christ returns and raises from the dead the bodies of all believers for all time who have died, and reunites them with their souls, and changes the bodies of all believers who remain alive, thereby giving all believers at the same time perfect resurrection bodies like his own.*

A. New Testament Evidence for Glorification

The primary New Testament passage on glorification or the resurrection of the body is 1 Corinthians 15:12–58. Paul says, "So also in Christ shall all be made alive. But each in his own order: Christ the first fruits, then *at his coming* those who belong to Christ" (vv. 22–23).[1] Paul discusses the nature of the resurrection body in some detail in verses 35–50, which we will examine in section C below. He then concludes the passage by saying that not all Christians will die, but some who remain alive when Christ returns will simply have their bodies instantaneously changed into new, resurrection bodies that can never grow old or weak and can never die:

> Lo! I tell you a mystery. We shall not all sleep, but *we shall all be changed,* in a moment, in the twinkling of an eye, at the last trumpet. For the trumpet will sound, and the dead will be raised imperishable, and we shall be changed. (1 Cor. 15:51–52)

Paul further explains in 1 Thessalonians that the souls of those who have died and gone to be with Christ will come back and be joined with their bodies on that day, for Christ will bring them with him: "For since we believe that Jesus died and rose again, even so, through Jesus, *God will bring with him those who have fallen asleep*" (1 Thess. 4:14). But here Paul affirms not only that God will bring with Christ those who have died; he also affirms that *"the dead in Christ will rise first"* (1 Thess. 4:16). So these believers who have died with Christ are also raised up to meet Christ (Paul says in v. 17, "We . . . shall be caught up together with them in the clouds to meet the Lord in the air"). This only makes sense if it is the *souls* of believers who have gone into Christ's presence who return with him, and if it is their *bodies* that are raised from the dead to be joined together with their souls, and then to ascend to be with Christ.

In addition to these passages in 1 Corinthians 15 and 1 Thessalonians 4, several other New Testament passages affirm the reality of the doctrine of glorification. Jesus says, "The hour is coming when all who are in the tombs will hear his voice and come forth, those who have done good *to the resurrection of life,* and those who have done evil to the resurrection of judgment" (John 5:28–29).[2] Jesus also says, "This is the will of him who sent me, that I should lose nothing of all that he has given me, but *raise it up at the last day.* For this is the will of my Father, that every one who sees the Son and believes in him should have eternal life; and *I will raise him up at the last day*" (John 6:39–40; cf. vv. 44, 54).

Paul says, "He who raised Christ Jesus from the dead will *give life to your mortal bodies* also through his Spirit which dwells in you" (Rom. 8:11; cf. 2 Cor. 5:1–10). He realizes that Christians should live in eager expectation of Christ's return and of the change in our bodies to be like his own perfect body. He says, "But our commonwealth is in heaven, and from it we await a Savior, the Lord Jesus Christ, *who will change our lowly body to be like his glorious body,* by the power which enables him even to subject all things to himself" (Phil. 3:20–21).

B. Old Testament Support for Glorification

Sometimes people have claimed that the Old Testament has little if any evidence of hope in a future resurrection of the body, but there is in fact more Old Testament evidence for this than we might realize. First, even before Jesus was raised from the dead, the New Testament indicates that many Jewish people living at the time of Christ had some hope of a future bodily resurrection. When Jesus comes to the home of Lazarus after he had died and says to Martha, "Your brother will rise again," Martha responds, "I know that he will rise again *in the resurrection at the last day*" (John 11:23–24). Moreover, when Paul was on trial, he said to Felix that he had a "hope in God which these themselves [his Jewish accusers] accept, that *there will be a resurrection* of both the just and the unjust" (Acts 24:15).

As for the beliefs of those living in the time of the Old Testament, Hebrews 11 tells us that Abraham "looked forward to the city which has foundations, whose builder and maker is God" (Heb. 11:10). We also read that many Old Testament saints "all died in faith, not having received what was promised, but having seen it and greeted it from afar, and having acknowledged that they were strangers and exiles on the earth. . . . But as it is, *they desire a better country, that is, a heavenly one.* Therefore God is not ashamed to be called their God, for he has prepared for them a city" (Heb. 11:13–16). The author even says that Abraham "considered that God was able to raise men even from the dead" (Heb. 11:19).

When we look at the actual teachings of the Old Testament itself, there are indications that Old Testament authors had a strong expectation of the resurrection to come in the future. Job says: "I know that my Redeemer lives, and that in the end he will stand upon the earth. And after my skin has been destroyed, *yet in my flesh I will see God;* I myself will see him with my own eyes—I, and not another" (Job 19:25–26 NIV).[3]

We read in the Psalms, "But God will redeem my soul from the grave; he will surely take me to himself" (Ps. 49:15 NIV; cf. 73:24–25). And we read in Proverbs, "Do not withhold discipline from a child. . . . If you beat him with the rod you will save his life from Sheol" (Prov. 23:13–14). Isaiah says, "*Your dead shall live, their bodies shall rise*"

---

[1]Murray J. Harris argues for the possibility of an alternative view, based on his understanding of 2 Cor. 5:1–10: that Christians receive their resurrection bodies immediately after they die. See Harris, *From Grave to Glory: Resurrection in the New Testament* (Grand Rapids: Zondervan, 1990), pp. 207–10. But this view is exceptionally difficult to reconcile with 1 Cor. 15 and 1 Thess. 4: see the discussion in D. A. Carson, "Unity and Diversity in the New Testament: The Possibility of Systematic Theology," in *Scripture and Truth,* ed. D. A. Carson and John Woodbridge (Grand Rapids: Zondervan, 1983), pp. 85–86.

(Isa. 26:19). Daniel has a very explicit prophecy that *"many of those who sleep in the dust of the earth shall awake,* some to everlasting life, and some to shame and everlasting contempt" (Dan. 12:2). (Cf. also Ezekiel's vision of the dry bones in Ezek. 37:1–14.)

Although Old Testament believers certainly did not have as much detail about the nature of the resurrection or the way it would come about through the resurrection of the Messiah, and although they did not have as clear a basis for confidence in the resurrection as we do in the actual event of the bodily resurrection of Christ, nonetheless there was certainly, as we have seen, an expectation of a future day of bodily resurrection. People who for years had meditated on and believed these statements of Scripture (such as Martha in John 11:24) were prepared to receive the full-fledged New Testament teaching on the resurrection eagerly, for it simply provided more detail and more assurance for what they already had believed.

C. What Will Our Resurrection Bodies Be Like?

If Christ will raise our bodies from the dead when he returns, and if our bodies will be like his resurrection body (1 Cor. 15:20, 23, 49; Phil. 3:21), then what will our resurrection bodies be like?

Using the example of sowing a seed in the ground and then watching it grow into something much more wonderful, Paul goes on to explain in more detail what our resurrection bodies will be like:

> What is sown is perishable, what is raised is *imperishable.* It is sown in dishonor, it is raised *in glory.* It is sown in weakness, it is raised *in power.* It is sown a physical body, it is raised a *spiritual body.* . . . Just as we have borne the image of the man of dust, we shall also bear the image of the man of heaven. (1 Cor. 15:42–44, 49)

The fact that our new bodies will be "imperishable" means that they will not wear out or grow old or ever be subject to any kind of sickness or disease. They will be completely healthy and strong forever. Moreover, since the gradual process of aging is part of the process by which our bodies now are subject to "corruption," it is appropriate to think that our resurrection bodies will have no sign of aging, but will have the characteristics of youthful but mature manhood or womanhood forever. There will be no evidence of disease or injury, for all will be made perfect.[4] Our resurrection bodies will show the fulfillment of God's perfect wisdom in creating us as human beings who are the pinnacle of his creation and the appropriate bearers of his likeness and image. In these resurrection bodies we will clearly see humanity as God intended it to be.

Paul also says our bodies will be raised "in glory." When this term is contrasted with "dishonor," as it is here, there is a suggestion of the beauty or the attractiveness of appear-

---

[2]Some evangelical Christians hold that believers and unbelievers will be resurrected at the same time (this is the position taken by amillennialists). Others (especially premillennialists) hold that the resurrection of believers occurs before the millennium and the resurrection of the unbelievers for judgment occurs 1,000 years later, after the millennium.

[3]Several words in this passage are difficult to interpret, and there is scholarly debate over the question of whether Job is looking forward to seeing God in this life (as he does in 42:5) or after his death (note that Job expects his Redeemer to stand upon the earth "in the end," and expects to see God "in my flesh" but this will be "after my skin has been destroyed"). For a

ance that our bodies will have. They will no longer be "dishonorable" or unattractive, but will look "glorious" in their beauty. Moreover, because the word "glory" is so frequently used in Scripture of the bright shining radiance that surrounds the presence of God himself, this term suggests that there will also be a kind of brightness or radiance surrounding our bodies that will be an appropriate outward evidence of the position of exaltation and rule over all creation that God has given to us. This is also suggested in Matthew 13:43, where Jesus says, "Then *the righteous will shine like the sun* in the kingdom of their Father." Similarly, we read in Daniel's vision, "And *those who are wise shall shine like the brightness of the firmament;* and those who turn many to righteousness, like the stars for ever and ever" (Dan. 12:3, in a passage talking about the final resurrection). Now both of these statements might possibly be understood metaphorically, and in that case they would not indicate that an actual brightness or radiance will surround our resurrection bodies. But there is no reason in the context of either of them that would cause us to see them as metaphorical, and other pieces of evidence argue against doing so. The hints of the age to come that were seen in the shining of the glory of God from the face of Moses (Ex. 34:35), and, in a much greater way, the bright light that shone from Jesus at the transfiguration (Matt. 17:2), together with the fact that we will bear the image of Christ and be like him (1 Cor. 15:49), combine to suggest that there will actually be a visible brightness or radiance that surrounds us when we are in our resurrection bodies.[5]

Our bodies will also be raised "in power" (1 Cor. 15:43). This is in contrast to the "weakness" which we see in our bodies now. Our resurrection bodies will not only be free from disease and aging, they will also be given fullness of strength and power—not infinite power like God, of course, and probably not what we would think of as "superhuman" power in the sense possessed by the "superheroes" in modern fictional children's writing, for example, but nonetheless full and complete human power and strength, the strength that God intended human beings to have in their bodies when he created them. It will therefore be strength that is sufficient to do all that we desire to do in conformity with the will of God.

Finally, Paul says that the body is raised a "spiritual body" (1 Cor. 15:44). In the Pauline epistles, the word "spiritual" (Gk. *pneumatikos*) seldom means "nonphysical" but rather "consistent with the character and activity of the Holy Spirit" (see, for example, Rom. 1:11; 7:14; 1 Cor. 2:13, 15; 3:1; 14:37; Gal. 6:1 ["you who are spiritual"]; Eph. 5:19). The RSV translation, "It is sown a *physical* body, it is raised a *spiritual* body," is misleading, and a more clear paraphrase would be, "It is sown a *natural* body subject to the characteristics and desires of this age, and governed by its own sinful will, but it is raised a *spiritual* body, completely subject to the will of the Holy Spirit and responsive to the Holy Spirit's guidance." Such a body is not at all "nonphysical," but it is a physical body raised to the degree of perfection for which God originally intended it.

---

summary of the exegetical issues and a persuasive defense of the view that Job is looking forward to a physical resurrection after he dies, see Francis L. Andersen, *Job,* TOTC (Leicester: Inter-Varsity Press, 1976), pp. 193–94. The view that this passage looks forward to seeing God in this life only is largely based on some scholars' convictions that the idea of a future bodily resurrection was not found in Judaism until long after Job was written (but see Heb. 11:10, 19, commenting on Abraham's faith in the resurrection).

In conclusion, when Christ returns he will give us new resurrection bodies to be like his resurrection body. "When he appears *we shall be like him*" (1 John 3:2; this statement is true not only in an ethical sense but also in terms of our physical bodies; cf. 1 Cor. 15:49; also Rom. 8:29).

In spite of this strong New Testament emphasis on the similarity between our bodies and Jesus' body after the resurrection, some have objected that we will not have physical bodies because Paul says, "*Flesh and blood cannot inherit the kingdom of God,* nor does the perishable inherit the imperishable" (1 Cor. 15:50). This is in the very section in which he has been discussing the resurrection of the dead. But it is surely a misunderstanding to say that this verse implies that we shall not have physical bodies. When Paul says, "flesh and blood cannot inherit the kingdom of God," what he means by "flesh and blood" is *our present human nature,* particularly our physical bodies, as they are now existing in the likeness of Adam after the fall—that is, subject to weakness, decay, and ultimate death. This is the point he has made in the previous four verses (1 Cor. 15:45–49), in which he has been contrasting Adam with Christ. He explains, "As was the man of dust, so are those who are of the dust" (that is, we ourselves in this present age, 1 Cor. 15:48). Then he explains, "Just as we have borne the image of the man of dust, we shall also bear the image of the man of heaven" (1 Cor. 15:49). By "flesh and blood" here Paul means "*flesh and blood in the present state of existence* with a body like Adam's after the fall, a body that is subject to decay and death." He does not mean that we shall exist in a nonphysical state, for the entire heaven and earth will be made new and renewed for us to live in (Rom. 8:18–25), and we ourselves "shall all be changed, in a moment, in the twinkling of an eye, at the last trumpet" (1 Cor. 15:51–52). We will not cease to exist in physical bodies, but we will be changed and we will have an imperishable body, "For this perishable nature must put on the imperishable, and this mortal nature must put on immortality" (1 Cor. 15:53).

Moreover, the repeated instances in which Jesus demonstrated to the disciples that he had a physical body that was able to be touched, that had flesh and bones (Luke 24:39), and that could eat food, show that Jesus' body, which is our pattern, was clearly a physical body that had been made perfect.

What kind of continuity will there be between our present bodies and our future resurrection bodies? Will our bodies look exactly the same and have exactly the same characteristics, or will they be somewhat different, or will they be almost entirely different? Moreover, will our resurrection bodies be made of the same molecules of which our earthly bodies consist, or will they be an entirely new creation from God, or will they be some combination of old and new?

Several passages indicate that Paul expected a considerable measure of continuity between our present earthly bodies and our future resurrection bodies. Paul said, "He who raised Christ Jesus from the dead will give life to *your mortal bodies* also through his Spirit

---

[4]The fact that the scars of Jesus' nail prints remained on his hands is a special case to remind us of the price he paid for our redemption, and it should not be taken as an indication that any of our scars from physical injuries will remain.

[5]Jesus' body did not have a bright radiance surrounding it immediately after his resurrection, but when he returned to heaven and received from God the Father the glory that was rightfully his, then "his face was like the sun shining in full strength" (Rev. 1:16). Jesus at his transfiguration gave his disciples only a brief glimpse of the glory that was rightfully his and would be his again in heaven.

which dwells in you" (Rom. 8:11). He said that Jesus "will change *our lowly body* to be like his glorious body" (Phil. 3:21). And when Paul spoke about the nature of the resurrection body he gave an example of a seed sown in the ground: "What you sow is not the body which is to be, but a bare kernel, perhaps of wheat or of some other grain. But God gives it a body as he has chosen, and to each kind of seed its own body" (1 Cor. 15:37–38). In this example, he draws on common human knowledge that there are differences between what is sown and what is raised (vv. 42–44), but there is also continuity—just as a seed grows into a larger plant, retaining the matter that was in it but taking to itself other materials from the ground as well, so we will have continuity and differences as well. On this analogy we can say that *whatever remains in the grave from our own physical bodies* will be taken by God and transformed and used to make a new resurrection body. But the details of how that will happen remain unclear to us, since Scripture does not specify them—we are to affirm this because Scripture teaches it, even if we cannot fully explain how it can happen.[6]

Another indication of significant continuity between our present bodies and the bodies that we will have is seen in the fact that those believers who remain alive on the day Christ returns will "be changed"—yet their bodies will not be replaced: "We shall not all sleep, but we shall all be *changed,* in a moment, in the twinkling of an eye, at the last trumpet. For the trumpet will sound, and the dead will be raised imperishable, and we shall be changed. For this perishable nature must put on the imperishable, and this mortal nature must put on immortality" (1 Cor. 15:51–53).

We must also clearly note that Christ's own resurrection body, though it differed somewhat from the body he had before he died, so that the disciples did not immediately recognize him in every situation, was similar enough in appearance for the disciples to know who it was rather quickly. There were some instances when they did not immediately recognize him, but this may in part be accounted for by the fact that during his earthly life and ministry he had no doubt aged considerably, since he was "a man of sorrows and acquainted with grief" (Isa. 53:3). After his resurrection, Jesus would have been restored to full and perfect strength and youthfulness of appearance. Just as we sometimes do not immediately recognize a friend who has aged considerably since the last time we saw him or her, so the disciples may have had initial difficulty in recognizing Christ because the opposite of aging had occurred. On the other hand, significant continuity between Jesus' body before and after the resurrection is seen in the fact that even the nail prints in his hands and feet and the wound in his side remained in his resurrection body (John 20:20, 27).

Another piece of evidence indicating continuity between our earthly and heavenly bodies is the fact that apparently people will recognize and know one another in heaven. Jesus says that people will come from east and west and "sit at the table with Abraham, Isaac, and Jacob in the kingdom of heaven" (Matt. 8:11). Moreover, Elijah, who had been taken up to heaven in his earthly body, was somehow recognizable to the disciples on the Mount of Transfiguration (Luke 9:30, 33)—of course, the disciples had not known Elijah or Moses in the flesh, but somehow these men retained their personal identities in such a way that the disciples believed that they were there and that they were just as real as Jesus was (see Luke 9:33). Finally, Matthew tells us that when Jesus died, "the tombs also were opened, and many *bodies* of the saints who had fallen asleep were raised, and coming out of the tombs after his resurrection they went into the holy city and appeared to many" (Matt. 27:52–53). The fact that these people's actual bodies were raised, and the fact that they appeared to many in Jerusalem, indicates again that there was some continuity between their dead bodies that were in the graves and the bodies that were raised up. Since they came out of the tombs "after his resurrection" we may assume that these also were saints who had received resurrection bodies as a kind of foretaste of the final day of glorification when Christ returns.[7] The fact that these people "appeared to many" suggests that they were recognizable—that people knew who they were. Again the evidence is suggestive rather than conclusive, yet it points in the direction of continuity between the body that existed before the resurrection and the one that existed after it.

There is today some hesitancy on the part of many evangelicals to affirm clearly that there will be a "resurrection of the body," or at least that the body that is raised will be a material, physical body that is in some way continuous with the body that was placed in the grave. To some measure, this may be due to a sense of inability to understand how God could raise the same bodies from the grave, especially when some of those bodies have been dead for many centuries. Yet some of this hesitancy is probably also due to the continuing skepticism of unbelievers who challenge the Christian view with exactly the kind of problems just presented—does this not seem like a fantastic, unbelievable position? How could God bring about such a thing?

In both cases—whether the hesitancy comes from the honest questioning of the believer or from the hostile skepticism of the unbeliever—we should realize that our inability to understand or explain something should never be a reason for rejecting it if it is clearly taught in Scripture. The many passages cited above indicating that God will raise *our mortal bodies from the grave,* just as he raised Jesus' body from the grave, indicate quite conclusively that there will be a definite continuity between our present bodies and the bodies we have in the resurrection. And if that is what Scripture teaches, then, even though we may not understand exactly *how* God will bring this about in every case, we should still believe it. The God who created the universe and created each one of us, and who sovereignly rules over every bit of this creation at every moment, and who carries along all things by his word of power, can certainly keep track of the parts of our physical bodies that he wishes to preserve and use as the "seed" from which a new body will be made.

It is important to insist on the resurrection of a real, physical body, not only for the reasons above, but also because this provides a clear affirmation of the goodness of God's physical creation. We will live in bodies that have all the excellent qualities God created us to have, and thereby we will forever be living proof of the wisdom of God in making a material creation that from the beginning was "very good" (Gen. 1:31). We will live as resurrected believers in those new bodies, and they will be suitable for inhabiting the "new heavens and a new earth in which righteousness dwells" (2 Peter 3:13).

---

[6]Someone may object that some bodies completely decay, are absorbed into plants, and then eventually into other bodies, so that nothing of the first body can be found. But in response we must simply say that God can keep track of enough of the elements from each body to form a "seed" from which to form a new body (see Gen. 50:25; Job 19:26; Ezek. 37:1–14; Heb. 11:22).

D. The Entire Creation Will Be Renewed As Well

When Adam sinned God cursed the ground because of him (Gen. 3:17–19), so that it brought forth thorns and thistles and would only yield food useful for mankind by painful toil. But Paul says that "the creation itself will be set free from its bondage to decay and obtain the glorious liberty of the children of God" (Rom. 8:21). He explains that this will happen when we receive our resurrection bodies—in fact, he says that the creation is somehow longing for that day: "For the creation waits with eager longing for the revealing of the sons of God. . . . We know that the whole creation has been groaning in travail together until now; and not only the creation, but we ourselves, who have the first fruits of the Spirit, groan inwardly as we wait for adoption as sons, the redemption of our bodies" (Rom. 8:19, 22–23). In this renewed creation, there will be no more thorns or thistles, no more floods or droughts, no more deserts or uninhabitable jungles, no more earthquakes or tornadoes, no more poisonous snakes or bees that sting or mushrooms that kill. There will be a productive earth, an earth that will blossom and produce food abundantly for our enjoyment.

E. The Unbelieving Dead Will Be Raised for Judgment on the Day of Final Judgment

Although the emphasis of Scripture is on the fact that believers will experience a bodily resurrection, there are some passages that state that *unbelievers* will also be raised from the dead, but that they will face the final judgment at the time they are raised. Jesus clearly teaches that "those who have done evil" will come forth "to *the resurrection of judgment*" (John 5:29); Paul also said that he believed "that there will be a resurrection of both the just *and the unjust*" (Acts 24:15; cf. Matt. 25:31–46; Dan. 12:2).

QUESTIONS FOR PERSONAL APPLICATION

1. Paul says that the expectation of a future bodily resurrection is the "hope" in which we were saved (Rom. 8:24). Is the hope of a future resurrection of your body one of the major things you look forward to in the future? If not, why not? What could increase your hope in the future resurrection of the body?

2. So strong was Paul's longing for the future day of resurrection, and so aware was he of the hardships that we still suffer in this life, that he could say, "If for this life only we have hoped in Christ, we are of all men most to be pitied" (1 Cor. 15:19), and, "If the dead are not raised, 'Let us eat and drink, for tomorrow we die'" (1 Cor. 15:32). Do you have a great longing for the future resurrection that gives you this kind of sentiment in your heart as well? If not, why do you not have the same perspective on the resurrection of the body that Paul did?

[7]See discussion of this passage in D. A. Carson, *Matthew,* in EBC, 8:581–82.

3. What do you think might occur in your life to give you a greater longing for the resurrection of your body? If you have a grandfather or grandmother or other older friend or relative who has died and gone to be with Christ, what do you think that person will look like on the day of resurrection? Can you imagine what it will be like meeting that person and becoming acquainted again? How will your relationship be different from what it was in this life?

SPECIAL TERMS

glorification
spiritual body

BIBLIOGRAPHY

Gaffin, Richard B., Jr. *Resurrection and Redemption: A Study in Paul's Soteriology.* Formerly, *The Centrality of the Resurrection: A Study in Paul's Soteriology.* Phillipsburg, N.J.: Presbyterian and Reformed, 1978.

Grider, J. K. "Glorification." In *EDT,* pp. 442–43.

Gundry, Robert N. *Sōma in Biblical Theology.* Cambridge: Cambridge University Press, 1975.

Harris, Murray J. *From Grave to Glory: Resurrection in the New Testament, Including a Response to Norman L. Geisler.* Grand Rapids: Zondervan, 1990, pp. 185–287.

_____. *Raised Immortal: Resurrection and Immortality in the New Testament.* Grand Rapids: Eerdmans, 1983.

_____. "Resurrection, General." In *NDT,* pp. 581–82.

Hoekema, Anthony A. "The Resurrection of the Body." In *The Bible and the Future.* Grand Rapids: Eerdmans, 1979, pp. 239–52.

Murray, John. "Glorification." In *Redemption Accomplished and Applied.* Grand Rapids: Eerdmans, 1955, pp. 174–81.

Schep, J. A. *The Nature of the Resurrection Body.* Grand Rapids: Eerdmans, 1964.

White, R. E. O. "Resurrection of the Dead." In *EDT,* pp. 941–44.

SCRIPTURE MEMORY PASSAGE

1 Corinthians 15:42–44: *So is it with the resurrection of the dead. What is sown is perishable, what is raised is imperishable. It is sown in dishonor, it is raised in glory. It is sown in weakness, it is raised in power. It is sown a physical body, it is raised a spiritual body. If there is a physical body, there is also a spiritual body.*

HYMN

"Ten Thousand Times Ten Thousand"

This hymn was written by Henry Alford, a New Testament professor at Cambridge University, England, and one of the greatest Greek scholars of the nineteenth century. The hymn pictures thousands of glorified believers streaming through the gates of heaven on the day of Christ's return, and ends with a prayer that Christ would come back quickly.

> Ten thousand times ten thousand in sparkling raiment bright,
> The armies of the ransomed saints throng up the steeps of light:
> 'Tis finished, all is finished, their fight with death and sin:
> Fling open wide the golden gates, and let the victors in.
>
> What rush of alleluias fills all the earth and sky!
> What ringing of a thousand harps bespeaks the triumph nigh!
> O day, for which creation and all its tribes were made;
> O joy, for all its former woes a thousand-fold repaid!
>
> O then what raptured greetings on Canaan's happy shore;
> What knitting severed friendships up where partings are no more!
> Then eyes with joy shall sparkle, that brimmed with tears of late;
> Orphans no longer fatherless, nor widows desolate.
>
> Bring near thy great salvation, thou Lamb for sinners slain;
> Fill up the roll of thine elect, then take thy pow'r, and reign:
> Appear, desire of nations, thine exiles long for home;
> Show in the heav'n thy promised sign; thou Prince and Saviour,
> come.

AUTHOR: HENRY ALFORD, 1867

Chapter

UNION WITH CHRIST

*What does it mean to be "in Christ"
or "united with Christ"?*

EXPLANATION AND SCRIPTURAL BASIS[1]

Although we have now completed our study of the steps in the application of redemption, one other subject is so frequently mentioned in Scripture and so wide-ranging in its application to our lives that it deserves a separate treatment here. That is the concept of union with Christ. As we shall see below, *every aspect* of God's relationship to believers is in some way connected to our relationship with Christ. From God's counsels in eternity past before the world was created, to our fellowship with God in heaven in eternity future, and including every aspect of our relationship with God in this life—all has occurred in union with Christ. So in one sense the entire study of the application of redemption could be included in this subject. However, in this chapter we can simply summarize the incredible richness of the scriptural idea of union with Christ. John Murray says:

> Union with Christ has its source in the election of God the Father before the foundation of the world and has its fruition in the glorification of the sons of God. The perspective of God's people is not narrow; it is broad and it is long. It is not confined to space and time; it has the expanse of eternity. Its orbit has two foci, one the electing love of God the Father in the counsels of eternity; the other glorification with Christ in the manifestation of his glory. The former has no beginning, the latter has no end. . . . Why does the believer entertain the thought of God's determinate counsel with such joy? Why can he have patience in the perplexities and adversities of the present? Why can he have confident assurance with reference to the future and rejoice in hope of the glory of God? It is because he cannot think of past, present, or future apart from union with Christ.[2]

We may define *union with Christ* as follows: *Union with Christ is a phrase used to summarize several different relationships between believers and Christ, through which Christians receive every benefit of salvation. These relationships include the fact that we are in Christ, Christ is in us, we are like Christ, and we are with Christ.*

As this definition indicates, four different aspects of our union with Christ may be specified from the biblical material. We will look at each of these four in turn:

1. We are in Christ.
2. Christ is in us.
3. We are like Christ.
4. We are with Christ.[3]

A. We Are in Christ

The phrase "in Christ" does not have one single sense, but refers to a variety of relationships, as indicated below.

1. In God's Eternal Plan. Ephesians 1:4 tells us that, God *chose us in Christ* "before the foundation of the world." It was "in Christ" that we were "destined and appointed to live for the praise of his glory" (vv. 1:11–12). Later he "saved us and called us" because of "his own purpose" and because of the grace which he gave us "*in Christ Jesus before the beginning of time*" (2 Tim. 1:9 NIV).

Since we did not exist before the foundation of the world, these verses indicate that God, looking into the future and knowing that we would exist, thought of us being in a special relationship with Christ. He did not first choose us and later decide to relate us to Christ. Rather, while choosing us, he at the same time thought about us as belonging to Christ in a special way, as being "in Christ." Therefore, he thought about us as eventually having the right to share in the blessings of Christ's work.

2. During Christ's Life on Earth. Throughout Christ's entire life on earth, from the time of his birth to the time of his ascension into heaven, God thought of us as being "in Christ." That is, whatever Christ did as our representative, God counted it as being something we did, too. Of course, believers were not consciously present in Christ, since most believers did not even exist yet when Christ was on earth. Nor were believers present in Christ in some mysterious, spiritual way (as if, for example, the souls of thousands of believers were somehow present in Christ's body during his earthly life). Rather, believers were present in Christ *only in God's thoughts*. God *thought of us* as going through everything that Christ went through, because he was our representative.

When Jesus perfectly obeyed God for his whole life, God thought of us as having obeyed, too. "By one man's obedience many will be made righteous" (Rom. 5:19). So Christ is our source of righteousness (1 Cor. 1:30; Phil. 3:9).

[1]The material in this chapter is taken from an essay written for Tyndale House Publishers (Wheaton, Ill.). Used by permission.

[2]John Murray, *Redemption Accomplished and Applied* (Grand Rapids: Eerdmans, 1955), p. 164.

Because God thought of us as being "in" Christ, he also could think of our sins as belonging to Christ: "God made him who had no sin to be sin for us" (2 Cor. 5:21 NIV), and "the LORD has laid on him the iniquity of us all" (Isa. 53:6). These were sins we had not yet committed, but God knew about them in advance, and thought of them as belonging to Christ. Thus, it was right that Christ should die for our sins. "He himself bore our sins in his body on the tree" (1 Peter 2:24; see also Rom. 4:25; 1 Cor. 15:3; Col. 2:14; Heb. 9:28).

But it was not just our sins that God thought of as belonging to Christ: it was we ourselves. When Christ died, God thought of us as having died. Our old self was *crucified with him* (Rom. 6:6). "I have been crucified with Christ" (Gal. 2:20). "One has died for all; therefore all have died" (2 Cor. 5:14; see also Rom. 6:4–5, 8; 7:4; Col. 1:22; 2:12, 20; 3:3; 2 Tim. 2:11).

In the same way, God thought of us as having been *buried* with Christ, *raised* with him, and *taken up to heaven* with him in glory. "God *raised us up with Christ* and *seated us with him* in the heavenly realms in Christ Jesus" (Eph. 2:6 NIV; see also Rom. 6:4–11; 1 Cor. 15:22; Col. 2:12–13).

When Christ returned to heaven, therefore, all the blessings of salvation were earned for us. God thought of these blessings as being rightfully ours, just as if we had earned them ourselves. Nevertheless, they were stored up for us in heaven—in God's mind, actually, and in Christ, our representative—waiting to be applied to us personally (1 Peter 1:3–5; Col. 3:3–4; Eph. 1:3).

3. During Our Lives Now. Once we have been born and exist as real people in the world, our union with Christ can no longer be something just in God's mind. We also must be brought into an actual relationship with Christ through which the benefits of salvation can be applied to our lives by the Holy Spirit. The richness of our present life in Christ can be viewed from four slightly different perspectives:

    1. We have died and been raised with Christ.
    2. We have new life in Christ.
    3. All our actions can be done in Christ.
    4. All Christians together are one body in Christ.

a. Dying and Rising With Christ: The death, burial, and resurrection of Jesus now have real effects in our lives. "You were *buried with him* in baptism, in which you were also *raised with him* through faith in the working of God, who raised him from the dead" (Col. 2:12). Here Paul's references to baptism and faith indicate that our dying and rising with Christ occur in this present life, at the time we become Christians.

Paul sees this present death and resurrection with Christ as a way of describing and explaining the change that the Holy Spirit brings about in our character and personality when we become Christians. It is as if the Holy Spirit reproduces Jesus' death and resurrection in our lives when we believe in Christ. We become so unresponsive to the pressures,

---

[3]Union with Christ is also sometimes referred to as the "mystical union." This is because we do not fully understand the workings of these relationships with Christ, and because we know about them only through God's revelation in Scripture.

demands, and attractions of our previous, sinful way of life that Paul can say we are "dead" to these influences, because we have died with Christ (Rom. 7:6; Gal. 2:20; 5:24; 6:14; Col. 2:20). On the other hand, we find ourselves wanting to serve God much more, and able to serve him with greater power and success, so much so that Paul says we are "alive" to God, because we have been raised up with Christ: "We were buried therefore with him by baptism into death, so that as Christ was raised from the dead by the glory of the Father, we too might *walk in newness of life*" (Rom. 6:4). "So you also must consider yourselves dead to sin and *alive to God* in Christ Jesus" (Rom. 6:11; see also 1 Peter 1:3; 2:24). Because we died and rose with Christ, we have power to overcome personal sin more and more (Rom. 6:12–14, 19); we have come to "fullness of life" in Christ (Col. 2:10–13); in fact, we have become a "new creation" in him (2 Cor. 5:17, with vv. 14–15), and should therefore set our minds on things that are above, where Christ is (Col. 3:1–3).

b. New Life in Christ: These last verses suggest a second perspective on our being "in Christ." We can think not only in terms of Christ's past work of redemption, but also in terms of his present life in heaven, and his continuing possession of all the spiritual resources we need to live the Christian life. Since every spiritual blessing was earned by him and belongs to him, the New Testament can say that these blessings are "in him." Thus, they are available only to those who are "in Christ," and if we are in Christ, these blessings are ours.

John writes, "God gave us eternal life, and this life is *in his Son*" (1 John 5:11), and Paul speaks of "the promise of the life which is *in Christ Jesus*" (2 Tim. 1:1). We read that "*in Christ*" are "faith and love" (1 Tim. 1:14; 2 Tim. 1:13), "grace" (2 Tim. 2:1), "salvation" (2 Tim. 2:10), "all the treasures of wisdom and knowledge" (Col. 2:3), and God's "riches in glory" (Phil. 4:19). Paul says that it is because of God's work that Christians are "in Christ Jesus, whom God made our wisdom, our righteousness and sanctification and redemption" (1 Cor. 1:30), and that "God . . . has blessed us in the heavenly realms with *every spiritual blessing in Christ*" (Eph. 1:3).

In fact, every stage of the application of redemption is given to us because we are "in Christ." It is "in Christ" that we are *called* to salvation (1 Cor. 7:22), *regenerated* (Eph. 1:3; 2:10), and *justified* (Rom. 8:1; 2 Cor. 5:21; Gal. 2:17; Eph. 1:7; Phil. 3:9; Col. 1:14). "In Christ" we *die* (1 Thess. 4:16; Rev. 14:13) and "in him" our bodies *will be raised* up again (1 Cor. 15:22). These passages suggest that because our lives are inseparably connected to Christ himself, the Holy Spirit gives us all the blessings that Christ has earned.

c. All Our Actions Can Be Done in Christ: The foregoing changes within our individual lives are accompanied by a dramatic change in the realm in which we live. To become a Christian is to enter the newness of the age to come, and to experience to some degree the new powers of the kingdom of God affecting every part of our lives. To be "in Christ" is to be in that new realm that Christ controls.

This means that every action in our lives can be done "in Christ," if it is done in the power of his kingdom and in a way that brings honor to him. Paul *speaks* the truth "in Christ" (Rom. 9:1; 2 Cor. 2:17; 12:19), *is proud* of his work "in Christ" (Rom. 15:17; 1 Cor. 15:31), reminds the Corinthians of his *ways* "in Christ" (1 Cor. 4:17), *hopes* "in the Lord Jesus" to send Timothy to Philippi (Phil. 2:19), *rejoices* greatly "in the Lord" (Phil.

4:10), and "in the Lord" *commands, beseeches,* and *exhorts* other Christians (1 Thess. 4:1; 2 Thess. 3:12; Philem. 8). He says, "I can *do all things* in him who strengthens me" (Phil. 4:13).

Paul also writes to believers about their actions "in Christ." He reminds the Corinthians, "in the Lord your *labor* is not in vain" (1 Cor. 15:58). It is "in the Lord" that children are to *obey* their parents (Eph. 6:1), wives are to *submit* to their husbands (Col. 3:18), and all believers are to *be strong* (Eph. 6:10), *be encouraged* (Phil. 2:1), *rejoice* (Phil. 3:1; 4:4), *agree* (Phil. 4:2), *stand firm* (Phil. 4:1; 1 Thess. 3:8), *live a godly life* (2 Tim. 3:12), and have *good behavior* (1 Peter 3:16). "In the Lord" they *work hard* (Rom. 16:12), *are made confident* (Phil. 1:14), and *are approved* (Rom. 16:10). Paul's hope for Christians is that they *live* in Christ: "Just as you received Christ Jesus as Lord, continue to live in him, rooted and built up in him" (Col. 2:6–7 NIV). Then Paul will achieve his life's goal, to "present every man *mature* in Christ" (Col. 1:28). John similarly encourages believers to "*abide* in him" (1 John 2:28; 3:6, 24), echoing Jesus' words, "He who abides in me, and I in him, he it is that bears much fruit" (John 15:5).

d. One Body in Christ: We are not simply in Christ as isolated individual persons. Since Christ is the head of the body, which is the church (Eph. 5:23), all who are in union with Christ are also related to one another in his body. This joining together makes us "one body in Christ, and individually *members one of another*" (Rom. 12:5; 1 Cor. 10:17; 12:12–27). Thus, "If one member suffers, all suffer together; if one member is honored, all rejoice together" (1 Cor. 12:26). The ties of fellowship are so strong that Christians may only marry "in the Lord" (1 Cor. 7:39). In this body of Christ old hostilities disappear, sinful divisions among people are broken down, and worldly criteria of status no longer apply, for "There is neither Jew nor Greek, there is neither slave nor free, there is neither male nor female; for you are all one in Christ Jesus" (Gal. 3:28; cf. Eph. 2:13–22).

Because we are one body in Christ, entire churches can be "in Christ" (Gal. 1:22; 1 Thess. 2:14). And the church universal, the church made up of all true believers, is collectively united to Christ as a husband is united to his wife (Eph. 5:31–32; 1 Cor. 6:17). Christ's purpose is to perfect and cleanse and purify the church, so that it might more completely reflect what he is like and thereby bring glory to him (Eph. 5:25–27).

Yet another metaphor is used in 1 Peter 2:4–5, where believers, in coming to Christ, are said to be like living stones, built into a spiritual house (see also Eph. 2:20–22). Thus, they are unified and forever dependent on one another, just as the stones of a building are united to each other and depend upon each other.

But the boldest analogy of all is used by Jesus, who prays for believers "*that they may all be one; even as you, Father, are in me, and I in you, that they also may be in us*" (John 17:21). Here Jesus prays that our unity would be like the perfect unity between the Father and the Son in the Trinity. This is a reminder to us that our unity should be eternal and perfectly harmonious (as God's unity is).

But this analogy with the members of the Trinity is very important for another reason: it warns us against thinking that union with Christ will ever swallow up our individual personalities. Even though the Father, Son, and Holy Spirit have perfect and eternal unity, yet they remain distinct persons. In the same way, even though we shall someday attain *perfect unity* with other believers and with Christ, yet we shall forever remain *distinct persons* as well, with our own individual gifts, abilities, interests, responsibilities, circles of personal relationships, preferences, and desires.

B. Christ Is in Us

Jesus spoke of a second kind of relationship when he said, "He who abides in me, and *I in him*, he it is that bears much fruit" (John 15:5). It is not only true that we are in Christ; he is also in us, to give us power to live the Christian life. "I have been crucified with Christ; it is no longer I who live, but *Christ who lives in me*" (Gal. 2:20). The factor that determines whether someone is a Christian is whether Christ is in him (Rom. 8:10; 2 Cor. 13:5; Rev. 3:20). God's wise plan, hidden as a mystery for generations, was to save Gentiles as well as Jews. Therefore, Paul can tell his Gentile readers that God's mystery is "*Christ in you*, the hope of glory" (Col. 1:27).

It is important to maintain, on the basis of these verses, that there is a real, personal dwelling of Christ in us, and that this does not mean that we merely agree with Christ or that his ideas are in us. Rather, *he* is in us and remains in us through faith (Eph. 3:17; 2 Cor. 13:5). To overlook this truth would be to neglect the great source of spiritual strength that we have within us (1 John 4:4). To remember it destroys our pride, gives us a constant feeling of deep dependence on Christ, and gives us great confidence, not in self, but in Christ working in us (Gal. 2:20; Rom. 15:18; Phil. 4:13).

This indwelling of Christ affects our response to those in need. Whatever we do to help a Christian brother or sister, we do to Christ (Matt. 25:40). Keeping Jesus' commandments is an indication that he is in us, and the Holy Spirit also bears witness to us that Christ is in us (1 John 3:24).

C. We Are Like Christ

A third aspect of union with Christ is our *imitation of him*. "Be imitators of me, as I am of Christ," writes Paul (1 Cor. 11:1). John reminds us, "He who says he abides in him ought to walk in the same way in which he walked" (1 John 2:6). So union with Christ implies that we should imitate Christ. Our lives ought so to reflect what his life was like that we bring honor to him in everything we do (Phil. 1:20).

Thus, the New Testament pictures the Christian life as one of striving to imitate Christ in all our actions. "Welcome one another, therefore, *as Christ has welcomed you*" (Rom. 15:7). "Husbands, love your wives, *as Christ loved the church*" (Eph. 5:25). "*As the Lord has forgiven you,* so you also must forgive" (Col. 3:13). "He laid down his life for us; and we ought to lay down our lives for the brethren" (1 John 3:16). Throughout our lives, we are to run the race before us, "looking to Jesus, the pioneer and perfecter of our faith" (Heb. 13:2; see also Eph. 5:2; Phil. 2:5–11; 1 Thess. 1:6; 1 John 3:7; 4:17). By contrast, disobedience to Christ holds him up in contempt (Heb. 6:6).

Our imitation of Christ is especially evident in suffering. Christians are called to take suffering patiently, "because Christ also suffered for you, leaving you an example, that you should *follow in his steps*" (1 Peter 2:21). Paul's goal is to "share his [Christ's] sufferings, becoming *like him in his death*" (Phil. 3:10; see also 2 Cor. 1:5; 4:8–11; Heb. 12:3; 1 Peter 4:13).

Furthermore, our suffering is connected with sharing in Christ's glory when he returns: "we suffer with him in order that we may also be glorified with him" (Rom. 8:17). This is probably because it is through suffering and difficulty that God makes us more Christ-like and causes us to grow to maturity in Christ (James 1:2–4; Heb. 5:8–9). Also, since Christ perfectly obeyed his Father even in the face of great suffering, so our obedience, trust, and patience in suffering more fully portray what Christ was like, and so bring more honor to him. It gives us great comfort to know that we are only experiencing what he has already experienced, and that he therefore understands what we are going through, and listens sympathetically to our prayers (Heb. 2:18; 4:15–16; 12:11). As the outcome of a life of obedience, we are able to share in Christ's glory: "He who conquers, I will grant him to sit with me on my throne, as I myself conquered and sat down with my Father on his throne" (Rev. 3:21).

Our imitation of Christ should not be thought of as a mere mimicking of Jesus' actions, however. The far deeper purpose is that in imitating him we are becoming more and more like him: *when we act like Christ we become like Christ.* We grow up to maturity in Christ (Eph. 4:13, 15) as we are "being changed into his likeness from one degree of glory to another" (2 Cor. 3:18). The final result is that we shall become perfectly like Christ, for God has predestined us "to be conformed to the image of his Son" (Rom. 8:29; 1 Cor. 15:49), and "when he appears, *we shall be like him*" (1 John 3:2). When this happens, Christ will be fully glorified in us (2 Thess. 1:10–12; John 17:10).

Yet in all of this we never lose our individual personhood. We become perfectly *like* Christ, but *we do not become Christ,* and we are not absorbed into Christ or lost forever as individuals. Rather, it is we as real individuals who shall still know as we are known (1 Cor. 13:12); it is we who shall see him as he is (1 John 3:2); it is we who shall worship him, and see his face, and have his name on our foreheads, and reign with him for ever and ever (Rev. 22:3–5).

Just as the Father, Son, and Holy Spirit are exactly like one another in character (John 14:7, 9), yet remain distinct persons, so we can become more and more like Christ and still be distinct individuals with different gifts and different functions (Eph. 4:15–16; 1 Cor. 12:4–27). In fact, the more like Christ we become, the more truly ourselves we become (Matt. 10:39; John 10:3; Rev. 2:17; Ps. 37:4). If we forget this, we will tend to neglect the diversity of gifts in the church and will want to make everyone like ourselves. We will also tend to deny any ultimate importance for ourselves as individuals. A proper biblical perspective will allow each believer to say not only, "We Christians are important to Christ," but also, "*I* am important to Christ: he knows my name, he calls me by name, he gives me a new name which is mine alone" (John 10:3; Rev. 2:17).

D. We Are With Christ

1. Personal Fellowship With Christ. Another aspect of union with Christ concerns our personal fellowship with him. It makes little difference whether we say that we are with Christ or that Christ is with us, for both phrases represent the same truth. Christ promised, "Where two or three are gathered in my name, there am I in the midst of them" (Matt. 18:20), and, "I am *with you* always, to the close of the age" (Matt. 28:20). Once again, since Jesus' human body ascended to heaven (John 16:7; 17:11; Acts 1:9–11), these verses must speak of his divine nature being present with us. Yet it is still a very personal presence, in which we *work* together with Christ (2 Cor. 6:1), we *know* him (Phil. 3:8, 10), we are *comforted* by him (2 Thess. 2:16–17), we are *taught* by him (Matt. 11:29), and we live our whole lives *in his presence* (2 Cor. 2:10; 1 Tim. 5:21; 6:13–14; 2 Tim. 4:1). To become a Christian is to be "called into the *fellowship* of [God's] Son, Jesus Christ our Lord" (1 Cor. 1:9). Yet this fellowship can vary in intensity, since Paul's benediction on Christians, "The Lord be with you all" (2 Thess. 3:16; cf. 2 Tim. 4:22) can only express a hope for still closer fellowship with Christ and a deeper awareness of his presence.

Furthermore, in some sense yet imperceptible to us, when we come to worship we now come into heaven itself, to "innumerable angels in festal gathering, and to the assembly of the first-born who are enrolled in heaven, and to a judge who is God of all, and to the spirits of just men made perfect, *and to Jesus,* the mediator of a new covenant" (Heb. 12:22–24). This participation in heavenly worship is what the Apostles' Creed calls the "communion of saints," and what a familiar hymn calls "mystic, sweet communion with those whose rest is won."[4] Hebrews 12 does not seem to suggest that we have a conscious awareness of being in the presence of this heavenly assembly, but it may indicate that those now in heaven witness our worship and rejoice in it, and it certainly implies that we can have a joyful awareness that our praise is being heard in God's temple in heaven.

In all our prayers now we are heard by Jesus and have fellowship with him (1 John 1:3), our great high priest, who has entered "into heaven itself, now to appear in the presence of God on our behalf" (Heb. 9:24; 4:16). Our fellowship with him will be greater yet when we die (2 Cor. 5:8; Phil. 1:23; 1 Thess. 5:10), and even greater still once Jesus returns (1 Thess. 4:17; 1 John 3:2). It gives us great joy to know that Christ actually desires to have us with him (John 17:24).

Our fellowship with Christ also brings us into fellowship with each other. John writes, "That which we have seen and heard we proclaim also to you, *so that you may have fellowship with us;* and our fellowship is with the Father and with his Son Jesus Christ" (1 John 1:3).

2. Union With the Father and With the Holy Spirit. This last verse suggests a final aspect of union with Christ. Because we are in union with Christ in these several relationships, we also are brought into union with the Father and with the Holy Spirit. We are *in the Father* (John 17:21; 1 Thess. 1:1; 2 Thess. 1:1; 1 John 2:24; 4:15–16; 5:20) and *in the Holy Spirit* (Rom. 8:9; 1 Cor. 3:16; 6:19; 2 Tim. 1:14). *The Father is in us* (John 14:23) and *the Holy Spirit is in us* (Rom. 8:9, 11). We are *like the Father* (Matt. 5:44–45, 48; Eph. 4:32; Col. 3:10; 1 Peter 1:15–16) and *like the Holy Spirit* (Rom. 8:4–6; Gal. 5:22–23; John 16:13). We have fellowship *with the Father* (1 John 1:3; Matt. 6:9; 2 Cor. 6:16–18) and *with the Holy Spirit* (Rom. 8:16; Acts 15:28; 2 Cor. 13:14; Eph. 4:30).

These additional relationships are not blurred into a distinctionless, mystical ecstasy, however. Both now and in eternity we relate to the Father in his distinct role as our heavenly Father, to the Son in his distinct role as our Savior and Lord, and to the Holy Spirit in his distinct role as the Spirit who empowers us and continually applies to us all the benefits of our salvation.

QUESTIONS FOR PERSONAL APPLICATION

1. Before reading this chapter, had you thought of yourself as being united with Christ from the point of God's choosing you before the foundation of the world to the point of going to be with him in heaven forever? How does this idea change the way you think of yourself and your own life? How does it affect the way you think of difficulties that you may be experiencing at this time? In what ways can the ideas of having died with Christ and having been raised with him be an encouragement in your present efforts to overcome sin that remains in your life?

2. Have you previously thought of doing the actions that you do each day "in Christ" (see Phil. 4:13)? If you thought of doing the reading that you are presently doing "in Christ," how would it change your attitude or perspective? What difference would it make to think of doing your daily work "in Christ"? What about carrying on conversations with friends or family members? Or eating, or even sleeping?

3. How can the idea of union with Christ increase your love and fellowship for other Christians, both those in your church and those in other churches?

4. Do you have any awareness in your day-to-day life of Christ living in you (Gal. 2:20)? What would change in your life if you had a stronger awareness of Christ living in you throughout the day?

5. For one or two days, try reading some section of the gospels and asking how you might better imitate Christ in your own life. What effect will the idea of following in Christ's steps (1 Peter 1:21) and walking as he walked (1 John 2:6) have in your life?

6. Can you name some times in your life when you have sensed an especially close personal fellowship with Christ? What have those times been like? Can you think of anything that brought about that close fellowship with Christ? What can we do to increase the intensity of our daily fellowship with Christ?

7. In your personal experience, do you relate differently to God the Father, to Jesus Christ, and to the Holy Spirit? Can you describe those differences, if there are any?

SPECIAL TERMS

being raised with Christ	one body in Christ
dying with Christ	communion of saints
in Christ	union with Christ
mystical union	

---

[4]This phrase is taken from the hymn, "The Church's One Foundation," written in 1866 by Samuel J. Stone.

BIBLIOGRAPHY

Baker, J. P. "Union With Christ." In *NDT*, pp. 697–99.

Gordon, Adoniram Judson. *In Christ; or the Believer's Union with His Lord.* 1872; reprint, Grand Rapids: Baker, 1964. (First published in 1872.)

Murray, John. "Union with Christ." In *Redemption Accomplished and Applied.* Grand Rapids: Eerdmans, 1955, pp. 161–73.

Poythress, Vern. "Using Multiple Thematic Centers in Theological Synthesis: Holiness as a Test Case in Developing a Pauline Theology." Unpublished manuscript available from the Campus Bookstore, Westminster Theological Seminary, P.O. Box 27009, Philadelphia, PA 19118.

Smedes, Lewis B. *Union With Christ: A Biblical View of the New Life in Jesus Christ.* 2d ed. Grand Rapids: Eerdmans, 1983.

Walvoord, J. F. "Identification With Christ." In *EDT*, p. 542.

SCRIPTURE MEMORY PASSAGE

Galatians 2:20: *I have been crucified with Christ; it is no longer I who live, but Christ who lives in me; and the life I now live in the flesh I live by faith in the Son of God, who loved me and gave himself for me.*

HYMN

"Jesus, Thou Joy of Loving Hearts"

This hymn has been attributed to Bernard of Clairvaux (1090–1153), a monk known for his love of God and deep piety. Other hymns attributed to him are "Jesus, the Very Thought of Thee" and "O Sacred Head Now Wounded." Though written eight hundred years ago, this hymn remains one of the most beautiful expressions of love for Christ in the history of the church.

Jesus, thou joy of loving hearts,
    Thou fount of life, thou light of men,
From the best bliss that earth imparts
    We turn unfilled to thee again.

Thy truth unchanged hath ever stood;
    Thou savest those that on thee call;
To them that seek thee thou art good,
    To them that find thee all in all.

We taste thee, O thou living bread,
    And long to feast upon thee still;
We drink of thee, the fountain-head,
    And thirst our souls from thee to fill.

Our restless spirits yearn for thee,
    Where'er our changeful lot is cast;
Glad when thy gracious smile we see,
    Blest when our faith can hold thee fast.

O Jesus, ever with us stay,
    Make all our moments calm and bright;
Chase the dark night of sin away,
    Shed o'er the world thy holy light.

AUTHOR: BERNARD OF CLAIRVAUX, C. 1150

We want to hear from you. Please send your comments about this book to us in care of zreview@zondervan.com. Thank you.